CONDUCTING BUSINESS IN THE LAND OF THE DRAGON

Previous Book by Alan Refkin and Scott Cray

Doing the China Tango: How to Dance Around Common Pitfalls in Chinese Business Relationships

Previous Book by Alan Refkin and Daniel Borgia

The Wild, Wild East: Lessons for Success in Business in Contemporary Capitalist China

CONDUCTING BUSINESS IN THE LAND OF THE DRAGON

What Every Businessperson Needs to Know about China

ALAN REFKIN AND SCOTT CRAY

iUniverse LLC
Bloomington

CONDUCTING BUSINESS IN THE LAND OF THE DRAGON
WHAT EVERY BUSINESSPERSON NEEDS TO KNOW ABOUT CHINA

iUniverse books may be ordered through booksellers or by contacting:

iUniverse LLC
1663 Liberty Drive
Bloomington, IN 47403
www.iuniverse.com
1-800-Authors (1-800-288-4677)

ISBN: 978-1-4917-1253-5 (sc)
ISBN: 978-1-4917-1255-9 (hc)
ISBN: 978-1-4917-1254-2 (e)

Library of Congress Control Number: 2013920199

Printed in the United States of America.

iUniverse rev. date: 11/22/2013

Praise for *Conducting Business in the Land of the Dragon*

Drawing upon their years of experience "in country," Alan Refkin and Scott Cray have crafted a practical guide of how to succeed as a Western company in the promising yet pitfall-ridden Chinese market. Comprehensively referenced and meticulously constructed, they also address critical yet arcane issues, including intellectual property and cyber security, with the same ease and common sense that they bring to more traditional topics. The result is more than a primer. It's a plan for successful engagement for Western companies wishing to better understand and master business development in China.

Rob Durst, CEO, Silver Bay Technologies

Working in the Latin American market, I've constantly been around foreign investors who fail to understand the challenges they must work through, and connections they have to establish, in order to be successful in an unfamiliar country or market. When I went with Alan Refkin to China a few years back, I couldn't help but be utterly impressed by the way he made overcoming the aforementioned challenges look easy, despite the culture and language barriers. The speed at which he formed solid relationships with Chinese business owners, officials, lawyers, and accounting firms amazed me.

If you have to buy one book which teaches you about how to conduct business in China, make this that book. You'll never find a better guide to take you through the reality of conducting business in China. Period.

Jose F Sada, president of DS Capital Partners

Having done business in China, but now focusing on emerging Eastern European markets, I found much of the information contained in *Conducting Business in the Land of the Dragon* to be not only highly informative for someone conducting business in China, but it also had applicability to other emerging markets. This is a well-written book for anyone who wants to go under the covers and see how business is really conducted.

Tom Suppanz, director of investment banking, NESEC

Doing the China Tango is a keen twenty-first-century guide to China and makes excellent reading for both experienced Sinophiles and China novices. Offering insights in a wide range of issues, everyone will learn from Alan's fascinating experiences and understanding of China, its people, its culture, and its future.

John Lucas, director, Weinberg & Company

Praise for *Doing the China Tango*

I've been investing in, writing about, studying, and observing the world of small stocks and their associated successes, foibles, and failures for nearly twenty-five years.

I've been witness to a $3,800 investment becoming $4.2 million over a twelve-year time frame, and the demise of one of the great behemoths of all time—the pride of Rochester, New York. I'm referring to Kodak, the master of all things celluloid, whose complete failure to embrace the digital imaging revolution led to its total undoing.

So, as a serial small-cap investor, I thought I'd found nirvana when I began studying the financial performance of the small stocks of China, which had navigated their way to US investors by listing on our stock exchanges and accessing our capital-rich markets. The valuations, profits, and growth rates had me swooning like a teenage girl in the front row of a Justin Bieber concert. With a little homework, patience, and luck, I was on my way to early retirement, riding the wave of the largest emerging consumer class in the history of the world.

As I was trained to do in my early days, I dug into the SEC filings, blindly believing the great accounting institutions of the twenty-first century had my back.

Alas, a substantial loss of my personal capital, along with a significant beating to my ego, was the result of not realizing early on that there is an entirely different and unfamiliar set of rules for doing business in China.

Without the proper guidance, you will find yourself stripped bare of your money and your pride in short order.

Had I met Alan Refkin earlier in the process, I might have been better prepared to swim in China's great white-infested waters.

After working with and learning from Alan, I came to recognize that it's possible to do business in China, but only with the intrepid guidance of a grizzled veteran of the China business world.

Standards of integrity will evolve in China to a higher level over time. However, at present, China cannot be ignored; 1.3 billion people make for a very large global footprint. Very few of those citizens have much in the way of Western-style possessions, and the new generation of Chinese all want the same stuff we have. That's a lot of opportunity.

Consider *Doing the China Tango* your personal survival guide for doing business in China. Don't read it. Study it, and use what you have learned.

Had the aggressive investment bankers of the last ten years studied *Doing the China Tango*, a great deal of emotional and financial pain might easily have been avoided.

Larry Isen, editor and publisher, EmergingChinaStocks.com

Doing the China Tango quickly and succinctly explains what China's business culture is all about. It should be required reading for anyone who is doing, or plans to do, business in China.

Philip Abbenhaus, director, Asian Equity Research Institute

I knew Alan in his early beginnings in China's business environment. I believe *Doing the China Tango* reflects the disappointment, and the success, that a foreign investor faces in doing business in China.

This book targets the reality of conducting business in China and takes into account the country's culture, social outlook, mind-set, legal environment, accounting methods, negotiation efforts, follow-up, and finally . . . success. In my opinion, it's an excellent guide for anyone who wants to be aware of what's needed to be successful in working with the business and government in China.

Jose F. Sada, president, DS Capital Partners

Alan Refkin: I dedicate this book to my beautiful and talented wife, Kerry, whose warmth and kindness envelop all those who know her. Also to J. J. Keil, Cindy and Dr. John Cancelliere, and Aprille and Dr. Charles Pappas.

Scott Cray: I dedicate this book first to the Lord, who directs my steps and without whom, none of my Chinese experiences would have ever been possible. Also to my lovely bride, Peke Lina, for always encouraging me. Last, but certainly not least, to all of the special Chinese people who have touched our lives and enriched our life experiences.

CONTENTS

Chinese Provinces and Cities

PREFACE

In *Conducting Business in the Land of the Dragon*, we delve into the evolving fabric of Chinese business and share an intimate knowledge of how business is conducted in China. We'll guide you through the intricacies of how Chinese negotiate, discuss how to better protect yourself from the increased threat of cyberespionage and the theft of your intellectual property, show you how to litigate if necessary, take you through what's needed to successfully interact with government officials, and show you how you can be successful and reap the financial rewards from conducting business in China. Most fail in China because they don't have the knowledge to succeed. We want to change that. For more than a decade, we've assisted scores of companies that wanted to take advantage of the enormous growth enveloping China. This book encapsulates that decade of advice and will help provide you with the knowledge necessary to be successful in the land of the dragon.

China is as tough a business environment as you'll experience anywhere in the world. Ask any of the companies that have lost hundreds of millions of dollars there or have closed up shop and gone home. They believed they had it together and that their team of legal, accounting, and business experts, who had been successful in other areas of the world, would also bring this same success to China. That's not an assumption anyone should make. China is unique. Its business culture has been isolationist for thousands of years, and only in the last thirty-five years has the government permitted businesses to freely interact with the rest of the international community. As a result, what we know about China is all recent.

The temptation on the part of many businesspeople, therefore, is to ignore China and move on to a business environment that's more Westernized and easier to understand. That may work for some, but China is the world's number-two economy and, by most predictions, slated to be the world's largest within the next two decades. China can't be ignored. Most companies can't, or don't want to, walk away from the world's future number-one market. But that's exactly what some are doing because they don't understand how to conduct business in China and accomplish their goals. *Conducting Business in the Land of the Dragon* will give you the in-depth knowledge and understanding that will make you better able to adapt to the current business environment, accomplish your goals, dominate, and win.

Alan Refkin and Scott Cray

ACKNOWLEDGMENTS

We would like to thank David Dodge for his help and advice in understanding Chinese financial transactions. Dave is a world-class expert on Chinese forensic due diligence, and we frequently tapped into that expertise in compiling portions of this book. We've worked with Dave for over a decade, and he's without question the most qualified person we know on the subject of US and Chinese accounting practices.

We'd also like to thank Vincent Zheng for his advice and perspective on all things Chinese. We've worked with Vincent for so long that he seems like a member of our family. During this time, he's been our oracle and provided us with valuable counsel in analyzing corporate trends within China.

We'd like to thank Zhang Jingjie (Maria), whose research has enabled us to verify facts and provide more detail in our writings than would otherwise be possible. Many times her research entailed reading through stacks of Chinese documents and translating into English those that we required. This took a great deal of time and patience, and for that we're both very grateful.

Dr. Kevin Hunter has been extraordinarily generous with his time in providing us with advice on all things technical. You'll never find a more patient and humbler person than Kevin, nor in our opinion, someone who has a better grasp of all things technical. His counsel is greatly appreciated.

Our editorial consultant manager at iUniverse, Sarah Disbrow, has been a joy to work with. Her advice, counsel, and insights are greatly appreciated.

We'd also like to thank others who have unselfishly given us the benefit of their counsel. These include Jose Sada, Daniel J. McClory, Clay Parker, Doug Ballinger, Mark Iwinski, Mike Calbot, Lawrence Wan, Hao Yang, Yanfeng Chang, Cao Yan, Steve Zhu, and Tammy Fluech.

Lastly, and most importantly, we'd like to thank our wives. Writing takes a great deal of time. Most of this time is spent in an office typing on our computers, with books and other reference data piled high on our desks and on the floor. Our wives have been extremely patient and supportive during this "social blackout." They provided us with encouragement and more than a few cups of coffee to keep us going. For that, and much more, you have our love, gratitude, and admiration.

INTRODUCTION

Scarcely a day goes by when China is not in the news. Several decades ago, that wasn't the case. China was considered backward, not business-friendly, and even worse, communist. That's changed in the ensuing decades to the point where most Fortune 500 companies have offices in China and thousands of smaller companies have followed suit. Why China? As we'll discuss, China's economic growth is meteoric, and it's the economic high-speed train that most companies want to climb aboard. They want to reap the financial rewards of conducting business with the world's number-two economy.

But there are also many companies that have not purchased a ticket to board this train. They're afraid. They've read in the news stories about the country's pattern of stealing foreign intellectual property, cyberespionage, environmental issues, nonenforcement of laws, and similar disparities that we'll discuss in detail. They know little about the land of the dragon, and as a result, they decide to remain domestic or focus in other areas of the world that don't seem to have the problems they've heard about in China.

Conducting Business in the Land of the Dragon was written as a detailed guide for businesspeople who want to succeed in China. We wrote it because we wanted to provide you with the lessons we've learned in the almost eleven years we've conducted business there. During that time, we've had more than our fair share of business dealings that went wrong, those that succeeded beyond expectation, and those that went exactly as we envisioned.

What we lacked when we first went to China was a book such as this. If we'd had one, conducting business in China would have been easier, and we wouldn't have so many scars to show from our learning experiences. Not that there weren't business books on China at that time. There were. But few of these books went beyond what we considered to be the superficial, and even fewer were written by those who went through the school of hard knocks and provided their personal insights. This is the book we wished we had when we first came to China.

We divided *Conducting Business in the Land of the Dragon* into fourteen bodies of knowledge, or chapters, that we feel are essential for anyone conducting business in China. We selected these subject areas because, from our experience, these are the bodies of information you'll need in order to succeed. That's not to say that businesspeople who are unknowledgeable in one or more of these areas will fail. On the contrary, we're perfect examples of those who've succeeded without this initial knowledge. However, for us, conducting business in China wasn't initially a quick or painless process. Eventually, as we obtained these bodies of knowledge, our successes increased. We hope to spare you this learning curve by providing you with all the knowledge you'll need to conduct business in the land of the dragon.

CHAPTER 1

Why China?

Why China? Three decades ago that question would have required a great deal of thought. China had yet to prove itself economically, was only beginning to gain political acceptance in the international community, and had just adopted capitalism. The world didn't know what to make of China.

And China didn't know what to make of the world. Its corporations were largely unfamiliar with the conduct of international business. Its political leadership was unacquainted with the nuances of international diplomacy. Its domestic leaders were unsure of how to interact with foreigners and structure transactions for those who wished to invest in their emerging economy.

China's problems weren't unique. All developed economies at one time or another addressed and overcame similar issues to become the established socioeconomic societies they are today. Like countries such as the United States, China must undergo three phases in its economic development in order to complete its transition to a mature economy. According to ChinaGlobalTrade.com, a program of the Kearny Alliance, these are the three phases:[1]

- development of industry
- development of services
- technological innovation

Development of Industry

In a country's early stage of economic development, labor flows from the largely agrarian society into industry. The country's growth consequently begins to accelerate as a result of its transition from less-productive agricultural labor to more-productive manufacturing labor. This is what occurred in the United States in the 1800s, and it's what's occurred in China since 1978. The productivity gains in this type of transition are huge, especially in the case of China, which has a plentiful agricultural workforce that has been increasingly migrating to urban areas in search of higher-paying jobs. The vast size of China's agricultural workforce has allowed China to obtain the urban labor necessary to attain its high sustained rate of growth for the past three decades. For example, while China has averaged a 7 to 9 percent rate of growth for the past thirty years, the growth rate in developed economies, such as the United States, is approximately 2 to 3 percent.

Productivity gains are easier for economies transitioning from an agrarian society to one of manufacturing. If you're already a developed economy, such as the United States, and you're already at the leading edge of technology, productivity gains come much more slowly. This is one reason why China is economically catching up at such a fast rate to Western economies. As Art Blakemore, an economics professor at Arizona State University, explains, "the greater the technology gap, the greater is the potential rate of catch-up." But as China's economy continues to develop, the technology gap with the West will continue to narrow until it eventually becomes almost nonexistent.[1] This first stage of development for a country is about competing on the basis of its low labor costs. China is currently exiting this phase of economic development.

Development of Services

In this phase of a country's economic development, growth comes from transitioning from less-productive industrial labor to the more-productive labor of providing services. As the country's industrial-based economy becomes more sophisticated, it begins to manufacture higher-end goods. Eventually labor costs are so high that the country's manufacturing base is focused only on the highest value-added manufacturing and services. In this transition, productivity gains from industry into services are smaller than from agriculture to industrial production.[1] China is currently entering this phase of development. It's purchasing required technologies from other countries and effecting technology transfers to its domestic industries.

Technological Innovation

In the last phase of a country's economic development, labor costs have risen to the point that the country is no longer the low-cost manufacturer of goods. Competition in this phase will come from other countries in both the development of industry and the development of services phases of their economic transition. Countries in this last phase will give to countries in the first two phases of their economic development cycles the low-cost and low-wage assignments that they previously performed in their transition from an agrarian to an industrialized economy. When this happens, these countries will also experience the same high rate of growth exhibited by China during its development of industry phase.[1] When China enters this last phase, it will be richer than it is today, just as America became richer when it entered this phase of its economic development.

> There are three sources of demand in an economy: domestic consumption, domestic investment, and trade surplus. Together these comprise a country's gross domestic product (GDP). In 2011, China's GDP growth rate was 9.2 percent[2] and, in 2013, it's projected to be 8.2 percent.[3] In contrast, the United States projects a GDP growth rate of 1.5 percent in 2013.[4]

Part of this decrease in GDP growth is, of course, due to China entering the development of services stage of its economic growth while the United States is well into its technological innovation stage. Still, China's economic growth is expected to continue for at least the next two decades, making this economic high-speed train something we feel everyone must climb aboard. What makes this difficult for many businesspeople is that relatively few know much about China outside of what they've read or heard in news broadcasts and publications, especially the fact that it's referred to as the manufacturing hub of the world. As a result, many businesspeople want to become involved in China, but they just don't know how. In our experience, gaining a basic understanding of China and its business practices rapidly paves the way.

In the next decade, according to *Forbes* magazine, there should be a number of major trends in China. Understanding these trends will allow you to take advantage of business opportunities resulting from China's increasing prosperity. The following are China's major trends:

- consumption
- income disparity
- urbanization
- environmental protection

Consumption

As we mentioned earlier, a country's GDP comes from three sources: domestic consumption, domestic investment, and trade surplus. A country's growth can still be strong, even if one component of the GDP is relatively weak, as long as the other components demonstrate significant growth. If a country has low domestic consumption, for example, it will become more reliant on trade surplus and domestic investment to generate its growth. And that's exactly what's occurred in China. In the past, China's extraordinary growth has relied on net exports and investments rather than on domestic consumption. Household consumption in Europe is in the range of 60 to 65 percent of GDP. In the United States, it's generally between 70 and 72 percent of GDP. At present, China's domestic consumption only accounts for 35 percent of the country's GDP. The Chinese government knew that such a low amount of household consumption made the economy vulnerable, as maintaining the present levels of the other two components of domestic GDP, domestic investment and the high trade surplus, was proving unsustainable. As a result, the government decided to make an effort to rebalance the economy and increase consumption. Many now feel that household consumption in China is at its lowest point, given the growth of the economy and increasing personal wealth.

With increased wealth, particularly in its middle class, China's consumers will continue to increase their consumption and eventually achieve a closer consumptive parity with the West. This offers an enormous potential for both foreign and domestic companies to increase the sale of their products in China.

According to the McKinsey Global Institute, global spending on consumer goods is expected to increase by $4.8 trillion, from $7.3 trillion in 2010 to $12.1 trillion in 2020. China is expected to account for 36 percent of global growth in consumer spending during this period.[13]

In addition, by 2025, two cities in China, Shanghai and Beijing, are expected to have 14 million households with annual incomes above $20,000. This would rank Shanghai and Beijing as fourth and fifth in the world, respectively, in terms of household incomes above this benchmark.[5]

Income Disparity

There are presently 550 million people in China who have an income up to eight times greater than the remaining 750 million Chinese citizens. Many lower-income residents are from the rural areas of China and need improved access to health care and other services, which the government will need to provide in order to raise their standard of living.[5] Social harmony is extremely important to a government that stays in power largely because the people see their lives getting better and therefore have confidence in the government's ability to address their needs. Trying to cope with this disparity by providing increased social services and more jobs, and decreasing corruption, are major goals of the government. As the government tries to improve the lives of its 750 million have-nots, a tremendous opportunity exists for those companies that can provide equipment and services to assist the government in these efforts. An example of one such opportunity would be providing health care and equipment to rural areas of China, where access to medical facilities is notoriously behind that provided to urban residents.

Urbanization

As we've mentioned earlier, China has increasingly moved from an agrarian to an industrial base, thereby transforming its economy and generating tremendous economic growth. In the coming years, it's expected that an additional 260 million Chinese will move from rural to urban China. In fact, between 2007 and 2025, the world's top ten cities, in terms of population growth, will include six Chinese cities. In addition, within this same time period, six of the top ten cities in the world, in terms of GDP growth, will be Chinese cities. In these six cities alone, GDP growth is expected to total \$3.6 trillion from 2007 to 2025.[5] This growth offers a tremendous opportunity for companies whose products address the Chinese consumer.

Environmental Protection

The fourth major trend in China in the next decade will be environmental protection. And for good reason. China needs the world's technology, brainpower, and assistance to remediate its environmental problems. The fact that environmental issues have been ignored for so long, in favor of enhanced economic growth, has only compounded the seriousness of the situation. The air is polluted from power plants utilizing coal as their primary fuel. Water is polluted from untreated industrial effluent, as well as agricultural drainage containing large amounts of fertilizer and chemicals. The food chain is suspect due to irrigating with polluted water containing industrial and agricultural runoff. These problems have become so massive that China is recognizing the unsustainability of its growth model unless the nation's environmental issues are addressed. These issues will be addressed in more detail in chapter 9, "Rising from the Ashes: China Tries to Solve Its Environmental Issues."

Assisting China in its remediation of environmental issues offers tremendous opportunity for companies with the requisite expertise. The need in China is so large for people and equipment that can help turn the tide of environmental pollution that companies focused on this area have an opportunity to provide more than a generation of work.

An Economic Goliath

In 2010, China overtook Japan to become the world's second-largest economy and replaced Germany as the world's largest exporter of merchandise. It's also the world's largest producer of automobiles, has the world's busiest seaport (Shanghai) by tonnage and, and with an annual GDP growth of 9.9 percent in the thirty years since 1979, should continue its substantive growth and become the world's largest economy by 2030.

China's economic growth benefits not only China, but also its global partners. Many companies, countries, and individuals who have a business relationship with China have also experienced substantial economic growth.[6] For example, according to Justin Yifu Lin, chief economist of the World Bank, China has become a major driving force for the world economy.[7] From 2000 to 2007, two-thirds of the economies of Africa grew at an annual rate of 5.5 percent or better, and nearly one-third at 7 percent, due to the massive raw material purchases made by China. Substantial growth rates for many Asian and Latin American countries are also attributable to Chinese purchases. For example, Japan, Argentina, Brazil, and Chile have all benefited from China's massive world buying spree.

China has also been a significant driver of global economic growth. In the 1980s and 1990s, China's contribution to the growth of global GDP was 13.4 percent and 26.7 percent, respectively, of the contribution of the United States. Between 2000 and 2009, China became the top contributor to global GDP, exceeding the United States.

A Fondness for Foreign Goods

Despite such historic growth, China is still expected to continue substantive growth over the next two decades. According to Archana Amarnath of Frost & Sullivan, by 2025 it's estimated that 65.4 percent of China's population, or 921 million people, will live in cities.[8] This urbanization, along with a larger working-age population, will accelerate China's economic growth, as urban dwellers tend to earn and spend more than rural residents. This offers a great opportunity for foreign companies to accelerate sales to China's increasingly affluent urban consumers, who have a fondness for foreign goods.

> Your average Chinese citizen believes that the quality of Chinese manufactured and agricultural products is below average. Consequently they value foreign goods over domestically produced products.

One of the reasons for this is that domestic goods have traditionally been manufactured with a focus on keeping the selling price low for consumers. As a result, domestically produced products normally have a price advantage over foreign goods, but they also have a reputation for shoddy workmanship and a limited life span. This price advantage is becoming less important to the consumer as quality issues continue to plague domestically produced products. Issues with tainted milk, exploding watermelons, or modifying the appearance of food products to make them appear fresher have created a great deal of distrust among Chinese consumers. As the standard of living increases within China, the average person's purchasing power, and ability to purchase foreign goods, will also increase.

Food safety is the number-one concern for a Chinese consumer, especially in regard to food products for infants and children. As foreign goods have a reputation for scrupulous quality, this also provides foreign companies with an enormous opportunity in the Chinese marketplace.

The World's Manufacturing Superpower

China has long been regarded as the world's manufacturing superpower. Even though some countries may be able to manufacture items more cheaply than comparable products in China are able to be manufactured, China continues to be the world's factory, accounting for 11 percent of global exports. According to the 2013 Global Manufacturing Competitiveness Index prepared by Deloitte Touche Tohmatsu and the US Council on Competiveness, China is the most competitive manufacturing nation in the world and is expected to remain so for at least the next five years. The Chinese government, in its publication *China Labour Market*, indicates that Chinese manufacturing dominance will continue for another decade.[9]

For whatever the period of time China continues its manufacturing dominance, it still faces a number of challenges. Chief among these are rising labor and infrastructure costs, as well as labor shortages.[10] China's labor costs have increased over 400 percent in a little over ten years from $0.60 per hour in 2000 to $2.80 in 2011. This is 1.5 times Thailand's labor costs per hour, 2.5 times that of the Philippines, and 3.5 times that of Indonesia.[9] During the same period of time, domestic transport costs have also increased, further driving up manufacturing costs.

In addition, most young people in China don't want the factory lives their parents had, or may still have. They don't want to work in manufacturing facilities where they perform the same tasks day after day. Unlike their parents, the younger generation, who have in the past tended to follow their parents by working in factories, are now more entrepreneurial. They desire travel outside of China and a career that offers more challenges and economic rewards. They also want more free time. These challenges are not unlike the labor challenges experienced by Japan and South Korea as they transitioned from an emerging to a developed economy.

In spite of these increased costs, China's manufacturing companies continue to be globally competitive. According to *China Daily*, the country's manufacturing competitiveness is not only based on labor costs, but also on the infrastructure necessary to support a substantial manufacturing base.[10] China, with its significant resources, has established a large and reliable infrastructure for manufacturers that is difficult for smaller countries to replicate. While lower-cost labor may initially entice many companies, the lack of infrastructure often deters them from moving their manufacturing outside of China.

Manufacturing has traditionally been focused in China's coastal cities, where labor and infrastructure costs are now at their highest. These cities provide marine, air, and rail access and are relatively easy for Westerners to get to. However, labor and infrastructure costs in central and western China are considerably cheaper, and as a result, many Western companies have moved their manufacturing operations in China inland.[6] Moreover, labor costs in China still remain, on the average, lower than other industrialized nations. China's average labor cost, for example, is $2.80 per hour, compared to $12 per hour in Brazil and $35.40 an hour in the United States.[10]

China knows it can't retain its low-cost manufacturing advantage forever.[11] Therefore it wants to transform itself into a more technologically sophisticated manufacturer.

> As one government official told us, "We want to be the country that manufactures the machines that make toothpicks, rather than manufacture the toothpicks themselves."

In accomplishing this, China is focusing on increasing its advanced manufacturing capabilities. It's also increasing the number of mergers and acquisitions, which will give it access to advanced technology, management, and marketing skills. What China envisions is a future where it owns the technology, manufactures sophisticated systems, sells these systems globally, and utilizes its manufacturing sophistication to produce higher-quality value-added products for its expanding domestic market.

China Is Modernizing

Drive into downtown Shanghai, and all you can see in any direction are skyscrapers. They're modern and visually stunning, and they dominate the landscape. It's New York on steroids. Walk down a city street, and you'll see teenagers talking on their iPhones, wearing jeans, and walking in Nike shoes. You'll see Starbucks, McDonald's, TGI Fridays, Pizza Hut, Walmart, Carrefour, and other consumer-oriented businesses surrounding buildings with names such as Boeing, Caterpillar, EADS Group, or Microsoft emblazoned on the top. Spending the night in Shanghai, you may go to a domestic hotel or choose to stay at an international chain hotel, such as Starwood, Hyatt, Hilton, Marriott, Four Seasons, or Ritz-Carlton. Less than four decades ago, China wasn't in any of these companies' business plans. Today China is at the center of most of them. No other country in the world offers them the economic opportunities of a modernizing and economically expanding China.

China's business culture is also modernizing as many of the country's foreign students and younger corporate executives return from their studies in the United States and bring with them new skills and attitudes. China's modernization has also fueled its appetite for Western technology, management techniques, risk-management assessments, marketing strategies, and other facets of modern business that can be integrated into corporate China. This creates enormous opportunities for foreign businesses that can offer new products, technologies, and skills to Chinese companies or that want to import their existing products into China. *The*

Economist projects that China will become the world's largest importer by 2014 as China's economy reaches a level of domestic consumption commensurate with other industrialized nations.[12] In line with this, Credit Suisse projects that China will become the largest consumer market in the world by 2020.

CHAPTER 2

Taking Advantage of the Chinese Economy

China today is an economic powerhouse fueled by a capitalist-based economy, foreign investment, and export-oriented growth. It's the first economy that's ever been able to attain an annual growth rate of greater than 9 percent for more than three decades. This rapid economic growth has resulted in a significant increase in Chinese government influence, both domestically and internationally. Domestically, as living standards continue to rise, Chinese people are more confident in their government's policies. Internationally, China's increasing national wealth has allowed it to exert economic influence globally. As its economy continues to outpace other global economies, particularly in the West, its global influence and prosperity will continue to increase. This provides a tremendous opportunity for businesspeople who wish to conduct business in China.

Ready, Fire, Aim!

When a company realizes that China is important to its future, we often see a flurry of activity as it wants to *rush* into the Chinese marketplace. The lightbulb has finally gone off, and it doesn't want to be late or left behind. It wants to get into the Chinese marketplace quickly, either ahead of its competitors or close behind, in order to prevent them from dominating the market.

Many companies have failed with this strategy, which we refer to as the *ready, fire, aim* approach. In fact, this really isn't an approach as much as it is a leap with one's eyes closed. They've given little consideration to management teams, Chinese employees, vendors, local laws, the cultural issues, and a host of other factors that will ultimately determine whether or not their business is successful. Instead, they believe they can hire this expertise, as they've done before in other countries, follow their experts' advice, and be successful.

> As we've stated many times: *China is unique and unlike any other business environment we've experienced.* In China, the uninformed usually get carried out on their shields.

If these companies had taken the time to understand the Chinese market, they very likely would have participated in China's extraordinary growth toward becoming the world's number-one economy. The most common autopsy report for those that failed in China is *they didn't know their market.*

Know Your Market

Recognizing that China is still an emerging market with increasing domestic prosperity, foreign companies are increasingly finding ways to address China's 1.3 billion consumers. According to McKinsey & Company, in 2008 the number of wealthy households in China was 1.6 million. By 2015 that number is expected to grow to 4 million households. This would make China the fourth-largest country in terms of number of wealthy households, after the United States, Japan, and the United Kingdom. Even so, today's wealthy Chinese account for only 1 percent of urban Chinese households. However, that number is growing at a phenomenal 16 percent per annum.

Most of the wealthy are concentrated in the eastern and south central regions of China, and 30 percent live in China's four richest *tier-one* cities of Shanghai, Beijing, Guangzhou, and Shenzhen. However, the geographical distribution of China's wealthy is changing. In the future, wealthy consumers are expected to come from smaller cities, thereby lowering the percentage of China's wealthy in tier-one cities. In fact, 75 percent of the growth in the number of wealthy consumers will come from those who don't currently live in tier-one cities.[13]

We should note that there are many definitions of what constitutes a tier-one city. In China, a tier-one designation is normally attributed to cities that have a population of greater than five million people, strong economic growth, an advanced transportation infrastructure, historical and cultural significance, and a large provincial GDP.[14] In spite of the variance in definitions, Shanghai, Beijing, Guangzhou, and Shenzhen are considered by most to be China's tier-one cities.[15]

> The Chinese consumer market differs from other consumer markets in that most Chinese consumers are younger than their global peers. According to McKinsey & Company, wealthy Chinese consumers are, on average, twenty years younger than those in the United States and Japan. In fact, 80 percent of wealthy consumers are under forty-five, compared to 30 percent in the United States and 19 percent in Japan.[13]

China's affluent consumers differ from its middle-class consumers in that the affluent consumer is richer than the middle class, but not as wealthy as the superrich. As such, they have different spending habits. According to *China Daily*, this affluent class of consumers is the reason for China's rapid rise in consumer spending and a key market driver in the coming decade. Affluent consumers are defined as those having at least $20,000 of disposable income, although the average is actually double that. There are currently 120 million affluent Chinese consumers with an annual buying power of $590 billion. By 2020, this group will number 280 million, or 20 percent of the country's population, with an annual buying power of $3.1 trillion. This number in 2020 is projected to be equal to Japan's anticipated national consumption, 28 percent more than Germany's, and 300 percent more than South Korea's.

Affluent consumers have an affinity for premium products and services.[16] Ivy Funds, which develops investment strategies for its investors, estimated the 2010 luxury goods market in China at $12.4 billion. It also predicted that the luxury goods market in China would grow to an estimated $27.9 billion by 2015 and account for a fifth of all global purchases in a global luxury market.[17] According to Vincent Lui, a partner and managing director in the Hong Kong office of the Boston Consulting Group, China's affluent consumers differ from middle-class and superrich consumers in that affluent consumers seek higher-end products for the emotional gratification they provide. They enjoy life, want to shop for the very best products they can afford, seek status and recognition, and want to exhibit their socioeconomic position through the purchase of recognizable brands.[16] Middle-class consumers, on the other hand, tend to focus on functional items with tangible benefits.

Chinese consumers have an inherent trust in the quality of foreign brands, but because Chinese consumers are younger than their global peers, they tend to be less knowledgeable about foreign luxury goods. For example, except for a few leading brands, unaided brand awareness remains quite low in China, as Chinese consumers often confuse luxury brands with premium ones, such as Nike. In addition, the spending habits of wealthy Chinese consumers are also changing. In the past, wealthy Chinese have purchased a majority of their foreign luxury brands abroad. This is changing, and wealthy Chinese have now increased their domestic purchases to where 60 percent of luxury brands are now purchased in mainland China.[13]

Although luxury and heritage brands do well in China midrange brands, such as Gap and Abercrombie & Fitch, don't fare as well.[18] Midrange brands are confusing to the Chinese consumer. One reason for this is that Chinese consumers have a difficult time understanding this segment of consumer products. They understand best-in-class and they understand value, but not a product that's in-between. In China, a product has to either be high quality or cheap in order to succeed.

Tailored Products and Messages

Many companies have successfully tailored their products for the Chinese consumer. Hilton Worldwide Inc., for example, offers high-end Chinese world travelers services such as front-desk workers who are fluent in Mandarin, Chinese-language television channels, and a breakfast menu with familiar foods such as fried dough sticks and rice porridge. Starwood Hotels & Resorts Worldwide globally offers in-room teakettles, slippers, and translation services.[13] FedEx drivers in China will wait for a customer to inspect his or her goods, and if the customer declines the merchandise, the driver will send the item back.

In addition to products, corporate messages also have to be modified to effectively communicate the need for consumers to buy their products. Take, for example, Proctor & Gamble's Oil of Olay. According to Harjot Singh, China's strategic planning director for BBDO, a global advertising agency based in New York, Oil of Olay is marketed differently in China than it is in the West.

> In the West, Oil of Olay's message is for women to love their skin. In China, however, the message is that Oil of Olay will get you a handsome husband.[19]

The Boston Consulting Group notes that De Beers, a family of companies that dominates the diamond industry, has traditionally recognized large sales of its engagement rings to Western buyers. However, in China, the concept of a Western-style engagement ring prior to marriage doesn't exist. Therefore, De Beers has marketed this type of ring to Chinese buyers not as a gift from a man to his fiancée, but as a symbol of love and commitment. Subsequently, the sale of *engagement* rings has turned out to be very successful for De Beers in China.

In some cases, tailored products may not be the best course of action. Take, for example, Swiss watchmaker Longines. The company entered the China market in the 1980s with a China-specific product line. However, according to Longines's vice president of marketing, Li Li, Chinese consumers "felt suspicious when they discovered products on offer in other countries were drastically different from those being offered in China."[13] The company changed direction and sold the same products in China as it sold internationally. China is now Longines's largest market.

The Chinese Market, a Matrix of Microsegments

Many companies believe that their sales and marketing models, business management techniques, and organizational structure, which have proved successful outside of China, will also work in China with little or no modification. As a result, many companies enter the Chinese marketplace unfamiliar with local competitors, distribution systems, the culture, geographic preferences, individual mannerisms, and local marketing techniques that are necessary for them to successfully sell their products. This is an all too familiar theme for those who decide to just *go for it* and enter the Chinese market quickly and with little preparation. "Just get us into China, and our products will sell themselves," companies often tell us.

Companies know that China, with its over one billion consumers, is likely the holy grail of consumer markets.

> Some companies take the time to comprehend the country's culture, geography, mannerisms, and other unique factors. They want to know how they can understand the Chinese consumer's uniqueness and adapt their product lines accordingly. These companies almost invariably succeed. Other companies believe their dominance in the United States and in other global markets guarantees them success in China. All they need, they tell us, is the right connection in China, and their products will fly off the shelves. These companies almost invariably fail.

It's like building an outdoor ice-skating rink in Florida. Great product; wrong environment. Companies that succeed know the environment before they begin construction and therefore enclose the ice-skating rink in an air-conditioned enclosure.

Some companies also believe that Chinese consumers are largely unsophisticated. They argue that, outside of a small percentage of the country who are part of the middle class, affluent, or superrich, Chinese consumers are all the same. Their view is that a majority of the Chinese people aren't familiar with most consumer products unless they're exposed to them through marketing campaigns or by word of mouth. Consequently they're the same as every other global consumer, who only requires awareness and a value proposition in order to purchase a product. As a result, these companies believe that *one size fits all* and that shoppers on the streets of Beijing and Shanghai are similar to cosmopolitan shoppers in Chicago or Berlin. "Consumers need to be told which products to buy," they tell us. "With substantive and repetitive marketing, consumers will purchase the products that are presented to them."

Our experience has shown that these assumptions don't apply in China. The assumption that the buying habits of the Chinese consumer are on par with those of consumers in other nations can quickly turn into a costly mistake when companies find their goods failing to capture market share in the world's most dynamic economy. In an illustration provided by Accenture, a multinational management consulting company, a major US appliance manufacturer thought it had China figured out. It was one of the best-selling consumer products companies in the United States, had strong brand recognition, and had a reputation for excellence. But after three years in China, its sales remained minuscule. The problem, as it turned out, was that it had an American mind-set, instituted American business practices, and hired American managers in a market that was not monolithic. It wasn't America. Instead, the environment was uniquely Chinese.[20] Accenture went on to note that China is composed of a matrix of marketing microsegments. These microsegments are further broken down according to differences in consumer tastes that vary by geography, product category, and buyer segment.[21]

One size doesn't fit all in China. What works in Europe or the United States may not work in China. Moreover, what works in Beijing may be completely ineffective in Shenzhen.

The MZ-HCI Group, the world's largest independent investor relations firm, notes that the average consumer no longer exists and that customers increasingly see themselves as unique individuals. Marketing to these individuals often involves a knowledge of unspoken cultural and social patterns. This is particularly true in China.[22] Foreign companies that have been successful in China have accurately gauged the needs of Chinese buyers and have culturally and geographically customized their goods to the country's various microsegments.[21] They've understood how to adapt their products to satisfy individual needs.

Attracting the Consumer

Price point is not the motivating factor in a Chinese consumer's purchase of a product. Accenture's research showed that a brand's perceived contribution to the community, such as the creation of local jobs or support of important local issues, as well as perceived harmony with the buyer's personal values, can be more influential than pricing. A brand's national origin is also influential with Chinese consumers. German and French brands, for example, may have low consumer awareness, but the country of origin gives the goods a high level of consideration with consumers because the country of origin has a reputation for engineering precision and luxury goods, respectively.[21] Japanese brands, on the other hand, have a high level of awareness, but are sometimes low on consumer preferences because of China's historical conflicts with Japan and its current dispute over the Diaoyu/Senkaku islands in the East China Sea.

Methods for attracting the Chinese consumer differ from those in other countries. For example, word of mouth carries exceptional weight with Chinese consumers, more so than in most countries. Many companies institute brand loyalty clubs to help perpetuate word-of-mouth promotion of their products. Product reviews, particularly when coupled with endorsements, are unusually powerful in attracting consumers and promoting brand recognition.

Direct mail and cold calling may work well in some countries, but they don't work well in China. They are viewed as intrusive.[21] However, multimedia kiosks and video boards, which may be viewed as intrusive in the United States and Europe, have a significant impact on the Chinese consumer.

Most companies expect China's current love affair and demand for foreign products to continue through at least 2020. Chinese consumers, with an affinity for foreign goods, both in luxury brands and inexpensive products, have made China the biggest market for many foreign companies. This demand is increasingly driven by foreign manufacturers adapting their products to Chinese tastes in the various microsegments that comprise the Chinese marketplace.

Foreign Companies Dramatically Expand

Increasingly, foreign companies are realizing that their future is in China. Even though Chinese brands generally enjoy a 90+ percent awareness, the average Chinese citizen has a greater degree of trust in a foreign brand. Take automobiles, for example. All premium and exotic car manufacturers expect China to be their largest market. Many forecast the Chinese super-car market to grow by 20 to 30 percent per year for the next five to ten years. Rolls Royce estimates that it will sell eight hundred cars in China in 2013, surpassing the United States and making China its largest market. Audi sales in China have surpassed Germany's, to become its largest market. Audi expects to sell more than one million cars in China in the next three years, surpassing both BMW and Mercedes-Benz in China. Mercedes-Benz sales in China have increased by nearly 50 percent, and Porsche is on track to have China pass the United States as its largest market.

Chinese consumers have also shown an affinity for foreign retailers. UK-based Tesco, the world's number-three retailer, believes that its current expansion program will quadruple its existing annual revenue in China to $7 billion over the next five years. Japan's Familymart plans to increase its current one thousand stores in China to forty-five hundred by 2015, and to eight thousand outlets by 2020. In apparel, Ralph Lauren plans to open sixty stores in China in the next three years, and Michael Kors plans to open fifteen stores in China the first year and one hundred stores in the next three to five years. Hugo Boss plans to add fifty stores to its existing eighty-six, and Prada plans to open 160 stores in China by 2016, given that 40 percent of its growth and 72 percent of its increase in profits comes from China. Sweden's H&M chain recently opened its one hundredth store in Nanning, and European fashion company C&A plans to expand from eleven stores to 150 stores throughout China by 2015.[23] The list of companies expanding in China continues to grow as companies want to take advantage of China's love affair with foreign goods and products.

Logistical Challenges

Among the challenges foreign companies face are the logistical challenges inherent with conducting business in China. Supply chain effectiveness is a challenge for foreign companies, especially where customers may be a distance from China's ports and major air hubs. As a result, logistical costs can be up to three times higher than those of the United States, the United Kingdom, or Japan. Part of the reason is that there's more demand for rail, ports, air, and river services than current capacity permits. In addition, the Chinese rail system, although it's undergoing improvement, is primarily geared to move bulk commodities, such as coal, over long distances.[21] It doesn't have the same efficiency in moving containers from ports to inland cities. Moreover, roads in some regions of China are not well-maintained and prove to be a challenge for the overland transport of goods. The government knows about these bottlenecks and is increasing infrastructure investments in an effort to try and address these issues.

E-Commerce

According to *The Economist,* China's e-commerce sales will soon surpass those of the United States. E-commerce in China is dominated by Alibaba, a family of Chinese Internet-based businesses; two of Alibaba's portals in 2012 handled $170 billion in sales, more than eBay and Amazon combined. Alibaba also accounts for more than 60 percent of all parcels delivered in China. The Boston Consulting Group indicates that apparel is the most popular e-commerce buying category, comprising 50 percent of all online sales in China, compared to 20 percent in the United States.[18] Digital content makes up one-third of all online sales.

> By 2020, China's e-commerce market is expected to be larger than the combined e-commerce markets of the United States, Great Britain, Japan, Germany, and France.[24]

China currently has an estimated 193 million online shoppers, more than any other country.[18] The Boston Consulting Group predicts that e-commerce could account for more than 8 percent of all retail sales in China by 2015. The primary reason for online shopping's popularity, according to the Acquity Group, a digital marketing and global branding e-commerce company, is that it's convenient. In addition, consumers find that online shopping gives them greater product selection and provides the ability to compare prices across various vendors.

Lauren Indvik, of Mashable, indicates that there are a number of factors driving China's e-commerce growth:[18]

- government-subsidized Internet
- low shipping costs
- growing middle class

The spread of government-subsidized high-speed Internet access and Internet-connected cell phones provides e-commerce companies with a potential shoppers' pool of 513 million, or 40 percent of China's current population. Broadband Internet access in China is relatively inexpensive, around $10 per month, compared with $30 per month in India and $27 per month in Brazil.[18]

Another factor driving China's e-commerce growth, according to the Boston Consulting Group, is that shipping costs for Chinese companies are about one-sixth those of their American counterparts. This makes ordering goods online relatively inexpensive for the average consumer and gives Chinese e-commerce companies an advantage not enjoyed by those in many other countries.

A third factor driving e-commerce growth, according to the Acquity Group, is that China's middle class is rapidly expanding and is expected to grow from 200 million to 800 million in the next twenty years. Middle-class shoppers have shown the highest affinity for e-commerce transactions.

Combined, all these factors allow those willing to become involved in China's growing economy the opportunity to participate and prosper in what will become the principal global economy for at least the next two decades.

CHAPTER 3

Government Subsidies and the Home-Court Advantage

What's made China the export powerhouse it is today is that it's able to produce its goods cheaper than anyone else, or on a scale in which smaller countries find it difficult to compete.[25] Most assume that this lower cost of goods is due to an inherent in-country economic benefit of cheaper labor, as well as less expensive infrastructure costs, such as electricity and water. And that's, for the most part, true. However, Chinese government subsidies for many industries have allowed many companies to produce their goods at an artificially low cost.

A subsidy is a direct or indirect transfer of resources from the government to a producer or exporter. In other words, a subsidy exists if there's a financial contribution or price support by the government where a benefit is conferred.[26]

According to a study performed by Capital Trade Incorporated and submitted to the US-China Economic and Security Review Commission, a financial contribution can be

- a direct transfer of funds, such as a grant, loan, or equity infusion;
- a potential direct transfer of funds, such as a loan guarantee;
- forgoing or not collecting revenue that is otherwise due, as with tax credits or deductions from taxable income;

- providing goods and services other than general infrastructure; or
- purchasing goods.

In the above examples, foreign companies may benefit from these subsidies in a number of ways:

- The interest rate on the loans they receive may be less than comparable commercial-rate loans.
- The government buys shares at a higher price than other investors or invests in a company in which other investors would not invest.
- The government forgives principal and/or interest.
- The tax paid by the company is less than that paid by a comparable company without a tax program.
- The goods or services provided are at costs below prevailing market conditions.
- Government-provided assistance replaces some of the corporate obligations of the company.
- Export transport or freight costs are less than domestic transport or freight costs.
- The terms for the products or services produced are more favorable for export than for domestic consumption.

A Lack of Transparency

Not all subsidies are easy to spot. They're not transparent. For example, municipal and local governments routinely provide water and electricity to companies whose products are exported, thereby allowing a company to manufacture its products at an artificially low cost. In addition, the government can subsidize a company by providing low or free rent. It can also provide land at no cost or at a price substantially below market value. All these methods for subsidizing a company lack transparency and are difficult to substantiate. But the end result is still the same. Due to government subsidies, China is able to manufacture goods at a price that makes the manufactured products of other countries uncompetitive.

In addition to subsidies, many provinces and municipalities relax enforcement of labor laws and environmental standards for companies in key economic sectors.[25] These subsidies are very difficult to document, yet they give Chinese companies a substantial economic advantage.

One of the most difficult subsidies to document are loans by China's banks to state-owned enterprises (SOEs). According to Peter Navarro, a professor of economics and public policy at the Paul Merage School of Business, University of California, Irvine, these loans are often issued at little or no interest rate and without expectation of repayment. Many of these SOEs are in heavy industries, such as petroleum and steel, and employ a great number of people.[27] As a result, the government is loath to allow them to go bankrupt, even if they lose a great deal of money, because of the loss of jobs and social unrest that would ensue.

The Home-Court Advantage

In what's considered by many to be a subsidy, China uses a value-added tax (VAT) rebate system for export industries.

> A value-added tax is a form of consumption tax where the seller charges the VAT to the buyer and then pays this tax to the government.

In China, a VAT tax is imposed in the domestic production and distribution process. However, in many cases, the government simply collects and then rebates this tax for exports.[27] In other cases, exporting firms are simply exempt from the tax. These practices create an uneven playing field in that the VAT rebate acts as an export subsidy and therefore violates World Trade Organization (WTO) rules, which prohibit export subsidies.

Subsidies make Chinese firms more competitive in the world market. Since China joined the WTO in 2001, government subsidies have annually financed over 20 percent of the expansion of the country's manufacturing capacity. These subsidies give China the ability to not only be competitive, but to also dominate markets in which it has no labor-cost advantage. In solar, steel, glass, paper, and auto parts, Chinese labor was 2 to 7 percent of production costs. Imported materials and energy accounted for the remainder of the manufacturing cost.[28] Yet the cost of Chinese auto parts was substantially below that of other industrialized countries with equally efficient manufacturing processes!

Taking autos and auto parts as an example, according to the Office of the United States Trade Representative, the Chinese government provided auto and auto parts manufacturers, between 2009 and 2011, more than $1 billion in subsidies. Autos and auto parts have been an increasing focus of the Chinese government, and between 2002 and 2011, China's exports of autos and auto parts increased more than ninefold, from $7.4 billion to $69.1 billion, catapulting China from the world's sixteenth-largest to the fifth-largest autos and auto parts exporters.

Some may argue that giving consumers access to cheaper parts is good. After all, given the same quality, most, if not all, of us would choose the cheaper-priced product. That works for consumers. However, on a micro level, the production of autos and auto parts in the United States is a key component of our nation's manufacturing base. In 2011, for example, manufacturers in the United States produced over $350 billion worth of autos and auto parts. Typically this sector accounts for about 5 percent of the US GDP and 16 percent of all durable goods shipments. It also employed, as of July 2012, over 800,000 American workers.[29] The sale of autos and auto parts by Chinese companies at artificially low prices jeopardizes many of these jobs, as well as has a direct impact on the American economy.

The reason that China's goods are priced so low, compared to those produced by other industrialized countries, is not only because of China's cheaper labor rate. It's also, as we mentioned, because of government subsidies. In 2000, according to the *Harvard Business Review*, labor-intensive products constituted 37 percent of all Chinese exports. By 2010, they fell to 14 percent. Yet China's exports continued to grow. The difference was government subsidies, which now allowed China to produce technologically advanced products and undercut unsubsidized foreign manufacturers. In 2011, the United States imported 560 percent more technologically advanced products from China than it exported.[28]

The Harvard Business Review gives two examples of how government subsidies can create a dominant global position for the product that's subsidized. In 2000, China was a net importer of steel, with 13 percent of world imports and 16 percent of global output. By 2007, it became the world's largest producer, consumer, and exporter of steel. During this same period, government energy subsidies to China's steel industry totaled

$27 billion. Today China produces half the world's steel, which sells for 25 percent less than US or European steel, even though China has no technological advantages.

In a second example, China became the world's largest paper producer, selling its paper at a substantial discount to both European and US paper. This was largely the result of $33 billion in government subsidies to paper manufacturers from 2002 to 2009.[30] With a similar subsidy package, foreign firms would be much more competitive against Chinese companies and experience increased output, exports, workers' earnings, and enhanced growth. Inversely, without these subsidies, China would experience a decline in its economy.

Promises Broken

In 2000, prior to China joining the WTO, member nations informed China that subsidies were not permitted among WTO member nations and that they would have to discontinue this practice. China, eager to gain entry to the WTO, promptly agreed. According to Usha C. V. Haley, professor of management and director of the Robbins Center for Global Business and Strategy at West Virginia University, and George T. Haley, professor of marketing and director of the Center for International Industry Competitiveness at the University of New Haven, the WTO requires annual notification from members on subsidies they maintain. However, until April 13, 2006, there was a total lack of compliance on the part of China, as it failed to acknowledge subsidies to domestic producers.

Finally, on that date, China identified seventy-eight subsidy programs that existed from 2001 to 2004. However, it ignored WTO directives that dictate that members should provide sufficient information *to enable other members to evaluate the trade effects to understand the operation of notified subsidy programs.* Instead, China's report simply stated that several central government ministries and agencies distributed and monitored subsidies, and extensive legislation in China supported these subsidies. No data were provided for anyone to assess the trade effects of any subsidy or the amount of the subsidy. China's notification focused almost entirely on subsidies to foreign-invested enterprises (FIEs).

> A foreign-invested enterprise (FIE) is a legal structure that permits a company to set up its business in a foreign country.

China's notification, therefore, ignored subsidy programs supported by provincial and municipal governments, favorable lending policies by commercial banks, financial preferences for SOEs, providing electricity at below-market rates, and other forms of subsidies that reduced the financial burden on industry.[31]

Subsidies and State-Owned Enterprises

It's estimated that the Chinese government has spent in excess of $300 billion subsidizing its biggest SOEs between 1985 and 2005.[30] SOEs provide the Chinese government with an overwhelming economic advantage in international trade, as their price advantages all but eliminate foreign competition.

SOEs are also used by the government to maintain social stability, as they employ a greater number of people than non-state-owned businesses would find acceptable. Since SOEs are government subsidized, bankruptcy is not an option unless the government permits it.

Subsidies and Unemployment

Throughout China's history, a disgruntled citizenry has played a prominent role in leading social reforms. The government may be the face of China, but the real power behind the throne is the people of China. The government knows this, and the Chinese Communist Party (CCP or Party) remains in power largely because a majority of China's people believe that life is getting better and that their standard of living is increasing. And since 1978, that's been the case as the Chinese economy has experienced unprecedented growth.

Perhaps nothing creates social unrest more than unemployment, the inability to find a job. Mao Zedong knew this in the 1950s when he instituted the iron rice bowl, or guaranteed lifetime employment. As a result, everyone who was of working age knew they had a job working directly for the government or in a government SOE. This maintained societal stability, but at the same time, it was also bankrupting the country. Senior government officials soon demanded a change, and the country instituted a series of reforms geared toward making SOEs more efficient and less dependent on cheap labor. The problem with this was that less labor usage equaled unemployment, and with the government being the country's only employer, more and more workers were out of work. The government walked a fine line. It was the proverbial catch-22: cut labor to create more efficient SOEs, which used less labor and didn't overburden the country's financial resources, while at the same time, find jobs for unemployed workers so as to not risk an internal rebellion.

With layoffs, downsizing, and increased efficiencies within SOEs, the number of surplus state workers in China began to increase. According to the National Bureau of Statistics in China, employees in government collectives decreased from 36.21 million in 1992 to 31.47 million in 1995, and again to 11.22 million in 2002. In addition, the number of employees in state-owned units decreased from 112.61 million in 1995 to 71.63 million in 2002.[32]

In addition to increased unemployment, the government at this time also had the additional problem of workers migrating from rural to urban areas in search of better-paying jobs. This rural-to-urban migration further increased the number of people looking for work in China's cities. If a solution to the increasing unemployment wasn't found quickly, the Party feared it would lose control.

As it turned out, that solution came from the private sector, which was allowed to reemerge in 1978 by China's leader at the time, Deng Xiaoping. Expanding rapidly after prohibitions on private ownership were rescinded, private companies hired and trained many of the unemployed.[33] Today China's private sector is, and will continue to be for the foreseeable future, the primary driver for the creation of jobs in China.

Subsidies and Private-Sector Firms

Since the private sector assumed the role of China's largest employer, the government goes out of its way to make sure it receives all necessary support. According to *The Economist*, in a review by Beijing research house *Fathom China*, researchers examined fifty prominent private-sector Chinese firms and found that forty-five of these were subsidized by the government. Geeley Automobile, which purchased Sweden's Volvo, for example, received a government subsidy that amounted to 51.3 percent of its net profit; China Yurun Food's government subsidy was 36.1 percent of its net profit; and Uni-President's was 18.2 percent of its net profit. Respectively, they received $141 million, $84 million, and $9 million in subsidies.[30]

The United States is not alone in accusing China of providing subsidies to private companies. The European Union (EU) has also made such accusations. One such accusation made by the European Union alleged Chinese government subsidies to manufacturers of solar panels, solar glass, and mobile-telecommunications equipment. In a complaint lodged by the trade bloc's EU ProSun, the company alleges that Chinese glass sold in the European Union is below cost and thereby damages the bloc's solar glass industry. The bloc is investigating alleged dumping and Chinese subsidies of $27 billion per year for solar panels and various related components that China exports to Europe.[34]

The European Union has been responsive in past cases of alleged dumping by imposing an antidumping duty. For example, in a case involving Chinese bicycles, the European Union imposed a duty of 48.5 percent when it determined that the bicycles were being illegally dumped. In addition, the European Union is conducting a more far-reaching investigation as to whether Chinese bicycle makers have circumvented these antidumping duties by shipping bicycles to Europe via Indonesia, Malaysia, Sri Lanka, and Tunisia.[35]

A substantial amount of government assistance to China's private sector comes from local and municipal governments. Providing subsidies to local companies often provides big rewards for local governments, as it enables private companies to develop new products as well as hire additional local staff at little or no cost.

Some believe that local subsidized support for companies may be a big investment risk, as subsidized companies may not turn a profit and don't always have the access to bank loans that's been given to SOEs.[36] In addition, with the country's new emphasis on anticorruption, local politicians may be keeping their heads low and wanting to remain anonymous in arranging for private company subsidies. Beijing is increasingly looking closely at local governments for signs of crony capitalism and corruption.

In our opinion, it's extremely difficult to build a private company of any consequence in China without direct or indirect government support. The government is always in the background for all business transactions, whether approving or directing contracts, granting access to land, subsidizing utilities, approving permits and licenses, or other business-related costs. Nothing of substance is accomplished in China without tacit government approval. Moreover, the government views subsidies as a good business practice. If a private company can gain an economic foothold outside of China, can create employment, or can enhance China's national or international influence, then that company will almost certainly receive a government subsidy. Government officials are the linchpin for obtaining government subsidies. They arrange for, and maintain, subsidies. It's not unlike the US Congress in many ways, as politicians push for projects in their home districts where local resources can be employed.

Politicians in China, as in most other parts of the world, come and go. They're in favor at times and out of favor at other times. When a business owner finds a local, provincial, or national government official who actively supports his or her business, that official has an unknown time span in which he or she can exercise influence. If that person is reassigned, the official replacing him or her may or may not be as supportive of the private company as the predecessor was. SOEs don't have this issue, as they're owned by the government. This gives them the advantage of state ownership and sponsorship, as well as a more stable and predictable subsidy income stream than that experienced by private Chinese companies.

Subsidies and the Job Crunch

According to EconomyWatch.com, there will be an estimated 15 million new entrants into China's job market annually between 2003 and 2015, with only 8 million new jobs being created annually during this same period of time.[33]

BBC News reports that young and well-educated people are having a difficult time finding a job in China's increasingly competitive job market.

In 2013, there will be an estimated 6.9 million college graduates in China, and many of these graduates will be unable to find work in their chosen profession, if at all.[37] Furthermore, these numbers may actually be low. The government's unemployment numbers are based on standards that are narrower than Western countries might normally expect, as they only consider registered urban unemployment. People who work for SOEs, for example, are not taken into consideration in the government's figures, as the Chinese government considers them employees of the state. Rural workers and urban workers who have seasonal jobs are also not considered. As a result, many feel that the government's unemployment rate is inaccurate by the standards of most industrialized nations. As an illustration, the government published a national unemployment rate of 3.6 percent in 2001, while the actual number is believed to be between 8 and 9 percent.[33] In industrialized northern China, the unemployment rate is closer to 25 percent.

With such disappointing employment numbers and more people entering the workforce than there are available jobs, the government has taken decisive action. As a result, there have been increased subsidies to many SOEs and other large employers so that companies can hire more unemployed. The government has also provided or approved similar funding for private businesses at the local and provincial levels.

We've been a witness to the end result of many of these corporate hirings. We've gone to government offices and literally have seen half of the office staff sitting at their desks reading newspapers, or else viewed rows of empty desks, where employees don't even bother to come to work. In a meeting with a national government official, we asked about the apparent lack of work for such a large staff and the rows of empty desks that we'd seen. We expected the government official to tell us that we arrived during an employee break period or when employees were summoned to a group meeting. Those explanations would, on their face, seem halfway reasonable. But he was straightforward and told us that the government wanted a certain number of people working in his office and that he hired them in order to satisfy this employment directive. Since his budget was increased accordingly, he didn't have a problem with so many idle workers.

Subsidies and Currency Manipulation

It comes as no surprise that for decades the United States, as well as a great number of other countries, have accused China of currency manipulation. China simply undervalues its currency. According to attorney Elizabeth L. Pettis, by manipulating the value of its currency, China is able to keep the price of its goods low, as well as keep the cost of goods produced in other countries at a level that's too high for the average person in China to purchase.[38] China is then able to promote the growth of its exports, while protecting its industries from international competition. The mechanism used to accomplish this is fairly straightforward. The Chinese government prohibits all dollar-to-yuan exchanges except those to which it is a party, directly or through official forex banks.[39] In addition, the Chinese government requires authorized exchange transactions to occur at a government-determined and administered rate.

> This undervaluation by China of its currency meets the definition of subsidy in that it makes exported Chinese products less expensive than they would be without this government support. According to Paul Krugman, a Nobel-winning economist, government support of the Chinese yuan provides Chinese manufacturers with a large cost advantage and is responsible for China's huge trade surpluses.[39]

It's Not a One-Way Street

When someone mentions government subsidies to businesses, most of us think of China. After all, there's hardly a week that goes by when we're not reading something regarding China subsidizing its national and local industries. What we seldom hear, however, is charges of US subsidies to domestic businesses. However, such accusations have been made by China, which, in a complaint filed with the WTO, claims that the United States subsidizes its clean energy projects. Most feel that this complaint is in direct response to a US Commerce Department tariff of as high as 250 percent on Chinese solar cells, since China's complaint was filed eight days after the imposition of this tariff. The US government alleges that Chinese solar cell manufacturers gain an improper benefit from government subsidies and caused at least four US solar manufacturers to go bankrupt in 2012. China's complaint was the seventh against the United States, which has lodged fifteen WTO complaints against China,[40] more than half of all WTO challenges against the Chinese government.

Who's in Charge?

One of the problems in taking action against countries suspected of subsidizing their domestic industries is that no one seems to be in charge of initiating action against countries that make illegal subsidies. Surprisingly, it's not the WTO. The WTO is not structured, according to Clyde Prestowitz, president of the Economic Strategy Institute, to enforce its own rules, as it doesn't monitor the policies, practices, and actions of its members. It also doesn't gather data or issue warning letters. Instead, it relies on member countries to file formal complaints and enter a dispute-settlement process.

Once a complaint is filed, a formal dispute-settlement panel is appointed and an investigation conducted. The panel will then listen to arguments from the contending parties and render a judgment. As you might imagine, this can be a lengthy process, during which time the infringing country continues its subsidies. Therefore, many times, countries hesitate to even enter into the process. Furthermore, national governments don't proactively initiate cases before the WTO. Instead, they only take action after corporations file formal complaints with them. Most corporations, however, are hesitant to do this, because when they file such a compliant, they're initiating it against the very country whose market they wish to enter or where they wish to increase market share. If you were Caterpillar, for example, would you file a complaint against China, the very market you're targeting for your global expansion? Probably not. You'd let the US government do it and plead that it's out of your hands. Unfortunately, neither the WTO nor the US government works this way.

This dilemma doesn't get any better when you try to approach it from the political side. If you're the president of the United States and require China's help with North Korea or Iran, would you draw a line in the sand on subsidies? Probably not. Consequently, we're wholeheartedly in agreement with Clyde Prestowitz that the antisubsidy codes of the WTO are essentially unenforceable.[41] When the question is asked of us as to who's in charge, it's difficult to find a satisfactory answer. Seemingly no one is.

CHAPTER 4

Working as a Foreigner in China

A little over thirty years ago, Beijing would probably have been regarded as a tourist destination for the adventurous foreigner, rather than as a business destination. Today that's changed. Foreigners are becoming increasingly common in China. And why not? It has a booming economy, has a quarter of the world's consumers, and is the planet's manufacturing hub. To gain its economic prominence, China has had to adapt to outside cultures, establish rules of laws, acquire global expertise, and educate its citizenry in these socioeconomic changes in a relatively short period of time.

When we think of China, we generally have an image of a uniform society, where everyone speaks Chinese, eats somewhat the same food, and has basically the same philosophical outlook. However, below the surface, China is much more complex. It's all and none of these things at the same time. It's a blend of various cultures, languages, and ethnicities that can manifest itself in a single nationalistic voice, the voice of an ethnic minority, or that of a resident of a particular geographic area. Chinese society isn't homogenous, and although 92 percent of its population consists of an ethnic majority, the Han, 8 percent of its population is composed of fifty-five ethnic minorities.[42]

Outsiders and Insiders

Many times foreigners feel that, even though they've lived in China for many years, they're still never really accepted into Chinese society. To a great extent, that's true. The social, economic, and cultural aspects of China have interacted over thousands of years to produce a business environment unlike that in other parts of the world.

In the earliest days of China, intensifying lawlessness, as well as varying climates and natural disasters, created havoc with individual farmers. In response, these farmers started to form communes or villages where they could pool their resources and increase their chances of survival. In these communes, they developed a collectivist way of thinking, where the good of the village superseded the welfare of an individual. All members of the village were considered insiders.

Insiders primarily conducted business within their group for fear of being cheated by outsiders, who often didn't share the group's values. As such, insiders primarily trusted only those who lived within their village. Those who lived beyond those boundaries were considered outsiders and were looked upon with suspicion. This collectivist way of thinking spread throughout China over succeeding generations.

There are a number of reasons why collectivism, which focuses on the group, still exists in present-day China. The primary reason is that most Chinese believe that group membership maintains harmony through interdependence and cooperation, thereby avoiding conflicts within the group.[43] They correspondingly believe that functioning as individuals, they would have less of a support network and a decreased synergistic relationship with other members of society. This way of thinking has been passed down from generation to generation, and it's still a dominant part of the current Chinese culture.

A collective group may be any size and encompass any level of society. It may, for example, consist of employees of a company, members of an organization, or an entire ethnic group.[44] It also may encompass all of China, or a single city, such as Shanghai, where residents speak a dialect not found, for instance, in Hangzhou or Suzhou, cities close to Shanghai but where an altogether different dialect is spoken.

Collectivism, although currently strong in China, is starting to become less prevalent. One of the biggest reasons for this has been the globalization of China. As China has become less isolated and its inhabitants more affluent, there's been a trend toward individualism. This trend will better enable expats, or foreigners who live in China, to achieve some degree of socioeconomic acceptance.[45] However, it's rare that a foreigner will ever fully integrate into Chinese culture.

Americans Are from Mars; Chinese Are from Venus

To the average Chinese businessperson, we're outsiders and they're insiders. According to Andrew Williamson, the relationship between China and the West has been described by one Chinese commentator as "Americans are from Mars; Chinese are from Venus. We are ready to be your friends, while keeping our characteristics."[46] Foreigners are seen by Chinese businesspeople as individualist outsiders, with few moral overtones. Chinese, on the other hand, view themselves as collectivist insiders, governed by pragmatism and wearing the philosophical shroud of Confucius. This philosophical belief is in the background of every business or personal discussion you'll have as a foreigner in China.

Confucius is the philosophical shroud that hangs over Chinese society. In fact, China and Confucianism are inexorably tied together. Like socialism, Confucianism promotes collective interests and community welfare.[47] It espouses social cohesion and ritual behaviors, rather than adherence to a strict legal code. Ritual behaviors can mean reciprocity, such as the Golden Rule: "What you do not want done to yourself, do not do to others." It can also mean filial piety, respect of children for their parents, or other forms of behavior that contribute to social cohesion.[48] As a result, China's Confucian society is less concerned with the strict legality of a situation than the effect it would have in their hierarchical society, such as on family and friends.

One Country, Many Languages

We frequently speak with businesspeople who tell us that they're learning Chinese. But *Chinese* is not a language. Instead, it's an umbrella term that covers a number of languages spoken in China that share a common writing system. China is linguistically fragmented, with numerous geographic areas having their own native dialect or language. Unless you live in that geographic area or learn the language or dialect spoken there, it's likely you won't understand what's being said. Overall, it's estimated that there are up to 250 separate languages spoken in China, such as Cantonese, some of which have dozens of different dialects.[49] Although Mandarin is the official language within China, and the one most foreigners learn, there are twenty separate dialects of Mandarin.[50] Complicating things even further for foreigners attempting to learn a Chinese language or dialect is the fact that most are tonal, meaning they use pitch to distinguish grammatical meaning.

The farther north you go in China, the fewer people will speak or understand English. This is more than likely due to one's proximity to Hong Kong, where English is understood and spoken throughout the city. In Shenzhen, a city in southern China, about a forty-minute car ride from Hong Kong, almost everyone speaks English. Beijing, in contrast, which is a three-and-a-half-hour plane flight north of Hong Kong, has relatively few people outside of those working in hotels, tourist attractions, and Western-style restaurants who speak English. We've gotten into more than a few taxis at the Beijing airport where the driver couldn't understand where we were going until one of us dialed the hotel's phone number and handed the phone to him. The hotel operator was then able to tell the taxi driver, in a language or dialect he understood, the name of the hotel and how to get there.

A Socialist-Capitalist-Communist Society

According to the current Chinese constitution, China is "a socialist state under the people's democratic dictatorship led by the working class and based on the alliance of workers and peasants."[48] In other words, China is a communist country under the leadership of the CCP, and its policies become national policies. Period!

Even though China's government is communist, China is every bit as capitalistic as the United States or other nations with a free-market system.

Understanding Chinese businesspeople's motivation isn't difficult. Their sole purpose in business is to make money, and if you're in a partnership with them and they're not making money, you're soon going to be rowing the corporate boat by yourself, as they'll move on to projects that do make them money. Capitalism is now an entrenched part of Chinese culture at all levels of society.

A Foreigner in China

Living as a foreigner in China gives one a good sense of perspective. It shows that individuals from two disparate cultures, with different historical socioeconomic legacies, ideologies, philosophies, and cultural guidelines, can effectively work together for mutual profit and benefit. Some find this surprising given that both countries are so different. For example, the United States is a country governed by laws that provide a rigid legal framework and code of conduct. China is somewhat similar in this respect in that it's enacted laws similar to those of the United States. But it also exhibits a marked difference in that it doesn't always choose to enforce these laws. Instead, it will selectively enforce laws in accordance with its national agenda. For example, China has very strict laws on environmental pollution. Yet because the country is growing so rapidly, the government doesn't enforce many of these laws. If it did, the end result might be that many power plants would have to be closed and therefore harm the country's national agenda for increasing the nation's energy supply. That's an unacceptable outcome in the eyes of the government.

Foreign companies are increasingly establishing offices in China. The Chaoyang district of Beijing, for example, an area on the east side of the city where foreigners tend to work and socialize, contains three thousand foreign businesses, with more than one hundred of the world's top five hundred companies having an office there.[51] Fueling this expansion is the fact that China continues to demonstrate sustained growth in the face of an economic downturn in the West.

With this expansion, most foreign companies have elected to import management skills from their corporate offices and fill less technical positions with local Chinese labor. As a result, there's been a rapidly increasing expat population. Over 600,000 foreigners,[51] or expats, legally work in China today, with many more working there illegally. According to *Shanghai Daily*, 173,000 expats live in Shanghai, a 6.7 percent increase from 2011. In fact, China's expat population has grown every year since 2000.[52] More adventuresome foreigners, as well as those who can't find employment in their native country, have gone to work for Chinese companies, which have an increasing thirst for foreign expertise.

In response to the growing number of foreigners working in the country, the Chinese government has introduced a green card system, allowing foreign citizens to gain permanent residency within China.[52]

Look before You Leap

Working in China can be both frustrating and rewarding. It will also, without question, be an adjustment. Knowing what to expect will make that adjustment easier.

Prior to making a decision to live and work in China, one should be aware of the following points:[42]

- Employment contracts are signed in both English and Chinese, but in a dispute, the Chinese version prevails. Therefore, have the translated Chinese document checked by an attorney or other competent professional prior to signing.
- Have medical insurance that can be used within China, as many of China's public hospitals don't accept foreign medical insurance.
- Check for the availability of Western hospitals in the area in which you expect to live, if you desire Western medical care. China is in many ways still immature, and the medical care you're used to may not be available in some areas. Also, some public hospitals, which are subsidized by the government, may refuse to treat foreigners.
- You won't be able to pay with a check in China. Instead, you'll be expected to wire funds, use a credit card, or pay with cash.

Finding a Job

When foreigners want to find a job in China, there are several things they can do to increase their chances for employment:[53]

- Visit China and get a feel for the environment.
- Try to make local contacts.
- Get some business cards printed, go to networking events, and meet HR consultants, headhunters, and employers.
- Become linked to expat, social, and professional networks, such as the following:
  - o Fortune Connection Club, or FC Club, is a high-level networking event, with different industry-specific gatherings.

- o Shanghai Connector, a marketing and communications company, hosts weekly networking events at different bars and restaurants.
- Send out resumes that have been translated into Chinese.
- Use a headhunting company.[54]
    - o best for comprehensive positions:
        - o Access People
        - o Antal International Asia
        - o China Team
        - o P-Infinity
        - o Consult Group
    - o best for legal talents:
        - o Best Talent
    - o best for management talents:
        - o Wang Li & Asia Resources
    - o best positions at multinational companies:
        - o Monster HK
- Use websites such as thebeijinger.com, Zhaopin.com, and www.ChinaHR.com to find relevant jobs, as well as social networks such as LinkedIn. These websites are also helpful:[55]
    - o best for teachers and engineers:
        - o eChinacities.com
        - o ForeignHR.com
    - o best for media and creative industries:
        - o CreativeHunt.com
    - o best for comprehensive hunting:
        - o Craigslist.com

Applicants for jobs in China should also be aware of common mistakes that often decrease one's chance of successfully obtaining employment.

When applying for a job in China and submitting a resume, follow these suggestions to enhance your chances:[56]

- Address your resume to the correct person within an organization.
- Don't appear in your resume to be a *jack of all trades* by trying to keep all your options open and appearing to be a master of none.

41

- Have a strong positioning statement in your resume, using descriptors such as *hardworking, self-motivated, driven*, or *excellent communicator.*
- Know what skills or position your target employer needs.
- Know the *must-have* criteria for the job you're applying for, or make an intelligent guess as to what those criteria may be.
- Showcase your skills, experience, and potential.
- Know what your services are worth in the local market for which you're applying, as asking for too much in a local market will limit your chances of finding a job.
- Indicate in your resume that you're *open to relocation,* as you'll probably be sending your resume from outside China and your potential employer will want to know that you're willing to work in China and not from your native country.
- Include recommendations that emphasize your key strengths and achievements.
- Include a portal, such as LinkedIn, or a website or web folio.

Requirements for Working in China

In order to work in China, you'll first need to have a job offer from a China-based company that's permitted to employ foreigners. Speaking Mandarin is not a requirement for employment by a Chinese company, but speaking Mandarin can increase your chances of securing a job, as the ability to communicate with other Chinese employees is considered highly desirable.

China is trying to curb the illegal employment of foreigners. Therefore, in order to legally work in China, you'll need a visa plus a work permit, or Z visa, issued by the Chinese Embassy in your home country. The Z visa only allows you to enter China for a period of time until you obtain work and residence permits, which will then allow you to work anywhere in the country. The term Z visa is derived from the Chinese word *zhíyuán* for *employee*.[57] To obtain a Z visa you'll need a Visa Notification Letter and either an Employment Permit, issued by a municipal office of the Labor and Social Security Bureau, or have official status as a foreign expert, as granted by the State Administration of Foreign Expert Affairs (SAFEA). Your employer will provide you with a government-issued Employment

Permit and the Visa Notification Letter. In addition, you'll need to bring your passport and three passport photos.

Under Chinese law, a work visa is a prerequisite before applying for a work permit. Foreigners who are working without a work permit or expert certificate, a license issued by the government to some foreign workers with a proven expertise in their field, would not have the protection of their labor rights in court. Those rights include social insurance, health care, and compensation for work injury.

As the global economy slows and manufacturing and exports decrease, the Chinese government has focused on protecting domestic jobs. Local governments have taken the lead and initiated a program of finding foreigners who have either illegally obtained employment without the requisite approvals or stayed beyond the employment period for which they were approved.[58] In Beijing, for example, the Beijing Public Security Bureau will check neighborhoods and carry out inspections in various areas of the city in an effort to ferret out *illegals* who work for Chinese companies with an L (tourist) or X (student) visa.

Obtaining Required Approvals

Obtaining required approvals in China is complicated and time-consuming. Many companies don't understand the process, and as a result, it becomes an ordeal that frustrates both the employer and the employee. It doesn't have to be that way. Although the process is somewhat complicated, if you know what's required and the order in which approvals are obtained, you can obtain requisite approvals in relatively short order.

A company first has to get permission from the government to hire a foreigner. The first place a company (employer) will start in hiring you will be the Administrative Center for Employment of Foreigners. This agency is responsible for issuing an Employment License to foreigners. The Employment License is also sometimes referred to as a *work license*. The company will have to submit the following documents in order to obtain a work license:[58]

- application form for foreigner's employment in China
- employee's resume (in Chinese, with the company's stamp affixed)
- certificate of employee's work experience

43

- report of reasons for employment
- proof of capability of the employee
- employee's degree certificate
- a copy of the employee's passport
- other legal documents required by related authorities, including a foreigner permit application card issued by the Labor Bureau, a stamped copy of the company's business license, and a stamped copy of the company's corporate code certificate

Once the employer successfully obtains this work license and sends it to you, proceed as previously mentioned, to the Chinese Embassy in your own country and obtain the Z visa. It should be remembered that the Z visa is only a method for you to enter China for a specific period of time and is not meant to be permanent or long-lasting. Once you enter the country you'll be expected to complete the required paperwork in order to obtain your work and residence permits.

After you obtain your Z visa and enter China, you'll next have to proceed to the Exit-Entry Inspection and Quarantine Center for a health check. You'll be required to bring the following to your medical exam:

- your passport along with a copy
- a copy of the company's business license with the company seal affixed
- three passport photos
- a completed application form, which can be obtained at the examination center

Upon successfully completing this check you'll be issued a health certificate, which you can then take to the Administrative Center for the Employment of Foreigners to apply for a work permit. The following documents are required for a work permit:[58]

- two copies of the work permit application with the company seal
- work license and a copy
- copy of the labor contract
- valid passport and Z visa (original)
- copy of passport and Z visa
- copy of your health certificate

- copy of the company business license
- copy of the company organization code certificate
- three passport photos
- copy of the registration form of temporary residence, obtained from the district Public Security Bureau station near your residence

Once you've been issued your work permit, you can then proceed to the Exit-Entry Administration Bureau of the local policy security bureau to apply for your residence permit. You'll require the following to apply for your residence permit:

- employment registration form of foreign employees in China
- work permit (original)
- visa and residence permit application form
- a passport photo
- original registration form of temporary residence and its copy
- original passport and visa
- original health certificate
- letter of application from the employer, with company stamp
- a copy of the business license (they may, on occasion, ask for the original document)
- original corporate code certificate and a stamped copy of such
- certificate of approval of business

Once this is completed, the employee can proceed to the Exit-Entry Administrative Bureau, where his or her passport will be returned along with a residence permit affixed inside.

As you can see, the procedures to obtain a work permit in China are complicated, and the permit is usually tied to one employer. Many smaller employers don't have the resources that exist at larger companies to complete the required paperwork.[51] According to Dan Harris in his *China Law Blog*, there may be procedures whereby an employee can go and work for a new employer without relinquishing his or her work permit. The first step in this process is to obtain a letter of release from the current/old employer, which should be provided as long as an employee has not violated his or her contract. This, of course, assumes the employee maintained a good relationship with the current/old employer. If the relationship is strained by the employee leaving the company, then it's possible for the old employer to strip the employee of his or her work permit so that he or she must leave the country within thirty days. Also, some employers keep an employee's passport and permits. This can create significant problems of their own.

However, assuming that the current/old employer is cooperative, here's a list of the documents the employee will need, along with actions that must be performed in order to work for a new employer without relinquishing the work permit:[59]

- a release letter from the current/old employer
- transfer or cancellation of the Employment Permit
- the employee's original diploma, which should show a bachelor's degree or above
- a simple resume, preferably in Chinese
- a letter from any ex-employers certifying that the employee has more than two years' working experience
- a passport and four two-inch white-background photos
- residence registration
- the business license of the prospective (new) employer and two copies with a chop (A chop is a seal bearing a name. Its impression is used in lieu of a signature.)
- chopped (stamped) application form

Although this process at first glance seems lengthy, it should only take two and a half weeks.

Work Experience

Satisfying the two years' work experience requirement, first legislated in 1996 as a requirement before becoming employed in China, is difficult for many foreigners. Documentation must be provided by a former employer as evidence that the applicant for a work visa has the required two years' work experience. Without this documentation, many foreign students desiring jobs after they finish studying in Chinese universities, for example, must leave China upon graduation.

This problem has given rise to a growing number of *consultation companies* that help people evade the two-year employment requirement.

Consultation companies in Shanghai and Beijing, for example, charge 1,500 yuan ($245) to 20,000 yuan ($3,263) to assist foreigners in meeting work visa requirements. The price variance is based on a client's nationality, age, and educational background. Many of the owners of these consultation companies are former government employees, whose continuing connections within the government allow them to obtain a work visa for foreigners who would otherwise not qualify.

There are quite a few consultation companies within major Chinese cities. The Xiangrui Business Consulting Agency in Shanghai, as an example, handles about sixty clients per month. From our observations, this is not an abnormally high number.

The requirement for two years' working experience probably has its greatest effect upon students who live, study, and begin to become assimilated within China, only to be forced to leave after graduation. This wasn't a problem during the time of Chairman Mao when, in 1950, there were only thirty-three foreign students in China. These students, all from Eastern Europe, were only allowed to study Chinese language and logistics at Tsinghua University, the only university in China approved to teach foreign students. By 2011, this number had grown to where 292,611 foreign students are currently studying agriculture, medicine, economics, and the arts.[60] Most likely upon graduation, however, these students will not be able to utilize their knowledge in China, but will be forced to leave and return to their country of origin to find work.

Legal Representative

When you're employed by a company conducting business in China, you should be aware that you may be asked to be the company's legal representative. As that representative, you'll have responsibilities relating to how your company conducts business in China. In fact, in the eyes of the Chinese government, as the legal representative, you're responsible for your company.

The *St. Louis Post-Dispatch* reported the story of a US citizen who was the CEO of a US company that used Chinese suppliers in the course of business. The company was owned at the time by a global private equity fund, which was trying to work through cash flow problems at the company. The company's CEO flew to China to attend a meeting he had called to explain to suppliers the company's current cash flow problems. During this meeting, the suppliers got angry, and the CEO, along with three other executives, had to barricade themselves in a conference room for thirty-six hours until riot police were able to extricate them. But shortly after, as the company's legal representative in China, the CEO was required to hand over his passport.

The reason, as this CEO later learned, is that every Chinese company must have a point person for litigation, corporate paperwork, and administrative matters. In addition, the point person is responsible for the company's debt.[61] Therefore, it's not unusual for a foreigner to be held in China pending payment of the company's debt. The US government can't intervene in Chinese commercial disputes, and passports can, therefore, be held indefinitely by the government until the debt is satisfied. Getting another passport from the US Embassy isn't an option as the Chinese government simply won't let the foreigner leave the country.

Working with State Secrets

China is also considering the approval of a law allowing foreigners to work in positions that involve handling China's state secrets. According to a draft proposal issued by the legislative affairs office of the State Council, the proposed change to China's Law on Guarding State Secrets divides state secrets into three levels according to the importance of the information.[62] Foreigners would be allowed to work with second- or third-level state secrets after the agency employing the foreigner receives approval from the central government or provincial and municipal governments.

Working as a foreigner in China can be challenging. China is very bureaucratic, and obtaining the necessary work approvals can be confusing and time-consuming. But for those who take the time, working in China can be an extremely rewarding experience. China's industrial and commercial sectors are still rapidly growing, and as they continue to grow, they'll need the increasing levels of expertise that foreigners provide. At a time when jobs in Western countries are decreasing, China's appetite for requisite foreign skills shows no sign of waning. Knowing what to expect as an expat in China will allow you to better plan and become successful as you immerse yourself in the most dynamic business environment in the world.

CHAPTER 5

Litigating in China

Many foreigners have heard that litigating in China is hopeless and that all court rulings are in favor of domestic companies and individuals. That's not true. Sometimes rulings do seem to defy logic and go in favor of the home team, especially when government interests are involved, but that's far from being the result of all court rulings in China. In fact, most court rulings are business-related and don't involve the government. In these situations, foreigners can prevail in a Chinese court of law. We did. And you can too.

Chinese laws are, in many ways, similar to those found in the United States and other Western countries. The reason for this is that China has taken what it considers to be the *best* laws from other countries and adapted them for domestic use. The difference between litigation in China and the West primarily doesn't come from the laws themselves, but from the interpretation and enforcement of those laws. The government, in many situations, tries to balance its interpretation and enforcement of laws with the resulting socioeconomic impact. The government therefore subjugates its laws to its domestic and international interests. As a result, it may choose at times to ignore or not enforce its laws when it feels it's in the public interest. However, as previously mentioned, most situations involving foreigners are business-related and don't concern the government's national and domestic interests. In these situations, foreigners can, and have, successfully litigated in China.

Prior to understanding how to litigate in China, it's necessary to understand the country's existing power structure. Understanding this will enable you to better comprehend how the judiciary is influenced by the government and is also the messenger of China's national policies.

The Constitution

The supreme law in China is the constitution. The Constitution of the People's Republic of China was adopted in 1954 and is still a work in progress. Since its adoption, there have been three additional constitutions, with the 1982 constitution being the most recent. That constitution has, in turn, been revised four times, the most recent of which was in 2004.

> The constitution sets out the structure of the state and includes the rights and responsibilities of various government organizations, as well as the rights of individuals. It also delineates individuals' civil, legal, and political rights.[63] These rights include a representative legislature; retirement benefits; the right to ownership of private property; freedom of speech, press, and assembly; and the right to work.

How Power Is Distributed in China

There are five main divisions of power in China:[64]

- The Chinese Communist Party (CCP) has the political power.
- The National People's Congress (NPC) has the legislative power.
- The State Council has the executive power.
- The people's courts have judicial power.
- The people's procuratorates have procuratorial power.

From the above, you might conclude that there's a diversity in the country's power structure, as there appears to be a separation of judicial and political power. But that conclusion would be wrong. The reason for this is that the highest power in China is the CCP. What the CCP wants is going to happen, irrespective of what any public law dictates. Going into court and fighting CCP policies is futile. In fact, the court will probably refuse to hear the case. That's the bad news. The good news is that the CCP's primary agenda is both political and economic. It's political in that its policies tend to bolster the CCP's grip on the country and, in doing so, maintain its political dominance as well as social harmony. It's economic to the extent that its policies also endeavor to enhance domestic prosperity. Hence, most businesspeople and business transactions fall below its radar.

Bureaucratically, the NPC is the country's legislative and lawmaking arm. The NPC Standing Committee supervises the State Council, the Supreme People's Court, and the Supreme People's Procuratorate, and also has the power to interpret laws. As a matter of practice, however, the NPC reflects the agenda of the CCP and, as such, tends to serve as a forum for resolving internal disputes between the CCP, various governmental agencies, and outside groups that reflect public opinion.

The State Council is the country's chief administrative authority and has the executive power within the government. It also forms a link between the country's provincial governments and the CCP. The premier of China chairs the State Council. Therefore, the State Council and the CCP are in lockstep and reflect the will of the CCP.

How Chinese Courts Are Structured

China's judiciary is reflected in its court system. There are four levels of judiciary courts in China:[65]

- the People's Court: established in each county and prefecture-level city
- the Intermediate People's Court: established in each prefecture-level city and provincial capital city
- the Higher People's Court: established in each province, autonomous region, or municipality reporting directly to the central government
- the Supreme People's Court: handles appeals from the Higher People's Court and issues juristic interpretations that have a legal and binding effect on the lower courts

To understand the structure of Chinese courts, you should first know how China is divided administratively. Not unlike in other countries, legal issues in China are resolved at different judicial levels.

Similar to the United States, which has states, cities, counties, municipalities, and districts, China has similar administrative divisions. China is divided administratively into[66]

- provinces,
- autonomous regions, and
- municipalities.

A province is the highest-level administrative division in China. There are twenty-three provinces in China, although the Chinese government openly refers to Taiwan as its twenty-fourth. An example would be Jiangsu province on the east coast of China, which includes Nanjing, Suzhou, and Wuxi, as well as other Chinese cities.

An autonomous region is a region that has a high ethnic population and that the government has elected to give separate legislative rights. An example of such a region would be Inner Mongolia.

A municipality, in China, is simply a higher-level city that reports directly to the central government. Examples would be Beijing and Shanghai. There are five municipalities in China.

Provinces and autonomous regions are further divided into

- prefectures, an administrative level between the province and the county,
- autonomous prefectures, an administrative level between autonomous regions and autonomous counties,
- counties, administrative units between prefectures and townships,
- autonomous counties, and a special class of county reserved for ethnic minorities and given more legislative power than regular counties,
- cities.

Administratively below them, counties and autonomous counties have

- townships,
- ethnic townships, and
- towns.

Judges

Until 2002, judges did not have to pass a standardized national bar exam in order to be appointed. Many of those who were appointed judges were army veterans who did not have any formal legal education, but received judicial appointments as a reward for their past services.

Today, anyone having a bachelor's degree, whether or not it's in law, can take the bar exam. In some of the more remote areas of China, three-year college graduates can sit for the bar exam.[65] However, for the Higher People's Court and the Supreme People's Court, passing the bar exam and having a degree in law are requirements. Also, current Chinese law requires judges to have a minimum educational background. If they don't have a degree in law, they can have a degree in another area, as long as they have a professional knowledge of the law. The degree must be from an institution of higher learning. In addition, the person must have been engaged in legal work for at least two years. If a person is to be a judge in the Higher People's Court or the Supreme Court, then a minimum of three years of legal experience is required. A person who's obtained a master's or doctorate degree in law, or a degree in another area from an institution of higher learning and has a professional knowledge of the law, can also be a judge. Such a person must have been engaged in legal work for a minimum of one year.[67] If that person is to be a judge in the Higher People's Court or the Supreme Court, then a minimum of two years of legal experience is required.

The minimum age for a judge or assistant judge is twenty-three years, and he or she must be a Chinese citizen. In addition, judges cannot have been criminally punished or dismissed from public office and must pass a judge examination administered by the Supreme People's Court.[67] A judge cannot be dismissed without cause or legal procedure, and a judge's performance is to be evaluated annually.

The Evolution of Lawyers in the Chinese Legal System

Only recently have lawyers become respected members of Chinese society. The reason for this was that lawyers were looked upon as people who caused problems. They rocked the boat, upset the social balance, and made people unhappy. Unhappy people caused revolutions, and that's not in the government's game plan.

As a result, in Imperial China prior to 1911, people who we now call lawyers could only give advice to their clients in how to draft papers so they could be heard and present their case in the Imperial Court. They were not allowed into the court or to speak on their clients' behalf.

The practice of law in China remained largely marginalized until 1982, when the *Provisional Regulations on Lawyers* set minimum professional qualifications for those referring to themselves as lawyers. Even then, it wasn't until 1986 that the Ministry of Justice initiated a bar exam for those who wanted to practice law in China. Consequently at that time, China had a mixture of people practicing law who had never passed a bar exam, who were more experienced at domestic laws applying to state-owned businesses than with private business practice, and who were largely ignorant of international law.

What caused China to increase the standards for its legal profession? The world did. China began in 1978 to interact with other nations, conduct trade, accept foreign investment, form joint ventures, and become involved in other sophisticated interactions with members of the international community, all of which required the knowledge of trained legal professionals. No longer able to rely on lawyers to just assist with domestic law and limited international interactions, the Chinese government realized that it now had to have sophisticated legal expertise to protect itself in the international community.

The government had a problem attracting qualified people to a profession that historically had been disdained and that paid terribly. As such, in 1982, China had only five thousand lawyers.

The reason that lawyers received such low pay was that they were state employees and were paid according to state wage scales. Legal fees in China were therefore set by the government and were uniformly low. For example, at that time, lawyers charged $3.75 to $19 for a criminal trial of first instance and about $0.14 to $0.70 for advising on matters not related to property. But attorneys did not get to keep this money, as they were technically state workers and were already being paid by the state.

That changed in 1990, when the Ministry of Justice and the Ministry of Finance realized that if they were to attract people to the legal profession, they would have to substantially increase legal fees. As a result, they issued joint guidelines on how lawyers were to be paid and allowed them to charge appropriately for their professional services. From that point forward, the number of attorneys began to increase, and by 2001 there were 117,600 lawyers in China for a population of 1.3 billion.[68] The United States, in contrast, had 950,000 lawyers for a population of 285 million.

With the setting of minimum standards for the legal profession, increased emphasis on the training of new attorneys, the establishment of a bar exam, and the changing of pay for lawyers, China was able to transform lawyers from being bureaucratic state employees to highly trained and talented business professionals representing national, domestic, and individual interests.

Differences between Litigation, Mediation, and Arbitration

Just as in the West, China also has litigation, mediation, and arbitration to try to resolve legal disputes. According to attorney Peter Zhu in his *China Lawyer Blog*, litigation is generally defined as when one party sues, or files a lawsuit, against another party. If the case is not settled and goes to trial, it can be extremely expensive and time-consuming for the parties involved. In contrast, mediation and arbitration are two cheaper, and possibly more expedient, alternatives to litigation. Mediation is a method of settling a dispute through the use of a neutral or detached umpire. It applies only to commercial and family disputes. On the other hand, arbitration is similar to a trial, where an arbitrator presides over the proceedings, makes findings of law and facts, and writes an opinion.[69] The arbitration may or may not be binding.

China's courts, looking for ways to clear their dockets, have pushed for mediation. For those who qualify, both parties are able to resolve the issues before them faster than going to trial. In addition, matters resolved in this manner are private and will not damage a company's reputation or reveal information the company wishes to keep confidential.

Arbitration is different. Successful arbitration, in our opinion, begins with the contract between parties. The contract would specify arbitration as the method for resolving disputes. This is preferred by many because the prevailing party in arbitration should be able to convert its arbitration award to a court judgment. At a minimum, an arbitration contract should include the following terms:

- Where would you like the arbitration to take place? A neutral city is preferable.
- If you desire a language other than Chinese, the default language for the arbitration, what language do you want?
- What nationalities would you like on the arbitration panel? In the opinion of many, having at least one non-Chinese on the arbitration panel is beneficial.
- What arbitration body would you like to use? In this process, select one that has handled foreign arbitrations in the past.

Your attorney can suggest additional terms that should be included in the arbitration contract. Be as detailed as you can. Ambiguity and making assumptions should be avoided at all costs, as Chinese businesspeople will hold foreigners to the letter of the contract, even though they might not feel the same obligation.

Evidence Collection

Unless both parties arbitrate or mediate, they're headed for litigation. One of the first things that you need to do in the litigation process is to collect evidence. In the United States, evidence collection generally centers on *discovery*, a process whereby each party can obtain evidence from the other party through depositions, the production of documents, and similar requests for information prior to a trial.

In China, there are no US-style discovery practices. In compliance with the *Civil Procedure Law* of the PRC, parties cannot make a discovery request of the opposing party.

According to Richard W. Wigley and Xu Jing of King & Wood Mallesons' Intellectual Property Group, evidence submission to PRC courts can take the form of[70]

- documentary evidence,
- material evidence,
- audio-video reference materials,
- testimony of witnesses,
- statements of parties,
- expert conclusions, and
- records of inquests.

Courts within the PRC have a preference for documentary evidence. Since US-style discovery is not permitted, the PRC courts have given attorneys two alternative methods of gaining access to information held by the other party. These methods include an Order for Evidence Preservation and a court-requested Expert Conclusions or Opinions.

The court can grant an Order for Evidence Preservation *when there is a likelihood that evidence may be destroyed, lost, or difficult to obtain later on.* When an Expert Conclusions or Opinions is ordered by the court, one or two persons with professional knowledge will appear in court to answer specific questions. However, no matter which of these methods is employed to collect relevant documentation, documentary evidence is required to be produced in as little as thirty days from the time the party receives the notice for evidence production. In foreign-related cases, this period may be extended to sixty days.[70] In addition, if evidence was formed outside of the PRC, then this evidence will have to be notarized according to PRC law and translated into Chinese, and the original documents or materials submitted to the court.

Starting Your Litigation

Since only Chinese nationals working for a Chinese law firm may appear in court, one of the first things one needs to do when initiating litigation in China is to find a reputable law firm. When selecting your law firm, try to get personal references from one of your friends or business associates. Many law firms will tout their capabilities and invincibility when interviewed, but not all will deliver. In addition, make sure the law firm you choose has an attorney working on your case who speaks your language. It's important. Many words in foreign languages don't easily translate into Chinese. If you're going to effectively communicate with your attorney, then it's a necessity that he or she speak more than just Chinese. Otherwise, you'll need an interpreter, and not all interpreters translate exactly what's said.

Once you've selected your attorney, you'll next need to address territorial jurisdiction. According to Steven C. Bennett of Jones Day, an international law firm, territorial jurisdiction is determined by venue, personal jurisdiction, and jurisdiction over property. It's also determined by factors such as domicile, place of business, place of alleged injury or conduct, location of property, and consent of the parties. Once sued in a Chinese court, if you fail to object to jurisdiction within thirty days for foreign companies, and fifteen days for local subsidiaries,[71] then this failure to object will constitute a consent to jurisdiction.

Cost of Litigation

We believe that litigating in China is generally less expensive than litigating in the United States. Part of the reason for this is that there's no formal discovery process in China. With this component missing, the cost of litigating in China tends to be reasonable.

There are three costs associated with litigating a case in China:[72]

- prelitigation costs
- attorney fees
- court and preservation costs

The first expense you're likely to encounter is prelitigation costs. Attorney fees, travel expenses, and time away from the office are certainly part of your prelitigation expenses. However, other expenses may include hiring a private investigator, since there is no discovery process. In addition, documents that are executed in the United States and that will be used in China require authentication by the Chinese government. In having documents authenticated, you have to bring or send the notarized document to the Chinese Embassy, or a consulate in the jurisdiction in which the document is notarized, pay a fee, and wait the several days it usually takes for the document to be returned. This can be both expensive and time-consuming depending on the number of documents for which authentication is required.

Attorney fees in China tend to be more reasonable than in Western countries. However, because virtually all foreign companies have domestic attorneys, what normally occurs is that clients will pay two sets of attorney fees: one in their native domicile and the other in China. Law firms outside of China will justify their fee on the basis that they're *overseeing* the Chinese law firm. This can prove to be expensive. We're not advocating abandoning your domestic law firm. What we're saying is that you should be aware of this potential expense when considering your legal expenses.

In civil disputes, court fees range from 0.5 percent to 2.5 percent of the amount of the claim. These fees could increase if you win your case and the other side does not agree to pay you your claim. In that event, you'd have to apply for enforcement of the judgment, which will further increase your costs.

If enforcement is necessary, you should immediately apply for preservation of your opponent's property. This may involve hiring a private investigator to ascertain your opponent's assets, as well as the payment of a preservation fee. Preservation fees cannot exceed 5,000 yuan ($816), and a deposit will have to be paid to the court to cover damages in the event there is a wrongful preservation. Deposits must be in the form of cash, a local bank guarantee, title to a property, or other meaningful collateral.

All court and preservation fees in China are generally prepaid by the claimant. But the court can apportion these costs, as well as prelitigation costs, such as notarizations and authentications. However, this is not guaranteed. Even if the claimant is victorious in his or her lawsuit, there's no guarantee of reimbursement for costs.[72] Reimbursement is at the discretion of the court. Attorney's fees, as a practice, are almost never reimbursed in China.

The Verdict

Local protectionism is frequently practiced in smaller cities where the company employs a meaningful number of locals. The greater the percentage of locals employed, the greater the possibility of local bias. Local and provincial governments want to employ the maximum number of people, and an increase in unemployment always causes concern. Therefore, giving large awards to foreign companies is discouraged.

You'll see large awards in China, but they'll almost always be in favor of Chinese companies. US companies that prevail in court, in contrast, receive much smaller awards. In addition, going to court in Beijing is quite different than going to court in a small province. The results may also vary widely, such as in the case of American Superconductor Corp. (AMSC), an American company that filed a lawsuit against Sinovel, a domestic Chinese company. AMSC filed its lawsuit in a number of jurisdictions, including Beijing and the small Chinese island of Hainan. The Hainan Higher Court dismissed AMSC's copyright infringement case, while the Beijing Intermediate Court ruled against Sinovel. The reason for these disparate outcomes is twofold.

The first is that local and provincial governments tend to be more protectionist than the national government. In other words, they exercise their home-field advantage and take care of their own. They don't want money that would otherwise go to pay workers, or expand a company's operation, to go to a foreign company. It doesn't make good business sense. Large foreign awards would also cause people in the local government's jurisdiction to feel that government officials lacked both good managerial skills and good judgment.

The second reason for this difference in judgments is that Chinese courts tend to base their decisions, especially at the local and provincial levels, less on the letter of the law and more on what they feel is right. Consequently, in our estimation, people tend to prevail less in China on technicalities than on the merits and impact of the case.

In the event that you've prevailed in Chinese court, your next hurdle will be to collect on that judgment. Enforcing a judgment in China is not easy.

Enforcing a Judgment

Unlike the United States, where a court judgment can be enforced with relatively little trouble, collecting on a judgment in China requires another set of procedures. According to Stan Abrams, a Beijing-based attorney and law professor, there can be a number of obstacles to enforcing your judgment, such as[73]

- defendant hides or transfers assets,
- political connections,
- local protectionism,
- bureaucracy, and
- corruption.

Applying for asset preservation will help to ensure that the other side's assets are available post-judgment. But you'll have to apply for it.[74] You're also unlikely to get any help from local or provincial governments, as they're usually on the side of the company since that's where their economic interests reside. However, once the court orders a freeze of bank accounts or other assets, the defendant cannot transfer or encumber those assets. When that occurs, local government and Party officials are less able to prevent enforcement of the judgment.

The defendant, especially in small jurisdictions, may have a good relationship with the local court. Therefore, even though you have a verdict, you may not be able to get it enforced by the local court because the defendant has a close relationship with one of the parties involved in the enforcement process. Preservation of assets, however, makes protectionism by local courts much more difficult.

Just as locals might try to protect a defendant with whom they have a relationship by not cooperating with the claimant or plaintiff, that lack of cooperation increases exponentially where the defendant is a large employer and taxpayer. A local government never feels that paying a foreigner is in its best interests, as there's no economic benefit to be gained by such cooperation.

Chinese bureaucracy makes the US government appear streamlined by comparison. It can make you feel at times like you're going in an endless circle. Part of the reason for this is that each local and provincial government has its own bureaucracy, biases, and method of operation. Consequently, getting two different government agencies to cooperate on enforcement is frequently difficult. That's because one or more government officials may simply choose not to be bothered by your request, or they may have a local bias and choose not to assist in the enforcement action. In addition, corruption is rampant in China. It's commonplace and it's used effectively in frustrating attempts to enforce a judgment, especially when a foreigner is involved.

> Attempting to enforce a US judgment in China is futile. If you obtain a judgment in the United States against a Chinese company that has no assets in the United States or another country that enforces US judgments, then you stand very little chance of receiving your money. Your judgment is not going to be enforced in China, as there's no agreement in place between China and the United States that recognizes each other's judgments. Your best alternative, when possible, is to obtain a verdict in China, go through the procedures of asset protection, and then enforce the judgment.

While litigating in China is less expensive than a similar legal process in other countries, local bias, protectionism, asset transfers, and corruption make it more difficult, if not sometimes impossible, for a foreigner to prevail. That being said, not every foreigner who sues in China has lost, and not every Chinese party to a lawsuit has prevailed. As we've previously mentioned, there are many instances when the factors above don't come into play or a number of compelling factors come together and allow you to prevail. It happened to us when we prevailed in a lawsuit against the CEO of a Chinese company. We went through the process discussed above, went to trial, and received the verdict. If we prevailed, you also can. Litigating in China isn't hopeless; it just takes an understanding of what's in front of you and the patience to navigate to a successful conclusion.

Lawsuits in China Increase

Litigation in China not only involves foreign companies suing Chinese companies and individuals; it also involves Chinese companies suing one another, an increasingly common practice. According to Simon Rabinovitch of the *Financial Times,* Chinese courts handled 376,000 financial lawsuits in the first half alone of 2012, an increase of 25 percent from all of 2011. This has created a huge challenge for courts, according to Jiang Dingku, chief partner at Zhejiang Great Strategy Law Firm, as judges in some cities now hear more than sixty cases a month, where once sixty cases a year would have been considered challenging for their schedule.

One way Chinese courts are addressing this rapid increase in domestic lawsuits is by providing better training at all levels of the court system, including judges, assistants, and other related judicial members. In addition, the government has created specialized economic and financial courts. According to Shahla Ali, a law professor at the University of Hong Kong, "this allows for judges within the courts to develop expertise and familiarity with a certain kind of dispute, whether lending, contract, or securities."[75]

CHAPTER 6

Protecting Your Intellectual Property

A report recently released by the US Department of Commerce indicates that intellectual property protections have a direct and significant impact on the US economy. The report, entitled *Intellectual Property and the U.S. Economy: Industries in Focus*, finds that intellectual property-intensive industries support at least 40 million jobs and contribute more than $5.06 trillion dollars, or nearly 34.8 percent of the US GDP. Moreover, the seventy-five industries that make the greatest use of patents, copyrights, or trademarks are responsible for supporting more than a quarter of all jobs in the United States. Twenty-seven million of these jobs are either on payroll or under employment contracts working directly for intellectual property-intensive industries.[76] Nearly 13 million more Americans are indirectly supported through supply chains that directly or indirectly service these industries.

Perhaps no foreign country impacts US intellectual property rights (IPR) more than China. According to Gary Locke, US ambassador to the People's Republic of China, the lack of enforcement of intellectual property rights in China is troubling to foreign firms. Especially troubling has been the protection of trade secrets, as previously this has not been the focus of enforcement campaigns.

Foreign companies have lost billions of dollars a year from all types of IP theft and misappropriation in China. Ambassador Locke gives the example of software, stating that in the United States, for every one dollar of computer hardware sales, there's about eighty-eight cents of software sales. But in China, for every dollar of hardware sales, there's only eight cents of software sales. According to the American Business Software Alliance, this difference is due to the fact that 80 percent of the software used in computers in China is pirated and therefore is counterfeit.[77] Software companies actually earn more from legitimate sales in Vietnam than they do in all of China!

The Four Types of Intellectual Property in China

Intellectual property in China is generally considered to fall into one of the following four types or categories:[78]

- patents
- trademarks
- copyrights
- trade secrets

The Chinese definitions for the four types of intellectual property are similar to those in the United States and other Western countries. In the United States we have the following definitions for intellectual property:

Patents are issued for inventions, designs, or utilitarian features of a product. A patent provides protection for a nonrenewable term of twenty years for invention, ten years for design, and ten years for utility model patents, which are not substantively examined before issuance.

A trademark can be a word, phrase, symbol, design, or combination of these identifying the source of goods or services. These are protected for renewable ten-year periods.

A copyright protects an original work in a fixed medium of expression, such as books, music, software, and so on. A copyright is protected for a nonrenewable term, for individual authors, for the life of the author plus fifty years. For foreign authors, the term of protection is fifty years.

A trade secret is a formula, pattern, device, or compilation of data that grants the user an advantage over competitors. This is covered by state, rather than federal law.[79] In order to protect a trade secret, a company must prove that it adds value to the company, that it's a secret, and that the company has taken appropriate measures to safeguard this secret, such as restricting the number of people within the company who have access to the formula.

Intellectual property infringement is rampant in China. According to the US Department of Commerce's International Trade Administration, 20 percent of all consumer products in the Chinese market are counterfeit. It's generally understood that patents, trademarks, and copyrights are good only in the country in which these rights are secured. For patents and trademarks to be enforceable in China, they must be registered with the appropriate Chinese agencies. Once registered and approved, China's patent laws extend patent protection for a period of twenty years from the date the patent application is filed.[78]

China has a *first-to-file* patent system in place, whereby patents are granted to those who file first, even if the person filing first was not the original inventor.[80] This is in stark contrast to the United States and the European Union, which have a *first-to-invent* rule.

If a patent application is made by a foreign company, the company must have a business address in China or utilize the services of an authorized patent agent. Patents are filed with the State Intellectual Property Office in Beijing, with administrative enforcement delegated to the provincial and municipal levels of government.

China also has a first-to-register system for trademarks that requires no evidence of prior use or ownership. As a result, the Chinese government has advised foreign companies seeking to distribute their products in China to register their marks and logos, along with Internet domains, with the Trademark Office. Foreign parties not having a business address in China must, in addition, utilize the services of an authorized trademark agent.

Copyrights differ from patents and trademarks in that they don't need to be registered between signatory countries to the Berne Convention. China and the United States are two of these signatory countries. However, registering copyrights does simplify ownership disputes. If a foreign party wishes to register its copyright(s) with the China National Copyright Administration, which evidences ownership, it would then be entitled to enforcement action in China.

Enforcement

Intellectual property enforcement is both administrative and legal. When parties feel that their intellectual property has been violated, they would either file a complaint at the local administrative office or through the court system. In addition, jurisdiction in an intellectual property case can go through a number of government agencies and offices. This has caused a great deal of confusion, as these agencies and offices are normally only given responsibility over one statute or a specific area of intellectual property law.[80] There may also be geographic limitations imposed on a case. In an administrative complaint, the infringer can only be fined and have goods or equipment used in the manufacturing process seized.

In a civil action, a claim for damages, or an injunction, can be issued by a civil court. Following a written complaint by the plaintiff, evidence will be presented at a trial and a verdict rendered. Judgments in civil actions may be appealed.

In a criminal action, complaints against infringers should be filed directly with the public prosecutor's office. The prosecutor will then conduct a raid, followed by a series of hearings, which may result in an indictment. A criminal conviction for intellectual property infringement can result in imprisonment of from three to seven years.

According to the US Department of Commerce's International Trade Administration, there are several factors that undermine effective enforcement action for intellectual property rights infringements in China:

- corruption and local protectionism at the provincial level
- reliance on administrative rather than criminal measures to combat intellectual property rights infringements
- limited resources and training available to enforcement officials

- lack of public education regarding the economic and social impact of counterfeiting and piracy

Chinese Agencies Charged with Administrative Enforcement

The US Department of Commerce lists the following Chinese government agencies as being the major players responsible for administratively enforcing China's intellectual property laws:[80]

- Administration of Quality Supervision, Inspection and Quarantine (AQSIQ)
- State Administration for Industry & Commerce (SAIC) Trademark Office
- State Intellectual Property Office (SIPO)
- National Copyright Administration (NCA) of China
- General Administration of Customs (GAC)
- Public Security Bureau (police)/Procuratorate (prosecutors)
- regional Intellectual Property Rights (IPR) Bureaus
- judicial system

Administration of Quality Supervision, Inspection and Quarantine (AQSIQ)

The function of the Administration of Quality Supervision, Inspection and Quarantine (AQSIQ) is to ensure the quality of Chinese products and standards. It's China's standard-setting and quality-control agency.[81] It also oversees entry and exit quarantines for animals and plants, certifies import and export for foreign manufacturers in regard to food safety, and is involved in administrative law enforcement.

> AQSIQ's primary mission is to protect the consumer against inferior or shoddy goods, which includes goods with a counterfeit trademark or those that are being marked in a package bearing another person's name and address.

69

The AQSIQ has an administrative enforcement arm by which it may take action against registered trademark infringers. As a matter of course, the main issue for the AQSIQ is quality, rather than the protection of intellectual property. According to the European Union's IPR2 Team, a complaint to the AQSIQ can only be based on two grounds: the goods are substandard or the goods are in a package that bears the name and address of another person. Most of the cases reviewed by the AQSIQ involve goods bearing a counterfeit trademark. In this case, the AQSIQ can fine those who produce fake or shoddy goods between two and five times the value of the goods. If the goods bear an incorrect place of origin, falsify the name and address of another factory, or forge quality marks such as certification marks, then *illegal profits* are seized and a *to-be-determined* fine is imposed. Administrative litigation can be instituted before the People's Court within fifteen days of notification of a decision by the AQSIQ.[82] If neither quality nor false name and address are an issue, and goods represent only a trademark infringement, then a claim would be filed with the SAIC instead of the AQSIQ.

State Administration for Industry & Commerce (SAIC)

The State Administration for Industry & Commerce (SAIC) is the largest of all IPR enforcement agencies and employs over 500,000 people. The SAIC is responsible for trademark registration, registration of businesses (individual and legal persons), administration of well-known trademarks, and trademark enforcement. The Fair Trade Bureau, as part of the SAIC, enforces the Law to Counter Unfair Competition Act, as well as violations of trade secrets.[80]

The SAIC investigates suspected infringements, and if it determines that an infringement has occurred, it can stop the sale of infringing items, destroy infringing marks or products, as well as impose fines and confiscate the machinery used to produce the counterfeit goods.

To lodge a complaint, a trademark owner would file the complaint with the local trademark bureau of the SAIC where the infringement was committed, give a copy of the trademark registration certificate, and provide evidence of the infringement, such as a sample of the infringing product. The SAIC does have some constraints on its power. For example, when it goes to the premises of the alleged infringer, it can't force the owner to open the premises if the location is on private property. Instead, it would have to call the police and also call the Public Security Bureau. Depending on the alleged infringer's relationship with the local police, the SAIC may or may not be granted access onto the premises.

Most infringers don't keep good documentation. As a result, invoices, contracts, and accounting books may not be available to use as documentary evidence. If, however, the SAIC is able to obtain entrance onto the premises of an alleged infringer and determines that an infringement has occurred, it will seize the goods, equipment, and seals used in the infringement. It may also impose a fine of up to three times the size of the illegal business, although this is not an easy number to calculate as Chinese authorities don't usually accept the price of authentic goods in determining the size of the illegal business. The maximum fine is 100,000 yuan ($16,313).[82] The SAIC can only act as a mediator in disputes. Legislatively only the People's Courts may apply Civil Procedure Law.

State Intellectual Property Office (SIPO)

> The State Intellectual Property Office (SIPO) is a national-level agency that examines foreign and domestic patents and can be thought of as the equivalent of the US Patent and Trademark Office.

The State Intellectual Property Office (SIPO) operates through a network of local provincial offices to administratively enforce patent complaints.

China has experienced tremendous growth in the filing of patent applications. In 2001, for example, it processed the filing of 40,000 patent applications.[80] This represented 5 percent of the global total.[83] In 2011 SIPO surpassed the US Patent and Trademark Office for the first time and became the largest processor of patent filings in the world. In that year, SIPO received 526,000 patent applications, a growth of 34.6 percent from the previous year. Globally China held a 24.6 percent share of patent applications in 2011.[84] According to Tian Lipu, Commissioner of the State

Intellectual Property Office (China), China's patent filings increased by 20 percent in 2012.[83] Part of the reason for this large increase is the country's transition from a manufacturing-oriented economy to an innovation-driven economy.[85]

National Copyright Administration (NCA)

The National Copyright Administration (NCA) is China's highest administrative agency for interpreting the country's copyright laws.

> The NCA is responsible for investigating and enforcing copyright infringements, managing foreign copyrights, and investigating significant national copyright infringement cases.[86]

Because of a chronic shortage of staff, the NCA generally does not take administrative action against infringers, but encourages both parties to utilize the court system to resolve disputes.[80]

General Administration of Customs (GAC)

> The General Administration of Customs (GAC) is responsible for controlling the transportation of inbound and outbound goods, combating smuggling, enforcing intellectual property rights, collecting customs duties and taxes, and collecting statistical data regarding goods in transit to and from China.[87]

The General Administration of Customs (GAC) is also responsible for collecting value-added tax, customs duties, excise duties, landfill taxes, air passenger duties, and insurance premium taxes.

Chinese law bans the import or export of goods that infringe on another's intellectual property. But in order to be enforceable by Chinese Customs, the holder of the intellectual property must record its intellectual property with Customs. Once recorded, a certificate will be issued by Customs and is good for a period of seven years. If the holder of this certificate then suspects that infringing goods are about to enter or leave China, it can submit an application to Customs at the suspected entry or exit point from China, asking Customs to investigate. If Customs determines that an infringement has taken place, it has the authority to confiscate or destroy the goods, and impose a fine.[80]

Public Security Bureau (police)/Procuratorate (prosecutors)

Commercial-scale piracy is considered a criminal offense. As such, administrative authorities and Customs have the authority to transfer these cases for investigation by police and prosecutors. They also can give an individual the right to prosecute, as a criminal offense, alleged infringers. The Ministry of Public Security's focus is currently in five areas:[80]

- fake and shoddy goods
- counterfeit luxury items
- high-tech products
- home appliances
- food and drugs

The Ministry of Public Security reports that, from November 2011 to August 2012, police *cracked* 72,000 cases of IPR infringement and the production and sale of fake and shoddy products. In these cases, more than 120,000 suspects were apprehended. The value of the goods seized, according to the police, was $6.4 billion.[88] It's not clear, however, if the value of goods seized is the market value of the genuine goods or the fake goods. Generally, criminal prosecution in instances such as these is rare, and most cases are handled administratively.

Regional Intellectual Property Rights (IPR) Bureaus

Some provinces and municipalities have established intellectual property rights bureaus and committees. However, enforcement at this level is limited and not always reliable, as regions and provinces in China tend to *protect their own*. This is because infringers contribute to the local economy, employ people, and pay taxes. As a result, actions against them will be minimal. As a general rule, the smaller the city, the less the IPR enforcement. In the event an infringer is found guilty, the fine is usually small in comparison to the offense.

Judicial System

Both civil and criminal actions can be taken against suspected infringers in the local People's Court. In a civil action, the first court to hear the case, at the subprovincial level, is the Intermediate People's Court. The Higher People's Courts hear IPR civil cases at the provincial level. Intellectual rights holders can also initiate a private proceeding against suspected infringers, although this rarely happens.

The burden of proof in a patent infringement suit lies with the IPR holder.[89] This can sometimes prove to be difficult, as there is no formal discovery process in China and it's therefore more difficult to obtain evidence from the infringer. Judges instead tend to rely on the opinions of outside experts in making their decisions as they try to understand the IPR and products in question.

Criminal actions are first heard by criminal tribunals in the People's Court following a Public Security Bureau investigation. A conviction for IPR infringement in the criminal courts can result in fines, as well as sentences of up to seven years, depending on the value of the infringed products. However, getting a criminal case into court can sometimes be a challenge in itself, as the courts have imposed a minimum value threshold for infringing goods. The threshold for trademark counterfeiting cases is 50,000 yuan ($8,157) for the value of the infringing products and 30,000 ($4,894) yuan in illegal income. For patents, the amounts are 200,000 yuan ($32,626) for the value of infringing products and 100,000 yuan ($16,313) in illegal income.[89]

The setting of minimal thresholds by the criminal courts may prevent criminal action from being taken against some infringers. In addition, although these threshold amounts may appear to be low, obtaining evidence to substantiate even these small sums may prove difficult. Infringers tend to diversify their products in a number of locations and keep their books and records hidden. Therefore, it may be impossible in some cases to prove that an infringer has exceeded the illegal income or product value minimums established by the courts.

Nevertheless, the main advantage of the judicial system over administrative proceedings is that it provides a stronger deterrent against IPR infringement. IPR infringement penalties in civil and criminal courts vary, with penalties in the civil courts being less than those imposed in criminal courts. In a civil court, for instance, an infringed party can only claim monetary damages for the loss of market share and revenue caused by the infringer. In criminal court cases, an infringer can receive a larger fine, as well as be sentenced to jail.

There are disadvantages to having a case heard in court versus an administrative proceeding. Court cases can easily take a year or longer to resolve and can be quite expensive since legal counsel is employed. Administrative proceedings, in contrast, usually reach resolution within a few weeks.[89] As a result, actions initiated through the judicial system are far fewer than administrative actions taken against IPR infringers. No matter what the venue for an IPR infringement case, judicial or administrative, damages are difficult to collect, and injunctions and limits on business activities are even more difficult to impose.

According to the *China Business Review,* the limited experience of many local judges in IPR cases, local protectionism, and low transparency in court cases are concerns in China. This is especially true when cases are heard outside of China's major cities. As an example, they cite a September 2007 court decision in Wenzhou, where a Chinese company, Chint Group Corp., filed a lawsuit against a French company, Schneider Electric SA's joint venture, Schneider Electric Low Voltage (Tianjin) Co., Ltd. Chint claimed that five of Schneider's circuit breakers infringed on Chint's patents. The court eventually agreed with the company's claim and awarded the Chinese company 334.8 million yuan, or about $49 million at the time.[89]

Foreign judgments, however, average far less. Typical damages awarded to foreign companies usually average less than $30,000 USD.[90] Often the cost of litigation exceeds the monetary awards made by a Chinese court when infringement against a Chinese company has been affirmed.

One reason we see such a disparity in judgments made against foreign companies versus those that are local is the impact such judgments can have on the community. As a result, justices are reluctant to fine a local company a large amount of money because it could cause financial hardship for the company and also result in workers being laid off. In China, which places a significant focus on social harmony and domestic contentment, unemployment and worker unhappiness are always concerns. The CCP is largely in power because they're able to maintain social harmony and provide economic prosperity. Consequently they avoid actions that could create social discord, bring about a loss of confidence in the Party's governing ability, or diminish economic prosperity.

US Government Agencies Charged with Enforcement

Intellectual property rights enforcement by the US government is coordinated through the following entities:[78]

- US Immigration and Customs Enforcement's (ICE) National IPR Coordination Center
- US Department of Justice's Computer Crime and Intellectual Property Section (CCIPS)
- www.stopfakes.gov
- US Embassy in Beijing, China
- US Customs and Border Protection e-Recordation website

US Immigration and Customs Enforcement's (ICE) National IPR Coordination Center

ICE has a task force that consists of member agencies that share information and coordinate enforcement actions. They also conduct investigations into the theft of intellectual property.[91] These investigations are conducted by the National Intellectual Property Rights Coordination Center (IPR Center), which is at the forefront of the US government's response to global intellectual property theft. According to the US government, the IPR Center shares information, conducts investigations, and coordinates enforcement actions with other global member agencies into the theft of intellectual property.[92]

US Department of Justice's Computer Crime and Intellectual Property Section (CCIPS)

The Computer Crime and Intellectual Property Section (CCIPS) is responsible for implementing the Department of Justice's national strategies in combating computer and intellectual property crimes worldwide. CCIPS prevents, investigates, and prosecutes computer crimes by working with other government agencies, the private sector, academic institutions, and foreign counterparts. According to the US government, the CCIPS law enforcement function is charged with investigating computer crime and IPR violations, including emerging computer and telecommunications technologies. It also litigates cases in these areas and provides litigation support to other prosecutors, as well as trains federal, state, and local law enforcement personnel.[93] In the changing world of technology, CCIPS will also propose new legislation to keep up with changes in technology, as well as intellectual property.

www.stopfakes.gov

The website www.stopfakes.gov, by the United States Patent and Trademark Office (USPTO), is intended to help small businesses protect their IP rights, both domestically and overseas. It was launched to serve as a one-stop shop for US government tools and resources on intellectual property rights by developing a number of resources to educate and assist businesses. It's especially focused on addressing the needs of small and medium-sized enterprises (SMEs), consumers, government officials, and the general public.[94] According to Bill Heinze, at the company I/P Updates, this website will provide guidance on whether someone should file for IP protection, and if they do, what type of protection to file for and how to go about it.[95]

US Embassy in Beijing, China

The US Embassy in Beijing provides information on China's current intellectual property rights environment, protection through prevention, China's intellectual property rights enforcement system, how the US government can help in infringement cases, and information resources. The Embassy will also provide information on legislation and what can be patented, copyrighted, or trademarked, and the registration process for each.[96] However, what the US government can't do is put any meaningful pressure on China to stop its companies from infringing on your IP, or give you legal advice. The best they can offer is to provide you with information.

US Customs and Border Protection E-Recordation Website

This is a tool that can be used for recording registered trademarks and copyrights with US Customs and Border Protection. Use of this website will greatly decrease the time and paperwork required to file your initial trademark and copyright recordation applications and thereby allow for more timely enforcement of your IP rights.[97] It will also help Customs prevent infringing imports from entering the United States.

US Government Assistance

As we've stated, if you think that the United States government will be able to help you with infringement on your intellectual property rights, you're wrong. It won't become involved.[78] Instead, it's up to you to hire local legal counsel and take action against alleged infringers. The reason behind this is that intellectual property is considered personal property, and the US government cannot serve as a rights-holder's attorney.[80]

US Lawsuits against Chinese Companies

Prevailing in an intellectual property lawsuit in a Chinese court can be difficult and very time-consuming. China's judicial system is not independent, and sometimes an anti-foreigner bias in local and provincial courts can favor homegrown firms. This bias manifests itself more in smaller cities than in major metropolitan areas such as Beijing and Shanghai. In addition to the Schneider Electric example provided earlier, another example of provincial bias can be found in the case of American Superconductor Corp. (AMSC). This company manufactured controllers/converters for Sinovel, a Chinese startup wind-farm company that had the financial backing of the Chinese government.

Sinovel was one of a number of wind-farm companies in which the Chinese government invested huge amounts of taxpayers' money. AMSC, a struggling US company based in Devens, Massachusetts, was anxious to have a Chinese partner, especially with the country's newly placed emphasis on wind farms. The deal between AMSC and Sinovel called for AMSC to make controllers in its Chinese subsidiary factory and then install them in Sinovel's wind turbines in northwestern China. Everything initially went well, but in 2010, Sinovel suddenly started rejecting AMSC's controllers, citing low quality.

AMSC, fearing oversights in their quality-control process, investigated. The investigation turned up some astounding facts. Investigators discovered that an employee/manager of Windtec, an AMSC subsidiary in Austria, had received a bribe of $20,000, plus an apartment and prostitute, for turning over AMSC's source codes to Sinovel. In addition, the employee was later found to be working for Sinovel and was helping the company modify AMSC's code in the controllers. Upon receiving the codes, Sinovel established its own subsidiary in China to make controller hardware, with its controllers now containing the modified AMSC code.

In Austria, the bribed employee was questioned by authorities and promptly confessed. He was subsequently sentenced by an Austrian court to several years in prison. Upon obtaining this information, AMSC instituted lawsuits in four jurisdictions in China for breach of contract and for copyright infringement, calculating damages at $1.2 billion. Sinovel immediately countersued for breach of contract and damages totaling $58 million. Two of the jurisdictions where AMSC filed its lawsuit were Hainan and Beijing. Hainan is a small island not far off the southern coast of China, in the South China Sea. In what was thought to be a case of provincial bias, the Hainan Higher Court dismissed AMSC's copyright infringement case. However, the Beijing Intermediate Court ruled against Sinovel.[98]

AMSC subsequently appealed the Hainan ruling to the Chinese Supreme Court, which agreed to review the case.[99] The date of the review still has not been set according to the most recent statement from AMSC.

Chinese Lawsuits against US Companies

Not all intellectual property lawsuits are by US companies suing Chinese firms. According to Jia Lynn Yang of the *Washington Post*, there are an increasing number of Chinese companies suing US firms, and this trend is expected to continue. *China Daily* indicates that intellectual property litigation cases rose to 66,000 in 2011, up 37.7 percent from 2010.[100]

Chinese firms are currently suing Apple for patent and trademark infringement, ranging from iPhone's voice assistant Siri to the Snow Leopard operating system. According to Peter Yu, a professor at Drake University Law School, for some foreign companies such suits can be a significant problem. This is especially true if their goods are manufactured in China. In that case, if a Chinese court issues an injunction on the production of its product, this will almost certainly have a significant impact on the company. However, in almost all cases, Chinese firms are looking for a monetary settlement as a means of resolving the dispute.

China Increases Its Patent Filings

China's patent office has surpassed Japan and the United States to become the busiest in the world, and the Chinese government is focused on continuing this explosive growth in patent filings. In an effort to make the economy less dependent on manufacturing, the Chinese government has set a goal for the filing of two million patent applications per year by 2015. The US patent office, by comparison, received 530,000 patent applications in 2011. However, in a recent report by the European Union Chamber of Commerce, the quality of Chinese patents was called into question, and the level of innovation was thought to be *overhyped*. China allows, as do Germany and Australia, a utility model, which is automatically approved by regulators without formal review. This is meant to encourage small inventors. But as the Chinese government is endeavoring to meet its two-million-patent-application goal, more and more utility model patents are being filed. Along with more patents has come more litigation. According to Chris Bailey, an executive at the intellectual property law firm Rouse, intellectual property lawsuits in China have nearly doubled from 2009 to 2011,[101] although observers feel that many of these claims are dubious.

Protecting Your Patents

On September 22, 2011, former Treasury Secretary Timothy Geithner told a forum in Washington that:

"They (China) have made possible systematic stealing of intellectual property of American companies and have not been very aggressive to put in place the basic protections for property rights that every serious economy needs over time.

"We're seeing China continue to be very, very aggressive in a strategy they started several decades ago, which goes like this: you want to sell to our country, we want you to come produce here . . . if you want to come produce here, you need to transfer your technology to us."[102]

China has for years adhered to the strategy Mr. Geithner mentioned in his Washington forum address. The Chinese government wanted technology, and it preyed on the greed of those who wanted to tap into the Chinese market, both as importers and exporters, to obtain the technology it needed. Recently, however, that's beginning to change, as China has indicated that it would drop its *indigenous innovation* rules. These rules specify that, in order to obtain a contract to sell equipment and technology to the government, the seller must transfer related patents and other intellectual property.

Many Chinese companies that work with foreign businesses, according to Dan Harris in his law blog *Protecting Your Intellectual Property in China, Part II*, are motivated to work with foreign businesses in order to acquire technology, trade secrets, and know-how via training from the owners of the intellectual property. In addition, most of these intangible assets have been lost to those who have been trained by the foreign businesses themselves. Once the information is stolen, it's difficult to prosecute those responsible, and nearly impossible to get the stolen information back. This loss most frequently occurs in[103]

- technology licensing products,
- joint venture manufacturing or services,

- OEM manufacturing,
- product design and development agreements,
- employee training, and
- distribution and sales agreements.

There are a number of steps a company can take to make the theft of intellectual property more difficult. A company should[79]

- educate employees as to what needs to be protected within the company so that they can better protect it. Inadvertent losses can occur from salespeople showing upcoming products, technical organizations describing research and development, publicity departments talking about new patent filings, and so on.
- perform a risk and cost-benefit analysis and determine what information, if lost, would hurt the company the most and which of these assets has the most risk of being stolen.
- place labels on information that is confidential, labeling it as such, and label it as proprietary on computer screens, indicating the importance of the information. This will support your argument, if the case gets to court, that you made it clear that the information was protected.
- ensure both physical and digital security. Restrict access to rooms where sensitive data are stored and use passwords to limit access to important databases.
- install software that tracks documents and intellectual property.
- analyze security breaches, both physical and digital, and put together a *big picture* of your company's security. An analysis of a single incident may not be sufficient to give you what's actually occurring within your company.
- analyze how you would go about stealing your intellectual property if you were spying on your company. This will give you the best indication of what preventative measures are needed to keep this from happening.
- beware of *social engineering*, where business intelligence gatherers elicit information from employees over the phone by implying that they're someone they aren't.
- beware of the conveyance of information in public places, such as conversations in an airport, a restaurant, or a bar. Also beware

of a competitor posing as a potential customer after a company presentation and attempting to get a demo of a new product.

The United States government is working on ways to protect intellectual property theft through the Internet. Senator Patrick Leahy, and eleven bipartisan cosponsors, introduced a bill in Congress called the Protect IP Act. The purpose of this law is to curb access to websites whose sole purpose is to sell infringing intellectual property or counterfeit goods. Currently, if a domain is registered in the United States, law enforcement has the right to seize a domain without trial via what's termed *asset forfeiture*.[76] The Protect IP Act will target domains registered outside the United States, giving the government the authority to force DNS servers in the United States to not carry such domains.

Summary

Intellectual property disputes between the United States and China have existed since the late 1970s, when China opened its doors to foreign trade. In the past, the United States had some degree of success by threatening China with trade sanctions, nonrenewal of its most favored nation's status, and opposition to China's entry into the World Trade Organization.[104] However, once China entered the WTO, things changed. When this happened, the United States had very little leverage over China and subsequently had to use the World Trade Organization's dispute-settlement process to resolve intellectual property disputes.

The real cost of intellectual property theft is not only the loss of jobs and decreased corporate profits, but also increased health risks from both counterfeit drugs and consumer goods. In fact, the World Health Organization (WHO) recently warned that as much as half the world's drug supply may soon consist of fake pharmaceutical drugs.

China is the global leader in the production of counterfeit goods. In 2010, 85 percent of the counterfeit goods seized in Europe and 76 percent of the counterfeit goods seized in the United States were believed to have come from China.[105]

While we've read that the United States and China have had numerous meetings on the subject of intellectual property infringement and that progress is being made, in point of fact, little real progress has actually been made in resolving key issues. One reason for this is that 8 percent of China's GDP comes from the counterfeiting of creative works, consumer goods, industrial products, and software. That's significant. Therefore, we don't believe that there will be an end to the production of counterfeit goods in China in the foreseeable future, because of the significant profits and number of people employed in the production process. The Chinese are not about to put thousands of their citizenry in the unemployment line, risk social discontent, and take a hit to their GDP. Why should they? Instead, the Chinese mind-set is that they must have an economic reason in order to give up profits that are this significant.

Unless there's a counterbalancing situation that would create an untenable situation, such as in the past where the United States threatened China with the loss of its most favored nation status, or an unacceptable political situation, there's nothing that will force the Chinese to balance the scales on intellectual property. It's simply not a level playing field, and the Chinese know it. In fact, the US government also knows it. Keeping a Chinese company from obtaining access to intellectual property seems, at this point, the most plausible way to prevent intellectual property theft.

CHAPTER 7

Chinese Employees and Employee Contracts

The face of Chinese employment has changed in recent years. Not that long ago Chinese employers valued graduates, who returned from studies in the West, to provide their companies with cutting-edge business and management techniques that would make them more competitive and profitable. Today that's changed. Chinese graduates returning from the West now find that employers are less interested in a Western education than in work experience. Many employers view employee work experience as critical for their corporate growth. As a result, the hiring and retention of experienced staff is of paramount importance to a Chinese company.

A Shortage of Skilled Workers

One of the toughest challenges for employers is finding and retaining qualified employees in China. This is contrary to the image of Chinese labor that most of us have. Most of us view China as having an almost limitless labor pool, where wages are cheap and demand for employment is abundant. However, that's not the case. China has a shortage of skilled labor, particularly in middle-management positions. In addition, wages are skyrocketing, with competition for talent increasing wages an average of 15 percent per year. With demand outstripping the supply of skilled laborers, it's not unusual for workers to job-hunt in order to obtain a better work package and develop more skills to increase their employment value.[106] One Chinese company reports that it loses about 10 percent of its workers after long holidays, such as the Chinese New Year. Some companies can lose up to 40 percent of their workers during holidays.[107] The reason that workers tend to leave during this time is that companies generally pay bonuses prior to a long holiday, such as the Spring Festival. Once employees receive their bonus, they'll try to find work at another company where they can earn more money or have better benefits.

The number of available workers across China has dropped in recent years due to China's one-child policy, which went into effect in the 1980s. In 2012, this resulted in the working-age population, ages fifteen to fifty-nine, falling for the first time in decades, thereby creating more demand for workers than there was supply.[107]

Many companies have instituted aggressive and innovative employee-retention programs. Kathy Chu of the *Wall Street Journal* reports that after years of offering production bonuses and other financial incentives to boost employee loyalty, employers are resorting to new methods to increase retention. For example, a Chinese clothing manufacturer held a sewing olympics. The company, which manufactures for corporations such as Burberry Group PLC and Brooks Brothers Group Inc., had employees race to cut, stitch, and fold raw fabric into high-end dress shirts. The winners received a small cash prize, but more importantly, had their life-size images placed outdoors, where they could be viewed by fellow workers. In a country that places a great deal of value on *face*, this was considered a substantial benefit.

Since boosting an employee's pay to compete with other manufacturers doesn't alone suffice to retain employees, some employers are resorting to other forms of incentives to increase retention. For example, some have sponsored dating events, constructed libraries and karaoke rooms on their work campus, and even held *American Idol*–type singing contests.[107]

Because of persistent labor shortages and the lack of required skills, some companies have moved their production from China to other countries that have the requisite labor and skills. For example, Crocs had 80 percent of its shoes made in China in 2012, but expects to have only 65 percent of its shoes manufactured there this year. Coach will similarly reduce its production in China, to about 50 percent by 2015, down from more than 80 percent in 2011.[108] Similarly, according to the *Wall Street Journal*, some companies have shifted their production from China to Vietnam. Lever Style, for example, moved part of its manufacturing to Vietnam and was subsequently able to lower costs to such an extent that they offered their clients a 10 percent discount per garment.[108] Since US retailers' profits generally average between 1 and 2 percent, the savings were significant.

Moving manufacturing operations to another country doesn't work for larger companies. According to Keith Bradsher of the *New York Times*, while some smaller companies are able to satisfy their manufacturing demands in other countries, multinational companies are finding that they can't entirely get away from China. One reason for this is that the labor force, economies, and even the electrical output in many Chinese provinces are larger than in all but a few Southeast Asian countries. If a larger company does decide to relocate to another country, it frequently finds that it quickly uses up local labor capabilities and thereby pushes wages up sharply. Therefore, only a relatively small number of companies, mostly in low-tech sectors like garment and shoe manufacturing, are seeking to leave China entirely. Many companies are finding it more efficient to build new factories in Southeast Asia to supplement their existing China operations.[109] In addition, productivity in China is rising almost as fast as wages in many industries. China's large population, huge industrial base, infrastructure, and increasingly sophisticated workforce still make it the manufacturing country of choice for most industries.

The Chinese government, for its part, considers the migration of some of its industries to other countries to be the natural progression of manufacturing and doesn't plan to replace the jobs that have moved offshore. China's exports are still rising at a double-digit rate, and they continue to be the largest recipient of foreign direct investment (FDI), attracting $112 billion of foreign investment in 2011.[108]

Increasing Employee Retention

In addition to the sewing olympics, karaoke, and other methods of retention mentioned earlier, there are a number of other ways in which a company can increase employee retention:[106]

- *Better internal promotion.* Employees frequently leave companies because they feel they have no upward mobility and their ability to increase their future earnings is limited. Creating a clear pathway for employees to become promoted will enhance corporate retention and decrease the number of employees who want to leave the company due to a perceived lack of future opportunities.
- *Training and travel.* The more training a Chinese employee receives, the more valuable he or she perceives himself or herself to be within the company. If this training is conducted overseas, it's viewed in a very positive manner by the employee and is a good retention tool. Even if training isn't conducted overseas, sending an employee on a trip as a reward for his or her valuable service to the company will be well-received by the employee and his or her fellow workers.
- *Recognition and rewards.* Everyone loves to be praised, and Chinese workers are no different. Rewards tell the recipients and their fellow employees that their work and accomplishments deserve special recognition. In China, public recognition is an especially effective form of praise and almost always increases employee loyalty.

Hiring Employees

Employment rules in China are different from those you're likely to encounter in other parts of the world. For instance, as a rule, Chinese citizens may not generally be hired directly by foreign companies. In addition, as we've discussed earlier, foreign workers may only be employed after they've completed the requisite documentation and obtained the necessary approvals. According to the law firm of Wang & Wang, Article 11 of *China's Regulations Concerning the Control of Resident Offices of Foreign Enterprises* states that the resident office of a foreign enterprise must entrust a *local service unit* to hire its personnel.[110] A company's subsidiary and branch offices must also engage a local service unit unless they obtain permission from the local labor office, in which case they can hire personnel directly.

This prohibition also applies to some professional services. As an example, unlike in most countries, a company in China can't unconditionally hire its own in-house attorney or accountant. Workers with special licenses, such as required by these two professions, must be employed by a recognized domestic professional firm.[110] However, as with most rules in China, there's a work-around, as many companies do employ these types of professionals. In doing so, companies have made special arrangements with the recognized employers of these individuals. The government knows this and considers the company's relationship with the paying employer to be private.

Termination of Employees

China has specific rules with regard to the termination of an employee. In all cases, it's important for the employer to thoroughly document an employee's performance and on what basis the employee was terminated, such as a violation of a specific rule or regulation. It's also important to document if the employee received the proper training for his or her position, as well as the results of any retraining if conducted.

> Employee contracts cannot be terminated if the employee is unable to work due to an occupational disease or injury suffered at work, or if the employee has not yet had a medical determination whether he or she suffered an occupational disease or injury. In addition, if the employee has at least fifteen years of continuous service and is less than five years from statutory retirement age, his or her contract cannot be terminated. Female employees who are pregnant, lactating, or in confinement can similarly not be terminated.

Gregory Sy, who is Of Counsel at Grandall Legal Group and a corporate/commercial lawyer, indicates that an employer may terminate an employee either without notice, with thirty-day notice, or with severance compensation for any of the reasons detailed below:[111]

Termination without Notice

- At any time during the probationary period if the employee fails to meet corporate standards.
- The employee materially breaches company rules and regulations.
- The employee is guilty of graft or corruption and damages the interests of the company.
- The employee goes to work for another company and fails to complete the tasks assigned by his or her original employer, even after he's been notified by his or her employer.
- The employee is the subject of a criminal investigation.
- The employee's labor contract is found to be fraudulent.
- The employee is absent without leave for fifteen days.[112]

Termination with Thirty-Day Notice

- After returning from medical leave or a non-work-related injury, the employee is unable to perform his or her current or newly assigned duties.
- The employee is incompetent or remains incompetent after training or adjustment of his or her position.
- The employer and employee cannot agree on a modified labor contract after there has been a major change in *objective* circumstances that were relied upon when signing the original labor contract.

Termination with Severance Compensation

- The employee is terminated after receiving a thirty-day prior notice.
- The employee is terminated due to a business restructuring or difficulties with the business.
- The employer wants to terminate the employee's labor contract, and the employee agrees.
- Expiration of a fixed-term labor contract, except where the employee refuses to renew the contract on equal or better terms.

- The employee's labor contract is terminated because the employer declares bankruptcy or loses his or her business license.

Severance is calculated by multiplying the number of years an employee worked by his or her monthly salary and adding half a month's salary for a partial year. There is a cap in that an employee earning more than three times the average monthly wage in the local employment area will only receive a maximum of twelve months in severance wages.[111] If the employee has less than one year of service, his or her termination pay is limited to a proportion of his length of service.[112] Severance is paid upon termination of employment.

Insurance

There are five mandatory types of insurance in the employment welfare system:[113]

- pensions
- medical insurance
- work-related injury insurance
- unemployment insurance
- maternity insurance

In addition, both the employer and employee mandatorily must contribute to a housing fund.

Pensions

A formalized retirement fund has existed in China since the mid-1980s, when state-employed workers were required to contribute a portion of their wages to a retirement fund.

> Employers usually contribute 20 percent of an employee's salary, but this rate varies and can be much lower in some cities. An employee's contribution is a uniform 8 percent nationwide.[113] Therefore, employees and enterprises jointly bear the cost of the insurance.

Once contributions have been made for a fifteen-year period of time, the employees are eligible at retirement age to start receiving their pension. The amount they receive is based on what they've contributed to their individual retirement fund. If this money is exhausted, the individual would be entitled to receive a pension from the public pool of funds, which is composed of employer contributions. If an employee dies before the amount in his or her individual fund is exhausted, then the remaining funds would pass to the employee's estate.[114] All contributions to the fund are not taxable.

China's pension system is likely to undergo future changes. Just as with the elimination of the iron rice bowl, the government is feeling increased economic pressure from its past social programs and is moving toward the eventual elimination of cradle-to-grave state-supported security.

Medical Insurance

> An employer will usually contribute between 7 and 12 percent of an employee's salary toward medical insurance. This percentage varies because some cities require a lower percentage. This is a shared system, where both the employer and employee make contributions. An employee normally is required to contribute 2 percent of his or her salary for medical insurance, but this amount will vary in some cities.

The amount of insurance coverage for different treatments varies according to the illness. Employees carry a medical insurance card containing the amount of contributions they've made, and these contributions can be applied to either purchase medicine or toward outpatient costs.[113] Employers' contributions go into a public pool meant to cover more expensive inpatient treatment.

Work-Related Injury Insurance

Employers contribute between 0.4 percent and 3 percent of an employee's salary toward work-related injury insurance. The amount paid depends on the company's location, as well as the occupational danger. Employees are not required to contribute.

If an employee is injured on the job, the employer is not required to pay for the employee's medical care, as this is covered by insurance. However, the employer is required to pay the employee's monthly salary for a period of time based on the average wage of the employee. During this time, the employer will gather proof of the injury, and fill out and submit required documentation to the insurance agency.[113] If the employee cannot return to work, the employer does not have to continue to pay the employee. Instead, the employee will apply to the social insurance fund for future payments.

Unemployment Insurance

Employers contribute as much as 2 percent of an employee's salary for unemployment insurance, but this amount can be much lower in some cities. Employees also make contributions to their unemployment insurance of approximately 1 percent. However, a few cities in China don't require this contribution.

Unemployment benefits last for a maximum of twenty-four months as long as the employee has made his or her contributions to the unemployment insurance fund for at least one year prior to filing for unemployment. The amount of unemployment insurance paid is fixed and unrelated to the individual's previous salary.[113] China's unemployment is highest in rural areas and in eastern coastal cities.[114]

Maternity Insurance

Employers contribute between 0.5 and 1 percent of an employee's salary, depending on the location of the company within China. No employee contribution is required.

Once maternity leave starts, an employer is no longer required to pay an employee's salary. Instead, the employee will receive her average monthly salary from the maternity fund. Maternity leave generally lasts three months, fifteen days before birth and seventy-five days after, but is permitted to be as long as five months in some cities. Difficult births or twins entitle the mother to an additional fifteen days of leave. In addition, one hour per day with pay is permitted for baby feeding until the baby is twelve months of age.[113] Fathers are entitled to paternity leave, also funded by the insurance fund. But paternity leave generally lasts only three days. The number of days permitted can vary by city, and longer leaves are allowed by some cities. During maternity and paternity leaves the employer is obligated to hold open the employee's position. Maternity leave is granted only once in a lifetime since China has a one-child policy.

Sick Days

Permitted sick leave in China can be quite long, depending on the number of years an employee has worked for an employer. The permitted sick leave period usually ranges from three and twenty-four months. If an employee is undergoing prescribed medical treatment and recuperation, he or she must be paid no less than 80 percent of the local minimum wage, unless another amount is specified by local law.[112]

Bereavement Leave

Bereavement, or funeral, leave is permitted when an employee's parent, spouse, or child dies. It's usually granted for one to three days, during which time the employee receives full pay.[115] Local rules may also permit bereavement leave when an employee's parent-in-law dies.

Marriage Leave

Marriage leave is permitted for up to three days. However, if the bride is at least twenty-three years of age and the groom at least twenty-five, then ten days is permitted.

Housing Fund

The purpose of the housing fund is to enable workers to save enough money to purchase a house or apartment. Contributions to this fund are from both the employer and employee and are mandatory. A number of cities, including Shenzhen in southern China, don't require an employee contribution.

> Employers contribute between 7 and 13 percent of an employee's salary. An employee's contribution varies by city, but his or her contribution usually matches that of the employer and the contribution is nontaxable.

Some cities don't set a limit on the amount one can contribute, but most do, with that limit generally being 500 percent of the average salary for an employee in the company's locale. Any portion over 300 percent is deemed to be taxable income of the employee.[113] When employees wish to purchase a house or apartment, they use their housing fund money to make the down payment. The housing fund can also be used at any time to pay back the loan to the bank. Upon retirement, the remaining balance in the housing fund can be withdrawn and used in any manner the retiree wishes.

Workweek and Overtime

China's labor law sets an average workweek at five days, eight hours per day, and forty hours of work time per week, with two rest days. If the employee works less than a standard eight-hour day, then this five-day limit doesn't apply. Overtime is permitted up to three hours per day and a maximum of thirty-six hours per month, with overtime pay set at 150 percent of normal wage, unless work is performed on weekends. If that occurs, the employee is paid 200 percent of normal wage. If employees work on a holiday, it's required to pay them 300 percent of their normal wage.[116] Women who are seven months or more pregnant or who breast-feed are not permitted to work overtime or at night.[112]

Holidays

There's a number of statutory holidays to which workers are entitled. The length of these statutory holidays is given below. Employers may also elect to give longer holiday periods or provide additional holidays. We know from personal experience that during Spring Festival, employees sometimes travel great distances to spend time with their families. During this period, we expect businesses to shut down for two to three weeks, rather than the three-day statutory minimum. Employees will normally receive a bonus of one to three months of their salary prior to the commencement of the Spring Festival.

Below is a list of official Chinese holidays. These are the minimum days an employee has off, but actual holiday periods provided by businesses will usually be longer. The following are China's statutory holidays:[112]

- New Year's Day—a one-day holiday held on January 1
- Chinese New Year/Spring Festival—a three-day holiday held the first day of the Chinese lunar calendar
- Woman's Day—a one-half-day holiday held for women on March 8
- Tomb Sweeping Day/Qingming Festival—a one-day holiday held the fifteenth day after the vernal equinox, which is either April 4 or 5
- Labor Day—a one-day holiday held May 1
- Dragon Boat Festival—a one-day holiday held the fifth day of the fifth month of the Chinese lunar calendar
- Mid-Autumn Festival—a one-day holiday held the fifteenth day of the fifth lunar month
- National Day—a three-day holiday held October 1

Vacations and Leave Days

Just as in many other countries, a worker's tenure determines the length of his or her paid vacation per year. Generally, workers start at a baseline of five paid leave days if their employment is less than ten years. After ten years, but less than fifteen years of accumulated employment, they're generally given ten paid leave days per year. If employees have more than fifteen years of accumulated employment, they generally receive fifteen paid leave days per year. We use the word *generally* because paid leave is set by local regulations in China's municipalities and provinces.[112] The leave periods provided are what we've found to be the generally accepted standard.

Employee Contracts

It's a requirement in China that all full-time workers have a written contract specifying

- the length of the contract,
- the employee's job description,
- the location of employment,
- working conditions,
- wages, and
- possible disciplinary actions to which the employee may be subject.

An employment contract must be provided within one month of the date the employment begins.[112] If the employer fails to receive a signed contract from the employee within this thirty-day period, he or she must pay double wages to the employee until a contract is signed.[117] An employer can avoid this liability, for failing to conclude a written contract with a reluctant employee, by terminating the employee before the thirty-day period has expired.

There are three types of Chinese employee contracts:

- fixed-term contract
- non-fixed term, or open-ended, contract
- project contract

While the fixed-term contract terminates on a specified date and the open-ended contract has no definitive termination date, the project contract is issued for employees who work on a specific set of tasks specified in the contract and terminates with the completion of those tasks.

The employer can establish a probationary period for the employee to determine if the employee's skills are in line with his or her expectations. The maximum length of this probationary period varies with the length of the contract executed by the employee. For contracts of between three months and one year in length, the maximum probationary period is one month. For contracts ranging between one and three years, it's two months. For a three-year or open-ended contract, it's six months.[117]

Chinese law requires the employer to inform employees of working and safety conditions before they sign their employment contract and prior to beginning their job.

According to Ronald Brown, a professor of law at the University of Hawaii, in his book *East Asian Labor and Employment Law,* all Chinese contracts must be in writing and should contain the following:[118]

- name, address, and legal representative of the employer
- name, address, and identification number of the employee
- duration of employment
- job descriptions and work site
- working hours, rest periods, and vacations
- labor remuneration
- social insurance
- labor conditions, working conditions, and occupational hazard prevention, as well as other matters stipulated by laws and regulations
- protection of confidential information, trade secrets, and intellectual property (if applicable)
- competition restrictions (limited to senior management and technical personnel)

Provisions such as performance, termination, severance pay, collective contracts (for a group of employees), and dispute resolution are addressed by applicable sections of local, provincial, and national law. If an employer places competition restrictions in the contract, they're obligated to pay the former employee post-employment compensation in monthly installments. This amount usually ranges from 20 percent to 60 percent of an employee's monthly salary. The limit for postemployment compensation is two years.

A part-time employee is defined as anyone who works for the same employer an average of not more than four hours per day and not more than twenty-four hours in aggregate per week. If these hours are exceeded, then the employee is considered to be working full-time and will then be governed by applicable regulations covering full-time employment. In the case of a part-time employee, the employer is not required to have a contract, as an oral agreement will suffice. The employer may terminate part-time employees at will and without severance pay.[119] There is no probationary period for a part-time worker.

CHAPTER 8

Corruption, Bribery, and Other Tools of the Trade

No society is exempt from corruption. It exists in every country. What makes corruption in China so different from that in other countries, in our opinion, is the Chinese government. The government, directly and indirectly, has tolerated various levels of corruption for millennia. As a result, understanding the relationship between corruption in business and corruption in the government is essential for any businessperson in China.

Government and Commercial Corruption

There are two types of corruption in China: government corruption and commercial corruption.[120]

> Corruption, for our purposes, includes nepotism, accepting bribes and kickbacks, lavish spending of public funds, laundering of profits, sending public money overseas, and receiving ownership in a company with little or no investment.

Most foreign businesspeople are exposed to commercial corruption. It's not unusual for Chinese members of your company to be working for suppliers or competitors. The Chinese mind-set for this is that employees believe they're working for themselves to a greater degree than they're working for their company. As an example, the China Market Research

Group reported that a vice president of marketing at a large company asked his Chinese employees to evaluate a new marketing agency for their company. The vice president invited a leading firm to make a competing presentation against the company that was currently doing their China marketing. Afterward, all eighty employees in sales and marketing were asked to vote and recommend who should represent the company. The challenger to the current marketing company made a strong presentation, whereas the incumbent's presentation fell far short. When it came time to tabulate the votes, the vice president was shocked to learn that the employees voted seventy-eight to two against the challenger. His only comment was, "Now I know why so many of them are driving BMWs and Mercedes when they only make $20,000 a year."[120]

A Westerner's view of corruption is usually black or white, while the Chinese view of corruption is usually gray. For the average Chinese, the circumstances dictate whether or not an act is corrupt. Depending on the circumstances, a kickback, bribery, or a fraudulent invoice may be looked upon as normal and expected, a part of doing business. Many Chinese believe the West is naive and unrealistic in the way business is conducted. Chinese businesspeople will tell you that their system works. Their economy is growing much faster than any economy in the West, their inflation is under control, and their standard of living continues to increase. As a result, trying to get a Chinese company to change the way they do business and accept Western standards of business conduct is difficult. The only way this usually happens is when a Western company refuses to do business unless the Chinese company complies with Western standards of conduct. Even then, the Chinese company will more than likely give lip service to the codes of business conduct dictated to them by their Western counterpart. Long-term compliance is unlikely without competent supervision.

Corruption Costs

Corruption within China carries a cost.

It's estimated that China loses $86 billion a year to corruption and that corruption is responsible for 2 percent to 15 percent in lost tax revenue and stolen government funds.

Minxin Pei, of the Carnegie Endowment for International Peace in Washington, estimates that 10 percent of Chinese government spending is lost to corruption, but that the chance of a corrupt Chinese government official going to jail for corruption is only about 3 percent. The last year that China's National Audit Office publicly issued its findings on misused or embezzled government funds was in 2005, when it reported that an estimated $35 billion in Chinese government funds were either misused or embezzled.[121] Following that revelation, the government ceased releasing similar figures.

Guanxi

Chinese business dealings between individuals and companies is governed by a special socio-business relationship called *guanxi*. What we would call inside information, a sweetheart deal, or corruption may in point of fact be guanxi or networking among family, friends, and business associates. With guanxi, individuals perform favors for one another regardless of one's social status within the group. It's a family affair among all parties. In performing these favors, reciprocity is considered obligatory. The more you request assistance from someone in your network, the more you owe reciprocal favors. There's also no expiration date on the request for a reciprocal favor.

In guanxi, the social and the personal have melded together and placed the relationship on a higher plane than mere friendship. There's a melding of family, friends, and business associates into a *communal group,* where a trusting relationship exists between parties.[122] This relationship takes precedence over all else, even laws. Guanxi is viewed as a long-term relationship, with trust as the cornerstone. Anyone outside your communal group is an outsider and is not to be trusted.

Friendships in China are action-based, rather than feeling-based. For example, a sign of friendship between parties would be receiving a sizable contract, even though you were not the most qualified or the lowest bidder. You, in return, would give a red envelope containing cash to your friend as a reciprocal gesture of that friendship. A red envelope with cash is how people traditionally present gifts to one another in China.

Other examples symbolizing friendship include a friend at your child's school gives your child high marks even though he's actually failed the class; a high-ranking professor at a business school presents you with your MBA, even though you're rarely at class; a government official provides you a two-year tax exemption, giving you a significant advantage over your business competitors; or you're given access to government land to expand your business beyond that of your business rivals. These are examples of what Westerners would consider corruption, but what your average Chinese would say is guanxi and what's expected in Chinese culture.

Not all corruption is associated with guanxi. Most corruption, in fact, is purely the result of greed. Chinese government corruption, for example, exists at all levels. According to the 2011 edition of the *Hurun Report*, the seventy richest parliamentarians in China have a combined wealth of approximately $75.1 billion. In contrast, the seventy richest members of the US Congress have a combined wealth of $4.8 billion.

Government corruption doesn't usually involve foreigners, as government officials are very uncomfortable with taking money from foreigners unless the projects are large real estate transactions or involve alcohol.[120] Government officials feel that foreigners don't know Chinese culture or how to play the game, and that the risks of being caught are just too high.

Can the Chinese Government End Corruption?

A question one might ask is why can't the government end governmental corruption? Since the government has an omnipotent power base, why doesn't it simply make public examples of corrupt politicians and conduct frequent internal audits on the use of government funds?

In our opinion, the primary reason is that the government doesn't want to rock the boat. It doesn't want to alienate or lose the support of local, provincial, or even national government officials. It wants these officials to keep the local citizenry content and prevent social unrest. As a result, the national government tolerates a certain level of corruption as a *cost of doing business*. If a local official wants to give a contract to his or her friend, give a passing grade to a friend's child, or get some money in return for a contract, then the government is generally fine with that within limits. As long as projects go smoothly, the foreign press doesn't print accusations of bribery or corruption, and the populace is content, then they'll likely turn a blind eye to what's happening.

Average Chinese citizens know of local government corruption and, for the most part, ignore it. As long as the corruption doesn't affect their daily life, they accept it as *the way it is*. However, when this corruption significantly affects the average Chinese citizen, there's usually a vocal or physical backlash by the citizenry that moves the government to take action. For example, an article written in the *Los Angeles Times* by Barbara Demick discussed the decades-old government perk of driving luxury cars. There are more than 100,000 Audi A6s in China, 20 percent of them owned by the government. In fact, government officials can be seen driving almost any brand of luxury automobile and have been photographed driving a Mercedes SUV, a Porsche Cayenne, a black Maserati, and even a Bentley. Since these cars are far beyond the means of the average Chinese citizen, most Chinese are unhappy that the country's money is being spent in this manner.

This unhappiness recently manifested itself after a recent spate of school bus accidents, with the worst one killing twenty-one kindergartners. In that accident, a group of sixty-two children were crammed into a van designed to carry six passengers. A microblogger calling himself Minxingdie summarized the outrage after this accident by blogging: "Every time I see a school bus accident and think about the great many Audi A6s on the street, I shake my head and sigh."[121] Another contributor to the website remarked, "No wonder there's no money left for school buses!" As a result of this accident, the government provided additional school buses and curbed the issuance and use of government vehicles in the area.

Examples of Corruption

Mark Magnier of the *Los Angeles Times* gave these examples of small-scale corruption in China:[121]

- giving doctors cash-stuffed red envelopes to do their best in the operating room
- passing a driving test even though you've never left the parking lot
- bribing reporters to print favorable newspaper stories
- drug dealers escaping arrest by paying off the police

- government officials demanding payment to award contracts and issue permits

Sometimes government officials will strongly suggest a *fee* to *expedite* a particular situation. Failure to pay this fee can have an adverse effect. For example, a routine inspection at a construction site may take only a short amount of time when a fee is paid. However, failure to pay this fee may result in many problems being discovered during the inspection process and required approvals being delayed for an indefinite period of time.

On a business trip a few years ago to Jiangsu province, we spoke with a local government official who wanted us to meet with a Chinese company the following day. The company, he told us, needed financial restructuring and was anxious to get its books and records in order. Since the government official's office was relatively close to our hotel, he volunteered to pick us up and drive us to his office for the meeting. When he pulled up in front of the hotel, we were both surprised to see him step out of a brand-new Buick. This is an expensive car in China, and this official wasn't of a high-enough rank to be provided with a government vehicle. On the drive to his office, he told us that he'd recently acquired this car, a top-of-the-line four-door version, and he was quite proud of it. Sensing our amazement, he told us that he had gotten a good deal on the purchase of the car or he couldn't have afforded it. We both thought that *free* could be categorized as a good deal.

Public officials such as we described in the above example earn around $450 per month. Corruption at this level is common, and most of these officials do indeed have nice cars. Even though this government official might be thought of as an example of egregious government corruption, he pales in comparison to Zhang Shuguang, the former deputy chief of engineering for China's Railway Ministry. In 2011, Zhang was arrested for corruption when an investigation turned up that he had accumulated $2.8 billion in foreign bank accounts.

According to Adam Minter of Bloomberg, the People's Bank of China posted a report, which was subsequently deleted, that stated nearly $120 billion in public funds has been taken by 16,000 to 18,000 public officials who have fled China since the mid-1990s.[117]

Corruption is not limited to the government. It exists, in one form or another, at all levels of Chinese society. Here are some examples of corruption that exist at the corporate level:[121]

- *False audits*. We routinely visit companies that hand us an audit that, upon close examination, turns out to be fraudulent.
- *Kickbacks*. A purchasing department taking kickbacks from suppliers.
- *Bribes*. Businessmen bribing government officials with real estate, cars, or ownership in lucrative businesses; secretaries getting paid to book their bosses' flights through a particular travel agency; receptionists referring calls to a rival firm; and teachers focusing on students whose parents give them money.

Living in Denial

The corruption we've previously described would, in most countries, be considered so immoral that it would make the evening news or be printed in the local newspaper. That seldom happens in China. That's because the media is controlled by the government, which doesn't want to create social discord and incite the people. Therefore, reports of corruption only appear in the local media if it's already surfaced on the Internet or knowledge of the corruption has spread so far by word of mouth that it's already widely known. In either case, an incident of corruption in the press is likely to be less of a revelation to the average Chinese and more of a documentation as to the government's view of the facts. In addition, the government may or may not decide to take action. Whether or not the government decides to act will, in large part, depend on the anger of the people over the incident and the political connections of the corrupt official.

The foreign press is another matter. When the government is embarrassed, things begin to happen. The government, always conscious of its foreign image, wants to let the world know that it doesn't condone the incident that's been reported, even though the incident might have tacitly been going on with the full knowledge of the government for quite some time. When the foreign press publishes an article on a corrupt official, a train crash, or a social injustice, for example, the Chinese government usually acts quickly and decisively to resolve the situation. Whoever the offender, even if supported by a local or provincial government official, will usually be dealt with harshly. The government wants to quickly get this incident out of the world press and put an end to investigative reporting of the incident.

Does Corruption Help the Chinese Economy?

In the first quarter of 2013, China's GDP growth posted a disappointing growth rate of 7.7 percent year over year, lower than expectations. While this growth would make economists in virtually every country in the world, except one, ecstatic if it occurred in their country, it disappointed China-centric economists, who expected a more robust GDP. One of the reasons for this lower GDP growth was the country's decreased industrial output.

While there are many theories as to why this decrease occurred, many rank-and-file Chinese blame President Xi Jinping's anticorruption campaign. They believe that the government's crackdown on corruption placed inordinate pressure on many Chinese to stay below the government's radar by avoiding the trappings of wealth and the gifting of luxury goods. Since people were buying less, they reason, industrial output had to be less. President Xi, for his part, tried to regain the country's trust in the CCP. The public has increasingly come to view the Party as self-enriching and corrupt. As a result, President Xi has instituted a series of reforms aimed at curbing corruption and extravagance within the government. According to *GlobalPost*, President Xi has initiated curbs on lavish dinners, high-end gift giving, extravagant banquets, liquor, flowers, travel, and the like. As a result, many restaurants, luxury retailers, and liquor stores have experienced a correspondingly sharp decrease in revenue. Shark-fin sales, for example, fell 70 percent,[123] and officials are no longer allowed to accept a Rolex as a thank-you for doing a favor.[124] Not even the military is exempt, as they've been ordered to clamp down on conspicuous consumption, including alcohol. Therefore, on the face of it, China's anticorruption campaign has had at least some impact on retailers and the economy.

The US Foreign Corrupt Practices Act

The Foreign Corrupt Practices Act (FCPA) of 1977, and subsequent amendments in 1998, prohibits the payment of bribes to foreign officials in order to obtain or retain business. The FCPA is divided into two major sets of provisions: the anti-bribery provisions enforced by the US Department of Justice, and the books, records, and internal controls provisions enforced by the US Securities and Exchange Commission (SEC).[125]

Under the anti-bribery provisions, any US company, its personnel, US citizens, foreign companies with shares listed on a US exchange or required to file reports with the SEC, or any person while present in the United States is prohibited from:[126]

> "Corruptly paying, offering to pay, promising to pay, or authorizing the payment of money, a gift, or anything of value to a foreign official, or any foreign political party official, for the purpose of obtaining or retaining business."

There is an exception to the FCPA known as the *grease payment* exception. This exception applies to payments that are used to expedite routine government actions by foreign officials. In authorizing this exception, Congress acknowledged the reality of doing business in developing countries, where business cannot effectively be done without such payments. These types of payments would include obtaining permits or licenses, scheduling inspections, or other ministerial tasks that involve no discretion.[125] An example would be paying a clerk to switch on the phones for a new business. The clerk has that responsibility to turn on the phone service but could delay this action for some period of time unless a payment is made. This obviously involves the payment of a small sum of money. However, there are no clear guidelines as to what constitutes an unacceptable amount of money.[125] For example, the payment of a much larger sum of money to a government official tasked with issuing a license or permit may be viewed as a bribe and not a grease payment.

According to Deloitte LLP, many companies now use third parties to help them establish operations in foreign countries. Third parties deal with local regulators for licenses and permits and may even function as sales channels for the company. This can lead to an increased amount of corruption tied to these third-party activities.[127] If a third party is guilty of corruption under the FCPA, then these actions may have an adverse effect on the principal company hiring them.

Joint ventures can also create problems for US companies operating in China. Take, for example, a US company, RAE Systems, that the US Department of Justice indicated it intended to prosecute. RAE Systems formed a joint venture with two local Chinese companies. Prior to the formation of the joint venture, the Chinese company bribed various Chinese agencies. They also made kickbacks to employees of government bureaus and gave lavish gifts to government officials. RAE Systems knew of these practices prior to the joint venture. In response, it set up a training program to educate employees on the FCPA and established controls to prohibit these practices from occurring in the future. However, these practices still continued. The Department of Justice concluded that the measures instituted by the company were *half measures*.[125] Since the company's sales force was an in-country direct sales force for its China operations, management could not effectively monitor or control the actions of its sales agents. Therefore, internal monitoring and control from outside of China was considered ineffective.

To establish an effective in-country FCPA program, one needs to have a local and trusted Chinese staff in charge of compliance.[125] A local Chinese staff is best qualified to monitor and detect FCPA violations, as well as educate employees as to acceptable business conduct under the FCPA. We don't believe an effective monitoring program can be established without in-country personnel, as each country has a unique business and cultural environment. China is no exception. Unless you have an experienced staff, who have substantive employment experience with Chinese companies, you'll be unlikely to detect and prevent FCPA violations. An experienced staff knows what to look for and can help foreign companies maintain compliance, while a foreigner simply has no clue.

In China, there's no cure for corruption. It's endemic. The government knows this and simply seeks to keep it at a level that's acceptable to the public. The problem isn't that the government doesn't want to end corruption. It does. The problem is that the cure may be worse than the disease. This means that the measures needed to end corruption could cause a substantial disruption of everyday life. Corruption has frequently been described as the oil that lubricates Chinese society and the economy. It's an entirely accurate statement.

Corruption is never going to decrease until a combination of measures is instituted. At a minimum, government wages should be increased to allow officials at all levels to earn a decent living. In addition, better internal controls and governance should be initiated, along with an increase in government transparency. Finally, there should be an increase in law enforcement. In most cases, anticorruption laws are already in place. However, the government chooses not to enforce these laws. Until there is a comprehensive enforcement program, combined with measures aimed at safeguarding the public from corruption, the oil that lubricates Chinese society and the economy is likely to continue its torrid flow across China.

CHAPTER 9

Rising from the Ashes:
China Tries to Solve Its Environmental Issues

China is beset by a multitude of environmental challenges caused by a combination of a lack of experience, poor planning, and an unwillingness to address the enormity of these issues until relatively recently. In addition, the massive amount of pollution in China today is, in some instances, getting worse due to the tremendous growth of the Chinese economy.

China has sixteen of the world's twenty most polluted cities, according to the World Bank.[128] The government estimates that environmental degradation cost it $230 billion in 2010, or 3.5 percent of its GDP.[129]

The Chinese government is currently in the process of playing catch-up and is now aggressively trying to solve its environmental challenges before the situation becomes substantively unresolvable. This attitude adjustment is a result of the realization that, unless environmental issues are addressed and resolved, the economic drivers that have been responsible for China establishing and maintaining the country's economic dominance and its political stability will, in time, eventually fade.

The natural resources that have helped sustain China's rise to be the economic superpower it is today have also been the biggest contributors to the country's pollution. The Chinese government is trying to change that and is aggressively seeking international expertise and technology in remediating its environmental issues. China's increasing emphasis on the environment has created enormous business opportunities for those who have the requisite technology and skills. Today no country spends more than China on creating alternative forms of energy, trying to remediate its environment, and implementing environmental controls.

Environmental Concerns

China has a number of pressing environmental concerns resulting from decades of failing to prevent, address, and remediate the country's pollution. The country's primary environmental concerns are[130]

- air pollution,
- water pollution,
- desertification,
- biodiversity,
- agricultural pollution, and
- waste.

Air Pollution: The Problem

Some would argue that air quality may be the most important environmental challenge facing China.

> The *New York Times* reports that air quality in China has deteriorated to the point that only 1 percent of the country's 560 million city dwellers breathe air considered safe by European Union standards.[131]

Edward Wong of the *New York Times* states that, in 2010, outdoor air pollution in China contributed to 1.2 million premature deaths, or 40 percent of the global total. By comparison, India, with 1.27 billion people, had 620,000 premature deaths in 2010 due to outdoor air pollution. The Paris-based Organization for Economic Cooperation and Development estimated that by 2050, more than 3.6 million people could end up dying prematurely from air pollution.[129] Most of those dying will reside in China and India.

In the past, the government generally ignored the specter of air pollution by acknowledging that there indeed needed to be steps taken to improve air quality, but that the actual quality of air wasn't as bad as people thought. No one actually believed this, of course, but this is what the government espoused. However, the most accurate information on the extent of at least one city in China's air pollution came from an unlikely source: the United States government. In Beijing, the US Embassy's Beijing Environmental Monitoring Center takes daily measurements for PM2.5 particulates, which is one of six components of the Air Quality Index (AQI) and a particulate tiny enough to enter the lungs. It's a by-product of, among other things, vehicle emissions.

The US Embassy also takes measurements of Beijing's air quality and then posts these readings. Not surprisingly, the American and Chinese AQI readings don't match. One reason for this is that the standards published by the two countries are different. According to US standards, if the PM2.5 density reaches 15.4 micrograms per cubic meter, the matching AQI figure is 50. According to Chinese standards, the AQI figure in this case is 35. In January 2013, the US Embassy reading in Beijing was 343, compared to the published Chinese government reading of 290. Although both the American and Chinese AQI technically stop at 500, individual readings can be higher. The main reason for this is that there's an international consensus that 500 is generally a number that can't be reached. However, the US Embassy in Beijing has measured readings as high as 886.[132]

The burning of coal is responsible for most of this air pollution. According to a study by Greenpeace and the Peking University School of Public Health, the burning of coal accounts for 19 percent of the country's total environmental air pollution. The next highest contributor to air pollution is vehicle emissions, which contribute 6 percent.[133] China consumes more coal than the United States, Europe, and Japan combined.[134] In fact, according to the *BP Statistical Review of World Energy* published in June 2011, China generated 77 percent of its electricity from coal and peat in 2010.[135] Therefore, it's not uncommon in China to inhale particles two to four times in excess of World Health Organization guidelines.[136]

Vehicle emissions continue to be a problem. With 2012 auto sales topping 19 million units and alternative fuel vehicles comprising only 0.6 percent of those sales, vehicle pollution is continuing to increase in China.[137]

Given the seriousness of air quality, one might assume that aggressive measures are being taken and that air quality improvements might be on the horizon. But the problem is so pervasive, and the cost to address these issues is now so enormous, that the government feels aggressive efforts at remediation will affect the economy, corporate profitability, and the sustainment of jobs. Consequently, air quality may actually get worse before it starts to get better.

> A Deutsche Bank report released in February 2013 estimated that, with the current trend of coal usage and automobile emissions, air pollution in China was expected to worsen by an additional 70 percent by 2025.[138]

On the numerous occasions that we've been to Beijing, the air has been so *thick* at times that you almost feel like you're in a cigar bar or a smoking lounge at the airport. We also believe this is why you're unlikely to see any automotive convertibles in China, especially in Beijing, as the faces of those riding in the car would likely be charcoal-colored by the time they arrived at their destination.

Air Pollution: The Solution

Bigger cities are addressing increasing vehicle pollution by instituting either a lottery or an auction system for acquiring license plates. Beijing, which has seen the number of vehicles within its city increase from 3.13 million in 2008 to 5.18 million in 2012, believes that its lottery system, along with other measures, has stopped 20 percent of the cars that would normally be driving into the city each weekday.[139] In addition, the government announced in February 2013 that it would begin to impose emission limits on six polluting industries, including coal-fired power plants and steel and petrochemical factories.[133] The government also announced it would set a 15-million-ton cap on coal consumption by 2015.

The Chinese Ministry of Environmental Protection (MEP) is trying to stay ahead of the increasing pollution within the country, but so far has been unsuccessful. Part of the reason is that China previously spent a great deal of money on infrastructure support for its industrial base and other expenditures that contributed to the success of its economy and increased overall employment. As a result, there wasn't much in the way of funding or governmental focus on environmental issues. That's beginning to change. Recently the government announced a $56 billion plan to reduce air pollution between 2011 and 2015.[136] In addition, the government is seeking more accurate information on the extent of pollution throughout the country. As an example, seventy-four cities are now required to release data on levels of particulate matter 2.5 micrometers in diameter or smaller,[129] a size that deeply penetrates the body's tissues.

Water Pollution: The Problem

Half of China's population lacks safe drinking water. In fact, whenever we're anywhere in China, we always drink bottled water. And we're not alone. Nearly all Chinese drink bottled water unless they boil local water first before consuming it. One of the reasons for this is that one-third of industrial wastewater, and more than 90 percent of household sewage, are released into China's rivers and lakes without first being treated.

> The underground water supplies in 90 percent of Chinese cities are now contaminated, according to sinologist Jeffrey Hays, in his website *Facts and Details*. In 2011 the Chinese government reported that 43 percent of state-monitored rivers were so polluted, they were unsuitable for human contact.[140]

In addition to industrial waste from thousands of factories and sewage discharge, agricultural pollution, resulting from the use of farm fertilizers, is also a significant contaminant to the country's water supply. It's estimated that 11.7 million pounds of organic pollutants are dumped into Chinese waters every day.[140] This compares to 5.5 in the United States, 3.4 in Japan, 2.3 in Germany, 3.2 in India, and 0.6 in South Africa.

An example of how China's rapid industrialization and growth have led to polluting the nation's water supply can be found in Rui'an, a small city near Shanghai. *Time* magazine reports that, prior to China opening to the world and beginning its incredible industrial growth, the people in this tiny city could swim and wash vegetables in the city's river. Now more than a hundred shoe factories discharge their chemical raw materials and industrial waste into the river, making its water undrinkable.

To demonstrate how his city's rivers had turned toxic, one resident in Zhejiang, a province in eastern China, wanted to make his point with government officials. He offered $32,000 to the chief of the local environmental protection department if he'd swim for twenty minutes in a nearby river.[141] The official refused the wager.

Water Pollution: The Solution

China's water pollution has proved difficult for the government to get its arms around. The government encourages domestic industrial growth and increased agricultural output. They're significant components of the country's economy and employ large numbers of people. They're also two of the largest contributors to water pollution. The inclination on the part of the government, therefore, is to leave well enough alone. The economy is booming, people are employed, and individual wealth is increasing across the nation. But the government knows it can't afford to be environmentally inactive. It knows that unless it enacts some manner of pollution controls on industry and agriculture, the country's current prosperity will slowly turn into a dead-end street. The citizenry, already unhappy with the nation's air pollution, will not also tolerate an increasingly toxic water supply. They expect their government to not only increase their standard of living but also their quality of life.

In the industrial sector, both local and national governments are increasingly having companies install water-treatment facilities at their manufacturing plants so that treated effluent being pumped into lakes, rivers, and streams is in line with international standards.

A more difficult problem for the government is the agricultural contamination of the nation's water supply. The government wants to keep farmers happy, as well as maintain the country's high level of agricultural production. Doing this while decreasing agricultural contaminants is an extremely difficult task. One of the methods employed to address this issue is to try to introduce various agricultural strains that don't require as much fertilizer, pesticides, or water. That's not possible with all agricultural products, but it's becoming increasingly prevalent. A parallel task is to try to educate farmers, something that's easier said than done, as farmers have traditionally resisted change. However, since fertilizer and pesticides cost money, a product that produces the desired crop yield with less growing expense attracts the attention of the nation's farmers.

The government is also stepping up construction of sewage-treatment facilities. A great many Chinese cities, unable to fund their expanding sewage-treatment needs, have simply dumped raw sewage into the country's lakes, rivers, and streams. The government knows this but can't prevent it, because many cities and towns don't have the funding to build or expand a sewage-treatment facility. As a result, the government is forcing local governments to address this problem.

Desertification: The Problem

Desertification, according to the *Oxford Dictionaries*, is *the process by which fertile land becomes desert as a result of drought, deforestation, or inappropriate agriculture*.[142]

The Gobi desert in central China expands and consumes 3,600 square kilometers of grassland per year. This expansion takes away farmland and forces many people to find other homesites, as the powerful sandstorms from the desert's incursion rob families of both their homes and their livelihood. In addition, one of the side effects of desertification is that many people have been relocated so that the government can try to forestall the desert's incursion by the planting of trees. According to the state-run Xinhua news agency, approximately 178,000 people have been relocated from grasslands and forests outside of Beijing and Tianjin in the past twelve years as 67,000 square kilometers of forest was planted.[143]

Desertification: The Solution

In an effort to stop the desert's invasion, the Chinese government is spending billions per year on an ecological project that they call the *Green Wall of China*. Launched in 1978, the ultimate goal of the project is to plant forests across four million square kilometers of the country by

2050. The government is currently restoring each year between 40,000 and 70,000 square kilometers of desertified land,[143] an area the size of Switzerland, by planting new trees and rejuvenating old forests.

The government is still addressing the problem of relocation of people in tree-planting areas. However, relocations will likely continue until the government feels it's attained its reforestation goals and that desertification has been sufficiently contained.

Biodiversity: The Problem

> Biodiversity is the summation of life on Earth to include the species, ecosystems, and genetic variations within an area

China contains a broad diversity of ecosystems. These include forests, deserts, grasslands, freshwater rivers, wetlands, coastal/marine, and agricultural ecosystems. Today most ecologists regard China as a biodiversity hot spot. Wetlands, for example, have declined in both quantity and quality. In the northeast, over 90 percent of the wetland plains have been drained and converted to farmland with funds provided by both the local and national government. The reason for this is fairly straightforward. Farmland produces jobs, revenue, and food. In China, it's difficult for the altruistic to compete when tax revenue and jobs are involved.

Grasslands have also suffered a similar fate and have been degraded due to a forty-year government policy of converting grassland to cropland.[144] This has resulted in the overstocking and overgrazing of the remaining grasslands. There continues to be a significant loss of habitat and ecosystems as China constructs dams and power plants to quench its insatiable need for energy.

Biodiversity: The Solution

China is taking steps to protect the country's biodiversity. According to J. Liu, Z. Ouyang, Stuart L. Pimm, Peter H. Raven, X. Wang, N. Han, and H. Miao's paper on *Protecting China's Diversity*, China has established 1,757 national and local nature reserves, which cover 13 percent of the country. In addition, the nation has set a goal to increase the number of reserves to 2,500 by 2050.[145] In accomplishing this, the government has implemented a bottom-up approach, where lower-level government organizations are now allowed to establish national and provincial reserves, with ultimate approval still coming from upper levels of government. This has allowed for a faster response to biodiversity issues throughout the country. However, this is not a perfect picture, as China's reserves are normally not located near major cities or affluent areas, where land prices are high. Instead, China's reserves tend to be in its poorer areas as residents and the local government view reserves as obstacles to human welfare and economic development. Still, the government realizes the extent of its biodiversity problems and is trying to strike a balance between local governments, who want to use land to create jobs and tax revenue, and environmentalists, who want to protect the country's resources.

Agricultural Pollution: The Problem

China's first national census on pollution in 2010 revealed that farms have become China's main source of water pollution, even topping the contaminated discharge from the nation's factories. Part of the reason for this, according to Greenpeace, is that China consumes 35 percent of the world's nitrogen fertilizer, and Chinese farmers typically use 40 percent more fertilizer than crops need. This overfertilization of crops has led to approximately 10 million tons of fertilizer being discharged annually into the nation's water resources. The government, for its part, has defended the nation's farmers, indicating that intensive farming methods are needed since China has only 7 percent of the world's land but feeds 22 percent of the world's population.[146] But according to *Xinhua* news, approximately 70 percent of China's arable land is heavily polluted.[147] The use of contaminated water is a major contributor to this pollution, as water contaminants eventually find their way into the soil and then into the food chain.

China's agricultural production contributes to a circular pollution cycle in that agriculture relies heavily on the use of fertilizers and pesticides, which in turn, seep into the existing water supply. This polluted water then combines with groundwater, as well as water from rivers and streams, which very probably contains industrial effluent and sewage. The end result is that crops in China are more than likely irrigated with heavily polluted water.

Knowing this, the question is why hasn't the government taken a more stringent stand on controlling agricultural pollution since many of these contaminants are known to enter the nation's food supply? From the government's point of view, there are two basic reasons. The first is that it doesn't want to alienate rural farmers, who rely on fertilizers and pesticides in order to grow their crops and make a living. Farmers believe that the faster and larger their crops grow, the more money they'll make. In addition, alienation of a large group such as farmers is not a good way to remain in power. As a result, the government is trying to balance the appeasement of farmers with the task of increasing the nation's crop production, while at the same time, instituting methods to decrease agricultural pollution.

Agricultural Pollution: The Solution

As mentioned earlier, the government has a tough road ahead of it in trying to decrease agricultural pollution. It's not easy. Telling farmers to use less fertilizer and pesticides and that, if they do, everything will be fine just doesn't work. No one's listening. In order for farmers to decrease the usage of these pollutants, there has to be a reason, and stemming the nation's water pollution isn't an acceptable reason. Instead, the only likely way to get them to decrease usage is to provide a better alternative. Barring a government subsidy that compensates the farmer for decreased production in order to stem agricultural pollution, the best alternative is to save farmers money without decreasing their crop yield. Agricultural strains that require less fertilizer, pesticides, and water offer an attractive alternative.

Waste: The Problem

The slow implementation of recycling programs within China has resulted in an increasing quantity of waste. China creates almost 360 million tons of waste annually, almost half of which is generated in cities. This number is growing at an average of 8 percent each year. In ridding itself of this waste, the government employs one of three primary methods. The first method is to bury the waste in landfills, which the government uses to dispose of 50 percent of the country's garbage. The second method is to burn the garbage in incineration plants, which accounts for 12 percent of waste disposal. The third method, at a little under 10 percent, is to use the waste as fertilizer. The other 28 percent of waste is left untreated and simply dumped.

Waste: The Solution

In the next five years, China expects to spend $22 billion to expand the country's waste-processing capacity.[148] A great deal of this money is expected to be spent on incineration plants, which also will generate electricity from the burning of the waste.

In addition, the government is attempting to get consumers to reuse many of the items that they would normally discard. Take, for example, plastic shopping bags given out at supermarkets and other retail and wholesale outlets. Beginning June 1, 2008, the government prohibited, except for takeout food at restaurants, giving out free plastic bags to customers. Instead, stores now sell ultrathin plastic bags. Customers are learning to bring their own bags with them when they shop, and as a result, there's been a 10 percent annual decrease in plastic bags that are thrown away.

Alternative and Renewable Energy

Many people use *alternative energy* and *renewable energy* interchangeably. But they're actually not the same. Renewable energy systems refer to those systems that utilize energy that comes from resources which are continually replenished. Examples include natural sources such as sunlight, wind, and geothermal heat.

Alternative energy refers to the source of the energy, or the equipment, which is an alternative or a replacement for conventional energy sources, such as oil or gas. An example would be a solar panel. The solar panel is considered both an alternative and a renewable form of energy because the construction of the solar panel is different from conventional systems and the solar panel is also powered by sunlight.

China wants to become a leader in both alternative and renewable energy. According to Meg Handley of *U.S. News & World Report,* Asia is now emerging as a leader in renewable energy initiatives and installations. Asia investments in alternative and renewable energy have grown 16 percent in 2012, to more than $100 billion, or 42 percent of the total global investment in the clean energy sector.[149] In comparison, spending in many countries has greatly decreased. US spending on renewable energy, for example, dropped 40 percent in 2012.[150] In Europe, clean energy investment dropped 51 percent in Italy and 68 percent in Spain. India also saw a decrease of 44 percent in its clean energy investments.[151]

Increasingly, China is becoming the world's alternative and renewable energy superpower. And for good reason. If China is to escape the immense pollution that plagues its air, water, and land resources, decrease its greenhouse gas emissions, and decrease its dependency on foreign oil, then developing its alternative and renewable energy resources may be the only way out. The country has established a national goal of having renewable energy account for 9.5 percent of the country's total energy consumption by 2015.[137]

However, that goal may be a stretch. Therefore, to satisfy the increasing demands of Chinese industry for power, the government continues to build conventional coal-fired power plants at the rate of one per week[128] in order to satisfy its energy needs. As a result, remediation of air pollution becomes increasingly more difficult.

There are three primary factors that impact China's renewable energy policies:[135]

- increasing demand for electricity
- decreasing reliance on coal
- greenhouse gas emissions

One of the ways that China intends to increase its electrical output, decrease its reliance on coal, and reduce its greenhouse emissions is through the use of wind power. In fact, China has become the world's largest wind-energy market, with 25 percent of the total global capacity for wind farms. But as large a market share as China now possesses, the country is still attempting to catch up with past policy lapses. This is because two years ago, China had an unregulated wind-energy market. According to Liu

Mingliang, an analyst from the China Wind Energy Association, wind-farm installations were approved at the provincial level, and the national government was out of the loop. However, even though the construction of wind-power farms was approved locally, they still had to transmit their power over state-owned power lines, whose planning and expansion was all done at the national level. As it turned out, the state and local governments were not always in sync. A substantial number of wind farms were being built that did not connect to the state grid. In other words, the national grid network planners were outpaced by the construction of provincially approved wind-power farms. Finally, with the wind-farm network quickly falling into disarray, the government stepped in. It restrained provinces from approving wind projects unless these projects were directly aligned with the planning of the state grid system. Still, over 30 percent of the total number of wind-power generators are awaiting connection to the grid.

Connecting to the state grid is only half the problem. The other half is that the state grid is not a state-of-the-art system and transmission interruptions are common. Because of the country's outdated grid system, wind farms lack the transmission-line capacity and reliability to effectively distribute electricity long distances from their rural farm locations to population centers. To solve this problem, the government will need to rapidly increase the number of long-range transmission lines capable of handling the electrical output from wind farms. Currently only 1 percent of China's total electricity is generated by wind power.[152]

Other forms of renewable energy, such as wind, rain, tides, waves, and geothermal heat, are actively being pursued by the government.

A Rocky Road Ahead

The Chinese government is beginning to take action. In its latest national policy doctrine, the twelfth Five Year Plan (2011–2015), the government addressed the country's environmental concerns and targeted a decrease in energy use of 15 percent per unit of GDP and a reduction of 17 percent in carbon dioxide emissions, by 2015.[135]

China also faces internal struggles over its energy policies. Just as in the United States, where large corporations and lobbyists can stifle even the best-laid plans, China also has special interest groups that try to change national policy for their own benefit. Large state-owned enterprises, especially those in the oil and power industries, who fear large cost increases, continually block government policies aimed at lowering pollutants.[153]

Lax enforcement of pollution laws and the levying of small fines for violations also contribute to China's pollution woes. For example, in February 2012, according to the *News-Herald*, a big electric power generator, Huaneng, switched off its coal scrubbers at its Pingliang power complex in Gansu. When this happened, emissions soared substantially past permitted levels. Huaneng was a repeat offender, and officials imposed what they considered to be an especially severe fine on the company: $13,000. Most estimate that the company saved more than this by not running its scrubbers.

In another example, one of China's biggest power companies, Huadian, turned off its coal scrubbers at its Datong plants, letting sulfur dioxide escape unchecked into the atmosphere at four times the government standard. Since Beijing is downwind from Datong, the city's Air Quality Index went off the chart. The utility, as it turned out, saved a substantial amount of money by turning off its scrubbers; in its view, scrubbers consume a great deal of power. In addition, in trying to hide this practice, utility employees falsified paperwork and sold its electricity at a premium rate, a practice the government allows power plants with low emissions.[154] Regulators finally caught the company and stopped this practice, but there was no mention of a fine or other action taken.

Some companies, such as China's refineries, are in a no-win situation. That's because the prices charged by China's refineries are controlled by the state, which at the same time mandates standards for cleaner fuels. Consequently, oil refineries have a difficult time funding the manufacture of cleaner fuels when the government has set a limit on the amount they can charge. In many cases, a loss is preordained. As an example, Sinopec, the world's second-largest refiner, reported $1.8 billion in operating losses from its refinery division in 2012. It was no surprise, therefore, when a government inspection board released a spot report on the quality of gasoline that found fifteen of 120 gasoline samples, and five out of sixty diesel samples, in thirteen provinces failed to meet government standards for sulfur, benzene, or other contaminants. It's estimated that China's gasoline contains twenty times the US limits on air pollutants.[154] In this situation, government policy on fixed pricing, and inadequate funding, contributed to increased pollution.

Regulation and enforcement of industry environmental laws for state-owned enterprises is difficult, as the company is irrevocably entwined with the government. For example, Chinese oil industry officials from state-owned enterprises dominate the boards that set fuel standards. In fact, a key standard-setting technical committee on petroleum products falls under the research institute of Sinopec. In addition, of the thirty-seven members on the committee, only two have backgrounds in environmental protection.[154]

China's citizenry, as a result of the nation's environmental pollution, is becoming increasing disillusioned with the government's inability to improve their daily life. Consequently, developing reliable renewable energy resources is not only necessary, but vital for the survival of the country's political leadership and global economic dominance. China wants to demonstrate to the world that it's now ready to become a leader on the world stage. To accomplish this, it will have to demonstrate that it's responsible and progressive in addressing its environmental problems.

The fact that China has substantial environmental challenges correspondingly provides substantial business opportunities for those with experience in the environmental sector. China is hungry to hire experts and purchase technology that will help remediate its environmental woes and enable it to sustain its economic growth and retain its global prominence.

CHAPTER 10

How Banks Operate and Implement Government Policy

China's banks play a significant role in both the Chinese economy and its economic policy. In fact, commercial banks are the dominant force in China's financial system. The key characteristic of China's banking system is what's been referred to by Carmen M. Reinhart, Jacob F. Kirkegaard, and M. Belen Sbrancia as *financial repression*.

Financial repression occurs when governments implement policies to channel to themselves funds that, in a deregulated market environment, would go elsewhere. Policies include directed lending to the government by captive domestic audiences (such as pension funds or domestic banks), explicit or implicit caps on interest rates, regulation of cross-border capital movements, and (generally) a tighter connection between government and banks, either explicitly through public ownership of some of the banks or through heavy "moral suasion."

Financial repression is also sometimes associated with relatively high reserve requirements (or liquidity requirements), securities transaction taxes, prohibition of gold purchases, or the placement of significant amounts of government debt that is nonmarketable. Financial repression issues come under the broad umbrella of the government efforts to ensure the health of an entire financial system.

Four banks in China account for 60 percent of the $15 trillion in financial assets held by state-controlled commercial banks: the Bank of China (BOC), China Construction Bank (CCB), Agricultural Bank of China (ABC), and China's largest bank, Industrial and Commercial Bank of China (ICBC). These four banks hold 58 percent of all household deposits and 50 percent of all corporate deposits. Moreover, according to Carl Walter and Fraser Howie, who have extensively studied the Chinese banking system, Chinese banks are the major force behind all capital raising in China. For example, in 2007, prior to the global financial crisis, Chinese equity financing raised $123 billion in funds. At the same time, bank loans totaled $530 billion and debt issued in the bond market comprised another $355 billion.[155]

> The nation's banks underwrite and hold more than 70 percent of all fixed income debt. In China, the banks are everything, and the government knows it.

Foreign Banks Make Money, but Are Not Relevant in China

Foreign banks constitute less than 2 percent of total domestic financial assets, and that number is likely to decrease as foreign banks have been liquidating much of their Chinese bank investments. The Bank of America, which in 2005 signed a $3 billion pact to acquire 9 percent of CCB, viewed its investment as a way for it to obtain access to tens of millions of Chinese investors. It was not alone. Between 2004 and 2009, foreign banks invested more than $33 billion in Chinese banks. However, that's changed. The Bank of America has sold down its holding in CCB to about 1 percent,[156] and the Goldman Sachs Group has sold its remaining stock in ICBC.

One reason for the recent unwinding of foreign investment in domestic Chinese banks is the more stringent capital rules, including that of Basel III, which established a global regulatory standard on bank capital adequacy. Introduced in 2013, Basel III makes a minority stake in financial institutions less attractive. As the *Wall Street Journal* explains, if the sum of a bank's minority investments in other financial institutions exceeds 10 percent of its core capital, then the amount in excess of that threshold must be deducted from its own capital.[157] Also, if the bank owns more than 10 percent of another financial institution, then up to 100 percent of the investment could be deducted from its core capital.

Overall, investments in Chinese banks and financial service companies have proved to be very profitable. The Goldman Sachs Group originally purchased a 4.9 percent of ICBC for $2.58 billion in April 2006, before the Chinese bank went public in Hong Kong. It later sold its remaining shares in May 2013 and raised about $10 billion in total from all sales of ICBC stock, more than triple its initial investment.[158] The Bank of America also made a handsome profit on its investment in CCB. HSBC purchased a stake in the Chinese insurance company Ping An, which subsequently increased by over 600 percent in the ten years it held its position in the company. Many foreign banks, as a pure investment, have held on to their stake in Chinese banks. HSBC, for example, continues to hold a 19 percent stake in the BOC, China's fifth-largest bank by assets. Spain's CaixaBank owns 16.1 percent of Hong Kong's Bank of East Asia Ltd.; Deutsche Bank owns 19.99 percent of Hua Xia Bank Co., a midsize Chinese lender; and BNP Paribas owns 14.7 percent of the Bank of Nanjing.[157]

However, in spite of these profits, banks are likely, over time, to sell much of their stakes in Chinese banks, especially since Basel III's January 1, 2013, implementation date. Banks have found that selling minority shares improves their capital ratios, especially since many feel that their investment may no longer experience the growth they've realized in the past.[157] In addition, the original reason foreign banks bought minority stakes in a Chinese bank, to get access to a large number of Chinese banking customers, never materialized. For these reasons, foreign ownership in Chinese banks is likely to decrease.

China's Central Bank

China's current banking system is administratively controlled by the People's Bank of China (PBOC), not to be confused with the Bank of China. The PBOC is China's central bank, which regulates financial institutions and controls monetary policy. Unlike its counterpart in the United States, the US Federal Reserve, the PBOC cannot make independent decisions regarding monetary policy. In order to finalize and publish those decisions, it needs the concurrence of the CCP, as any announcements it does make have to integrate into the government's economic and social planning.[159]

The People's Bank of China (PBOC) was established in 1948, and between 1949 and 1978, was responsible for both central and commercial banking. In 1979 the government decided to retain the central banking function with the PBOC and split off, from this *all-in-one* bank, into four specialized, independent state-owned banks:[160]

- Bank of China
- People's Construction Bank of China, later renamed China Construction Bank
- Agricultural Bank of China
- Industrial and Commercial Bank of China

The government determined that each of these four banks would have a specific focus. The Agricultural Bank of China would provide for rural financing. The Bank of China would provide foreign trade payments, settlements, trade financing, and shipping insurance. The People's Construction Bank of China, later renamed China Construction Bank, would provide large-scale infrastructure financing. The last bank to be split off from the PBOC was the Industrial and Commercial Bank of China (IBC), in 1983. The ICBC assumed responsibility for all industrial and commercial banking operations and services, including the savings business. It subsequently became China's largest bank. Therefore, in 1984, China had a central bank and four specialized banks. This created, at long last, stability in China's banking system.

Policy Banks

In 1989, China was in the midst of an economic metamorphosis on a scale it historically had never experienced. Growth at the local, municipal, and provincial levels was explosive, and these governments wanted to do all they could to ensure that nothing hindered their expansion. This sometimes put China's national and local governments in bureaucratic disagreement with one another. For example, while the national government wanted to put banking constraints on growth to control inflation, local and provincial governments wanted unlimited access to capital. To local governments, the more money they can borrow and spend on infrastructure, the more their commercial, labor, and tax bases would expand. This, of course, would result in higher employment and more tax revenue. But a by-product of this type of expansion is often inflation and higher prices, something the national government wanted to avoid.

It was at this time that three different areas of concern became apparent to the government. The first was that the country's present banking system, which for all practical purposes only established itself a little more than a decade before, was still transformational and in need of additional sophistication if it were to support a national growth initiative. Banking experience regarding exports, imports, and overseas financing was relatively new to a previously isolationist China. In the past, the state owned everything, and there was little need for international banking. When the government told a bank to make a loan, it made the loan. When the government told the bank to wire money overseas, it likewise did that. Now that China had a banking relationship with the outside world, sophisticated banking transactions were required for both international trade and investment. The nation's current banking laws were inadequate to deal with these newly expanded areas, and urgent banking reforms were now needed.

The second area of concern for the government was that if it were to control inflation, rapidly rising housing prices, and other consequences of its rapid growth, it would need to make further changes to the nation's banking policies that would allow for consistent financial directives and an orderly growth in line with national initiatives.

Thirdly, the government realized that the specialized banks that were previously created, and which operated at the direction of the CCP, were not what would be considered true commercial banks, as they didn't address the growing interaction and levels of sophistication required when working with foreign banks and in making overseas investments. The government desperately needed, therefore, to establish a commercial banking system to better support its growing international banking efforts, as well as provide needed economic controls and guidance. As a result, in 1994, the State Council for the People's Republic of China created three policy banks:

- China Development Bank (CDB)
- Export-Import Bank of China (Exim bank)
- Agricultural Development Bank of China (ADBC)

Policy banks are charged with promoting and financing the construction of China's infrastructure, as well as promoting exportation and food production.[160] They're widely regarded as the financial muscle, giving the government the ability to implement both its domestic and international agendas.

These banks were also attractive to the Chinese banking system, as the government transferred to them government-dictated loans, thereby allowing the specialized banks to now focus on commercial loans.

China Development Bank, the Muscle Behind China's Global Expansion

The largest and most influential of China's policy banks is the China Development Bank (CDB).[161] The government deems the financial health of the CDB as a critical component of its domestic policy, as well as its future plans to expand its influence internationally. In fact, the CDB is the linchpin of the country's expansion of its domestic infrastructure, as well as for obtaining the critical natural resources necessary to fuel its expansion. In this effort, the CDB provides the financing for projects the Chinese government deems to be in the national interest. It supports the government's macroeconomic policies, national economic development, and strategic structural changes in the economy. For example, when the government wanted to increase its access to international natural resources, the CDB provided the China National Petroleum Corporation (CNPC) with a $30 billion line of credit.[162] In doing so, it not only helped the government to better meet its increasing demand for energy, but also assisted the CNPC in becoming more globally competitive.

Over time, the policy banks' role as an extension of the country's international policy has continued to expand. Today China is a significant global lender, able to impose its political will and extend its economic influence through the CDB and its smaller policy banks. In fact, between 2009 and 2010, China lent more money to the entire developing world than was lent by the World Bank.[162] During this period, the CDB and, to a smaller extent, China Exim Bank, has lent $110 billion to developing-country governments and companies. The World Bank, during this same period of time, lent $100.3 billion.[163] The largest of China's policy banks, the CDB is also the world's largest development bank, with over $980 billion in assets. It's China's biggest lender, with over $210 billion in outstanding loans in over ninety countries and regions throughout the world.[164]

CDB also extends lines of credit to foreign governments and foreign energy companies. In doing so, it secures these loans with the natural resource reserves of the company or country and obtains repayment from the sale of these resources, such as the sale of oil and gas to one of China's national oil companies. It's a win-win for the Chinese government in that it secures long-term access to critical natural resources for its rapidly growing economy, provides it with low-risk loans that are secured by valuable natural resources, and extends the influence of the Chinese government and its associated SOEs globally.[162] In the event that the CDB lends money to a foreign government for infrastructure projects, the CDB will specify that most, if not all, equipment and labor be provided by Chinese firms.

One example of China extending its international influence through the CDB can be found in Venezuela. Since 2007, the CDB has lent Venezuela $42.5 billion, collateralized by the revenue of its oil reserves. According to Charlie Devereux of Bloomberg, Venezuela accounts for 23 percent of all of CDB's overseas loans, more than the $29 billion the United States has spent rebuilding Iraq from 2003 to 2006.[162] These loans give China a great deal of influence in Venezuela, where in addition to securing needed oil for its growing energy requirements, much of the money lent to Venezuela returns to China from contracts to Chinese state-run companies. Chinese oil companies in Venezuela include China Petrochemical Corp. and the country's biggest oil and gas producer, China National Petroleum Corporation (CNPC).

A similar oil-for-loans program is in place in Ecuador, where oil-backed loans account for $7.3 billion, or a third of the Ecuadorian government's budget.[165] CDB's energy-backed loans are closely coordinated with the Chinese government and its SOEs.[166] This is a well-thought-out and scripted long-term strategic plan designed to further the Chinese government's objectives in various geographic areas, enhance its access to energy, and support domestic Chinese firms.[164]

Another way in which the CDB is furthering the government's national objectives is by providing acquisition financing to acquire foreign technology companies. These acquisitions will subsequently give the Chinese companies, and by extension the government, access to the acquired company's technology and intellectual property rights. With wages continuing to increase in China, the government is intent on diversifying the country from simply being a source of low-cost manufacturing to a country that also provides technology and intellectual property to other countries.[164] In this effort, which is funded to a great extent by the CDB, Chinese companies are able to make strategic acquisitions globally and then integrate their newly acquired technology domestically.[166]

The CDB not only provides financing for overseas projects, but for domestic projects as well. CDB has provided financing for the Shanghai Pudong International Airport, the North-South Water Diversion Project, and the Three Gorges Dam, as well as other projects that offer economic stimulus, such as airports, roads, and high-speed rails.[162]

In the world of global finance, CDB is a game changer. Its sheer size and available capital give it the ability to dominate almost any market segment it chooses. Let's give you an example used by Frank Hochberg, the head of the US Exim Bank, which is a fraction of the size of the Chinese policy banks, to illustrate what keeps him awake at night. One of Hochberg's insomniac moments is caused by Huawei, a Shenzhen telecom company that was founded in 1987 by a retired military officer, but did not begin to export its equipment until 1996. In the late 1990s, the CDB provided Huawei with a $30 billion line of credit. Access to these funds allowed Huawei to reduce its cost of capital and offer financing to buyers at rates and terms better than their competitors. "None of the G-7 countries provided levels of financing anywhere near those of the CDB. That keeps me up at night," Hochberg said.[167] Today, Huawei is China's largest phone equipment manufacturer and the world's second largest after Ericsson AB, with 65 percent of its revenue coming from outside China.[168]

Henry Sanderson and Michael Forsythe, authors of *China's Superbank*, point out that CDB's credit lines are often used for vendor financing. They give as an example a transaction involving Tele Norte Leste Participacoes (TNLP), Brazil's largest landline company. When TNLP was shopping for equipment in 2010, Huawei had an immediate advantage over its competitors. It was able to provide TNLP with a two-year grace period on payments and an interest rate of 2 percent over the London Interbank Offered Rate (LIBOR). At that time, this gave TNLP an effective interest rate of approximately 4 percent, when other Brazilian companies were paying about 5.99 percent for their debt.[167]

China Development Bank continues to be the muscle behind China's global expansion. It's the financial arm for the Chinese government, promoting domestic as well as international growth. In doing so, it projects China's political and economic agenda and influence throughout the world.

Problems Persist

The Economist reports that there are two primary concerns in regard to China's banking system. The first is the possibility of bad local-government debt. The second concern is bad property loans. While many might believe that the Chinese economy is bulletproof, it isn't. The Chinese banking system is thinly capitalized, with a ratio of equity to assets, in 2012, of 6 percent.[169] This is low in comparison to the United States, which has a ratio of 11.3 percent, the Russian Federation with 12.4 percent, and Argentina with 12.1 percent. This low equity-to-asset ratio is an important indicator of a country's solvency.

Part of the reason for this low solvency ratio is that, in the aftermath of the world financial crisis, the national government initiated an infrastructure boom by permitting local government financing. It also permitted off-balance sheet entities to get around prohibitions on borrowing. As a result, local governments borrowed—a lot! Local government debt is now thought to be approximately $1.4 trillion, with 20 to 30 percent of that debt estimated to be nonperforming.[170] That's created a significant problem for the government, which doesn't want bad or nonperforming loans on its books. In attempting to solve this problem, the government decided the best way to deal with this vast amount of bad debt was to direct the banks to roll over these loans and issue local bonds in their place. By doing this, the government avoided the issue of a default by a local government.

This rollover, however, was only a bandage over the wound. Problems remain within China's banking system. These problems include

- bad loans to SOEs,
- loans to property developers,
- corruption,
- theft, and
- bad debt.

Bad loans to SOEs. The biggest problem for Chinese banks are bad loans to SOEs. On the face of it, one wouldn't think that loaning money to a business enterprise would be a problem. If the company doesn't repay the loan, the bank can always attach the company's assets to seek some degree of repayment. But loaning money to an SOE is essentially loaning money to the government. Moreover, SOEs weren't originally created to be moneymaking machines. Instead, they were designed to employ large numbers of people and create the basis of social stability. Therefore, loans to SOEs are often based on political rather than commercial criteria. In fact, the amount of loans to SOEs is so massive that it constitutes 90 percent of all Chinese banking loans.[160] Chinese banks are quite often used by the government as a funding agent for directed government subsidies to SOEs, rather than acting in the capacity of a prudent lender.[171] In addition, SOEs will often use loans from the bank to make investments outside the company.

> It's common for an SOE to obtain a loan from the bank and then relend the money to smaller companies that don't qualify for bank loans. Since SOEs loan money at a much higher interest rate than they're paying, they make a sizable interest rate spread on the borrowed capital, which can substantially improve their bottom line.

One of the problems with this scenario is that SOEs borrow so much money from China's banking system that the banks simply don't have enough capital to loan to all the companies that request a bank loan. Instead, these companies are often forced to borrow money from SOEs, shadow bankers, financial intermediaries who are not subject to regulatory oversight, or peer-to-peer lenders at a significantly higher cost than a traditional bank loan. As a result, many of these smaller companies have gone out of business, as their cost of capital makes it difficult for them to succeed.

Loans to property developers. Real estate loans is another problem area for the government. The government wants to regulate the ability of developers to obtain loans in an effort to control housing prices and inflation. With few investment options outside of a captive stock market, the Chinese people view real estate as their investment of choice. They'll buy as much as they can for cash and also borrow at the bank to purchase even more. The problem this creates is that property prices rise to the point where housing becomes increasingly less affordable. While developers love this scenario, the government wants to maintain an orderly real estate market, where prices don't skyrocket from year to year. Therefore, it directs banks to cut off loans to developers when it wants to rein in real estate construction. However, in spite of this, it's not uncommon for loans to continue to be made to property developers. These are primarily facilitated by local and provincial governments, which exercise influence over the banks within their jurisdiction. Many developers who obtained bank funding in this manner, so that they could start their projects, make money almost immediately from the presale of housing units. The developer will then then use this money as collateral to obtain additional real estate loans from the bank.[160]

This scenario works as long as you have a cooperating economy. But as an economy declines, as we saw after a world financial crisis, so does the demand for real estate. And that's exactly what happened. A pullback in the economy, coupled with the implementation of more stringent government laws that set limits on the purchase of a second or subsequent property by home buyers, resulted in many developers going bankrupt.[171] Local and provincial banks that made loans to developers at the direction of the government found themselves consequently holding worthless loans. This illustrates one of the vulnerabilities of the Chinese banking system: in addition to economic changes, bank loans and lending policies can be impacted virtually overnight by a change in government policy.

Corruption: Corruption remains prevalent in the banking industry.

The Chinese Banking Regulatory Commission reported that one bank alone issued 4,700 bogus mortgages worth over $169 million, and another reported 3,700 bogus mortgages worth over $95 million.[171] The Chinese system of business is particularly vulnerable to corruption since access to land, approval of licenses and permits, and just about everything else associated with business, and real estate in particular, require government approval. Consequently many bank loans are more subjective that they would be in the West.

On many occasions, we've spoken to companies that have said their bankers have told them what their financials must look like in order for them to obtain a loan. Bankers have privately confirmed to us that they'll tell a company what financial requisites their documentation needs to reflect in order for them to qualify for a loan. Favors are done, something of value is usually given, and magically the documentation submitted is what's needed to obtain the loan. Both the bank officer and the company executive know that, even in China, this violates existing banking laws. It's corrupt, and if made public, they may be made examples of. However, they also know that this practice is the norm and is unlikely to come to light. Therefore, making loans in this manner continues to persist and probably will long into the future, despite the government's anticorruption campaigns. Unless the banker suddenly starts driving a Bentley or the client takes the cash and runs, no one is going to be looking under the covers as to how the bank loan was made.

Theft: Theft is a major problem within the Chinese banking system. One would believe that banks would have solid controls in place to prevent theft of the assets of either a client or the bank. But that's not always the case, as internal controls and external audits are frequently lax.

In an example given by sinologists Harold Chee and Chris West, a Chinese JV partner took out a loan with a Chinese bank as a gesture of goodwill to the Chinese government, demonstrating their commitment to their joint venture project.[160] It wasn't that they particularly needed the loan; instead, it was to be seen as a gesture of their intent to remain in the community. The company intended to repay the loan over a number of years, and the bank assigned someone to handle this account. Eighteen months later, the bank called the company and asked when they intended to start to repay their loan. The company responded that they'd been making their payments all along, even though they hadn't met with the bank representative for some time. The bank came back to the company and told them they had no record of any monthly payments being made and that the loan manager had died some time ago. Since the company's payments had gone directly to the bank in care of the company's representative, the company concluded that the bank employee, and possibly someone else, had taken the company's repayments. The "dead" employee was later seen by one of the company's employees shopping in a local mall.[171]

Bad Debt: Some investors, such as Shoreline Capital Management Ltd. and DAC Management LLC, according to the *Wall Street Journal*, have seen China's bad loans as an opportunity. Shoreline had raised over $300 million at the end of 2012, and DAC is seeking to raise a similar amount, to buy and manage distressed loans on the part of investors. Typically, distressed debt investors purchase bad loans at a fraction of the amount the bank originally lent. Shoreline, for example, bought loans for 10 percent of their original face value. Still, purchasing distressed debt is risky. As the *Wall Street Journal* points out, government politics, a legal system that's subject to outside influences, and paperwork that's not as detailed as we see in the West all increase investor risk.[172]

It's estimated that 30 percent of the loans made by Chinese banks, or approximately $150 billion, is bad. However, some estimate that this figure is too low and the real number could be as high as $500 billion.[160] Canadian banks, as a comparison, average about a 2 percent nonperforming loan ratio.[171] China's regulators, on the other hand, claim that nonperforming loans account for less than 1 percent of total loans in the banking system.

Foreign Banks Are Still Foreign in China

When China became a member of the World Trade Organization, it agreed to open its financial markets to foreign competition by 2007. In anticipation of the opening of these markets to foreigners, many foreign banks invested heavily in expanding their networks within China, focusing largely on China's huge domestic consumer market. However, foreign banks did not receive their anticipated level of government support. Rather, they received less government support after the 2008 financial crisis, as the CCP now viewed foreign financial models as *nonresponsive*. Some would say that *nonresponsive* in China can be defined as not able to be manipulated.

The bigger picture is that the government has no intention of fully allowing foreign banks access to its domestic population.[155] Foreign banks are in China to make money. In contrast, domestic banks take direction from the government and the CCP, whether or not they make money on that directed transaction.[173] This is something foreign banks would never agree to.

The government believes that being able to provide direction to the nation's banks allows it to better control the economy and inflation, and maintain domestic tranquility.

Foreign Credit Cards

China is among the fastest growing credit card markets in the world. By 2020, it's expected that China will have issued over 900 million credit cards, overtaking the United States and making it the world's largest credit card market. According to Simon Rabinovitch of the *Financial Times*, 46 million credit cards were issued in China in 2012 alone.

If you're using a foreign credit card in China at an ATM or to make a purchase, UnionPay will be involved. UnionPay is a Chinese bankcard association that is under the auspices of the PBOC. It's currently owned by eighty Chinese banks and other state entities. It's seen its revenue triple between 2007 and 2011, to $978 million, as the Chinese people begin to move away from being a cash-only society and increasingly adopt the use of credit cards. With such huge growth in the use of credit cards, the Chinese government has been loath to give credit card organizations full access to its markets. In complaints filed with the WTO, foreign credit card companies allege that China has allowed UnionPay to monopolize yuan-denominated transactions. And the WTO has agreed with this allegation. But China has ignored the WTO and still has not permitted foreign credit card companies greater access to its markets.

In fact, it's done just the opposite. In June 2013, China blocked MasterCard from processing transactions in yuan and ordered EPayLinks, an online payment platform, to stop issuing yuan-settled credit cards in partnership with MasterCard. The PBOC further declared, "No payment institution is allowed to cooperate with foreign card companies in developing cross-border payment businesses involving yuan bank accounts or yuan payment accounts. Foreign currencies must be used when clearing and settling domestic acquisitions made by people holding foreign credit cards."[174] This doesn't mean that you can't use a foreign credit card in China. It just means that UnionPay has to be included.

When we're in China and insert our bank's ATM or credit card into a local ATM machine, or use one of our credit cards to pay for a transaction, we've never experienced a problem. The reason for this is that UnionPay is being paid by the merchant for the transaction. There are no competitors. UnionPay is a monopoly, and the government wants it to remain that way so that it can grow this market internally, without foreign participation.

The Government Exercises Control

The Chinese government knows that the stability of its banking system is directly related to the country's financial and social stability and its remaining in power. For all their wealth, Chinese banks are not aggressively expanding internationally. One reason for this is that Chinese banks simply don't operate like Western banks. Instead, they're largely controlled by the government, which wants to exercise a significant level of influence to enhance domestic stability and support economic growth. In addition, the repayment of loans takes on a wholly different meaning for a Chinese bank, as many loans are made at the direction of the government, and if these loans are not repaid, the banks are not called to task by a regulatory body because of the bad loans.

Bad loans are not always revealed publicly by Chinese banks.[155] Examples can be found in the fact that many nonperforming loans go unreported, causing bank balance sheets to look stronger than they actually are. The government, for its part, supports this. It wants to solve its financial problems internally, out of sight from the international community. What China's relying on is that its strong economic growth will resolve its banking problems and any issues it currently has will simply fade away with a growing economy. At its current 8 percent rate of growth,[171] they very well could.

CHAPTER 11

China's Growing Influence in Other Parts of the World

Within the last decade, China has grown to become a global power. Driven by a soaring economy, at a time when most Western economies are still recovering from a global recession, China has used its huge foreign exchange reserves, and internationally focused political policies, to expand its global influence.

China's growing participation in international affairs reflects not only a desire to be recognized as a global power, but also its desire to create a stable environment for its own economic development. In this regard China's strategy is to create a win-win scenario, where assistance is provided to foreign governments in areas that have mutual interest for the Chinese government.

Three global areas, in particular, have a strategic importance to China: Africa, Australia, and Latin America.

Why Is Africa Important to China?

Africa and China have conducted trade for centuries. This trade was initiated around the middle of the eighth century and reached its peak between the ninth and tenth centuries.[175] But only recently, beginning in the 1990s, has this trade accelerated and evolved to the point where China and Africa have created a mutual codependence on one another. China cannot grow without Africa, and Africa cannot prosper without China. Africa is China's third-largest trading partner.[176]

China's growth is fueled by its access to natural resources and having a stable long-term supply of raw materials. In this regard, Africa is essential to its national interests. Conversely, China's purchase of its raw materials has enabled Africa to invest these funds in the long-term development of its resources.[177]

In addition, China has further assisted many African countries by helping to establish their infrastructure so that it can take advantage of their resources. Examples of such assistance can be found in the construction funding of railways, roads, and utilities.

Prior to the 1990s, China relied on its domestic coal and oil resources to provide the energy necessary to fuel its growth. By 1993, that changed, and the country no longer had the ability to provide the natural resources necessary to fuel its expansion. As a result, for the first time, China became a net importer of oil. By 2003, its continued growth made it the world's second-largest consumer of oil behind the United States, accounting for 13 percent of the world's demand for petroleum. One of the reasons for this colossal increase in the demand for energy was the double-digit growth China was experiencing. Another reason was that ten of the eleven biggest oil fields in China had already passed their peak production,[178] and China needed to find a steady, long-term supply of oil to satisfy its future energy needs. Currently Africa, primarily the countries of Angola, Nigeria, and the Sudan, provides 25 percent of China's petroleum imports.

In addition to oil, according to Robert I. Rotberg, president of the World Peace Foundation, other African natural resources imported by China include[177]

- timber from Gabon, the Democratic Republic of the Congo (DRC), Equatorial Guinea, Cameroon, and Liberia;
- cotton from Benin, Burkina, Faso, Mali, Cote d'Ivoire, and Cameroon;
- copper from Zambia and the DRC;
- ferrochrome and platinum from Zimbabwe;
- diamonds from South Africa; and
- tin and Tantalum from the DRC.

Dot Keet, a fellow at the Transnational Institute, reports that China also conducts a number of other activities within Africa designed to enhance its access to natural resources. These include:[176]

- extractive mining, focused on fuel supplies, uranium, and industrial minerals;
- construction of infrastructural projects, such as roads, railways, dams, power lines, public housing, hospitals, clinics, schools, and sports stadiums;
- supplying capital equipment, such as heavy construction machinery, transport equipment, and telecommunications equipment; and
- large-scale interest-free grants to governments and *soft* loans attached to specified projects. A soft loan is a loan that's made on terms that are very favorable to the borrower.

China's influence has become dominant in continents such as Africa because of its ability to provide capital. It acts as a banker to a large number of African countries by providing low-interest loans, many times at zero or near-zero interest rates. Loan repayments are usually made through the escrow of oil or other natural resources.[177] This is one of the primary reasons that China has fared so well in securing natural resources in Africa. For example, according to Dot Keet, in Angola China offered $2 billion in aid for infrastructure projects, and in turn, secured a former Shell Oil block that was also being sought by India. In Nigeria China promised $7 billion in investments and the rehabilitation of power stations. In return, it received oil rights to areas sought by a number of multinational companies. In Gabon China pledged to build a rail line, dam, and deep-water port. In return, it received the rights to a $3 billion iron ore project that was also sought by Brazilian and French firms. And the list goes on.

This is referred to in Africa as the *Chinese model,* in which trade and investment play prominent and interlocking roles. In fact, the United Nations Development Program feels this model eases China's dependency on the West. The director for the UK Centre for Foreign Policy Analysis adds that, "The phenomenal growth rates in China and the fact that hundreds of millions have been lifted out of poverty is an attractive model for Africans, and not just the elderly leadership. Young, intelligent, well-educated Africans are attracted to the Chinese model, even though Beijing is not trying to spread democracy."[176]

Many Africans actually prefer the Chinese model to political-economic models employed by the West. A Nigerian official noted that the West is never prepared to transfer technology, while the Chinese seem to have no problem with technology transfers. And although Chinese technology may not be as sophisticated as that in the West, it's better to have Chinese technology than none at all. A Nigerian journalist also illustrates this differentiation in saying that China's strategy "is not informed by the Washington Consensus . . . They have not branded subsidy a dirty word."[176]

Chinese loans have enabled African countries to obtain the funds necessary for the construction of hospitals, utilities, low-income housing, roads, railways, and other facilities necessary to promote internal stability and growth.[177] The only country in Africa that has not received Chinese aid is Swaziland, which still has allegiance with Taiwan.[179]

In addition to purchasing raw materials, China also exports consumer products to its African trading partners. It supplies them with electronic goods, machinery, motorcycles, clothing, footwear, and other low-value consumer items.[177]

Things have not always gone smoothly for China in Africa. On the contrary, Chinese goods are perceived by some African countries, such as Zimbabwe, to be of inferior quality. They feel that China is taking advantage of them by supplying cheaply made products, yet charging them for higher-quality goods. Also, several Chinese companies operating in countries such as the Democratic Republic of the Congo and Gabon have been shut down for alleged environmental abuses. Since many Chinese companies are frequently able to get away with environmental abuses in China, many feel that they can employ the same environmentally insensitive manufacturing and construction techniques in Africa. And in some African countries, they can. However, many African nations are sensitive to environmental abuses and hold foreign companies accountable.

China's sourcing of its manufacturing supplies from domestic Chinese companies, for products that are sold in Africa, has caused a great deal of anger in many African companies, which feel that China should be buying from African vendors instead. They've also complained about the Chinese practice of importing Chinese labor for its infrastructure and factory projects, rather than employing African workers. These practices have angered many African countries, such as Zambia and Lesotho,[177] which feel that this lack of in-country sourcing, coupled with the flood of cheap Chinese goods, has contributed to the bankruptcy of local industries and the subsequent unemployment of many Africans.

In spite of these issues, China's relationship with Africa continues to flourish. According to the International Monetary Fund (IMF), between 2001 and 2006, Africa's exports to China rose 40 percent, and its imports from China rose 35 percent. During this same period of time, the average growth rate for world trade was 14 percent.[180] In 2012, trade between Africa and the BRICS countries (Brazil, Russia, India, China, and South Africa) amounted to $310 billion, an elevenfold increase from 2002. It's anticipated that this number will increase to $500 million by 2015, with 60 percent of that amount consisting of China-Africa trade. Although South Africa is part of these numbers, it only became a BRICS member in 2010 (forming the "S" in the acronym) and comprises only 2.8 percent of BRICS trade.[181]

Why Is Australia Important to China?

At first thought, you wouldn't believe that Australia and China would be closely aligned. After all, the two countries aren't synergistic by language, culture, or politics. But as it turns out, they are aligned by trade.

China is Australia's largest trading partner,[182] and trade between the two countries has grown fourfold in the last ten years.

Prior to President Nixon's trip to China, Australia had no diplomatic relations with China. Instead, its trade and foreign policy was focused on Europe and the United States. That changed in December 1972 when Gough Whitlam, the prime minister of Australia at the time, followed America's lead and established diplomatic relations with China. With the establishment of diplomatic ties, both the United States and Australia subsequently downgraded their relationships with the Republic of China on Taiwan.

Even though a formal relationship between Australia and China started only four decades ago, the Chinese people have taken a liking to the culture, people, and politics of Australia, and today there are large numbers of Australian-born Chinese and Chinese-born migrants/Australian citizens living in the country. Domestically, Chinese living in Australia primarily live in the major cities of Melbourne, Sydney, and Brisbane. However, you can usually find a Chinatown in every Australian capital city throughout the country.

China and Australia have not only linked themselves by trade, but also by education. Mainland Chinese send their children to be educated in Australia, and consequently, Chinese students studying in Australia have rapidly increased from the several thousand studying there in 1987 to more than 150,000 as of September 2011. They now comprise 26 percent of all foreign students in Australia. The number of university agreements between the two countries has risen by 75 percent in less than ten years, from 514 to 885.[183]

Trade, however, remains the dominant basis for Australia-China relations. As Australia's largest trading partner, most of the imports from Australia to China are minerals. They account for about 79 percent of all imports to China from Australia. Nationally, 15 percent of all Chinese mineral imports now come from Australia.

China exports over $37 billion of goods to Australia annually.[183] This is primarily machinery and electrical equipment. Total trade between China and Australia is steadily increasing and reached $122.3 billion in 2012, up 4.9 percent from the previous year.[183] As of 2011, China had a $50 billion trade deficit with Australia.[184]

Stewart Partners, a strategic advice and wealth management company, reports that trade with China has resulted in the following economic benefits for Australia:[185]

- Chinese exports now account for 4.6 percent of Australia's GDP.
- In the last ten years, the percentage of Australian exports to China has increased from 5 percent to 25 percent.
- Resources account for 58 percent of Australia's total exports, up from 35 percent ten years ago.
- The value of goods shipped from Australia to China in 2012 was $58 billion; $34 billion was iron ore.

- China's demand for Australia's natural resources is a contributing factor to a projected increase in tax revenue from $240 billion in 2012 to an estimated $300 billion by 2014 to 2015.

Australia's huge natural resource reserves, especially iron ore, are becoming increasingly important to China, which is struggling to meet its energy needs to sustain its economic growth. Moreover, Australia is geographically closer to China than Brazil, another large supplier of natural resources to China. Consequently, Australia can deliver the iron ore to China faster and cheaper. In addition, Australia's coking coal, used in the manufacture of steel, is of a very high grade and therefore sought after.[186] Similar-quality iron ore is mostly found only in Africa.

China requires increasing amounts of natural resources and is taking action to encourage other countries to give it favorable treatment in the shipment of oil and other energy- and industry-related commodities. Therefore, on January 1, 2012, it reduced import tariffs on over 730 products. Import tariffs were reduced to 4.4 percent, 50 percent less than the most favored nation tariff rate.[187] Australia's economy and natural resources industries have significantly benefited from this tariff reduction.

In Australia, according to Hilary Inglis, senior investment consultant for iPAC, resources and energy companies comprise 38 percent of the S&P/ASX 300 index. Correspondingly, the income produced by these companies has a trickle-down effect on the economy and helps to create a stronger Australian dollar. This makes Australian imports cheaper and puts downward pressure on inflation. It also allows the Reserve Bank of Australia more leeway on how it manages interest rates and ultimately enables their lowering.[186] Australia has enjoyed twenty-one years of uninterrupted economic growth, thanks in large part to China's voracious appetite for the country's natural resources.[188] It's estimated that trade and investment with China brought benefits of about $4,000 per Australian household in 2009, which has since risen to $10,500 per household per year in 2011.

China is a significant investor in Australia. According to the *Australian Financial Review*, apart from Hong Kong and tax havens such as the Cayman Islands and the British Virgin Islands, Australia is the largest recipient of China's overseas direct investment.[189] In a report released by KPMG and the University of Sydney, between September 2006 and June 2012, there were 116 transactions completed, totaling an investment of $45.1 billion by Chinese enterprises in Australian businesses.[190]

Investment between the countries is not a one-way street. In 2007, Australia's investment into China was on par with Chinese investment into Australia. But in each year since, China has increased its investment, so that now for every dollar Australia invests in China, China invests $21 in return.[191]

Although Australia exports large quantities of iron ore and coal to China, the country doesn't rely only on the sale of minerals to maintain its economic relationship with China. As China modernizes, there's been a growing demand for liquid natural gas (LNG), something that Australia possesses in abundance. China's demand for LNG is expanding rapidly, and in 2011 alone, it increased its demand by one-third. To meet China's increased appetite for LNG, as well as orders from other countries, Australia plans to quadruple its LNG capabilities by 2017.[191]

Australia plans to expand its food exports into China's growing market. Agriculture minister Joe Ludwig estimates that by 2050, world food consumption will be 75 percent higher than in 2007, with almost half of that increased demand coming from China. As a result, Australia has set a national goal to increase its agriculture and food-related exports 45 percent by 2050. Australia currently exports 55 percent of its food production.[192]

With so much of Australia's resource-based economy dependent on China, any change in China's growth significantly impacts the Australian economy. Yet most government officials are optimistic about their increasing economic ties since China's growth is projected by most economists to make China the world's largest economy by 2027, shifting economic dominance to the East for the first time in a hundred years.[191] By 2050, China's economy is projected to be the size of the United States' and India's combined.

China and Australia continue to get closer. In April 2013, the two countries signed a landmark currency agreement, allowing for the first time the Australian dollar and the Chinese yuan to be directly converted. This eliminates the need for companies and currency traders to first translate the yuan into US dollars.[188] China has also committed to annual leadership talks with Australia. Australia joins Russia, Germany, and Britain as the only four countries with whom China has committed to have these annual talks. China and Australia have also agreed to hold annual military exercises, although limited only to humanitarian assistance, disaster relief, and maritime engagement and peacekeeping.[190]

Why Is Latin America Important to China?

Latin America is important to China for two primary reasons:[193]

- China wishes to gain access to Latin America's natural resources.
- China wishes to attract political support from Latin American countries for its global agenda.

China Wishes to Gain Access to Latin America's Natural Resources

Latin America is an ideal region for China to obtain the raw materials and petroleum required to sustain its fast-growing economy. Latin America has vast reserves of natural resources, and most of its countries have a stable political climate.

China recognized the strategic role Latin America played in its economic future. It also knew that it had to secure reliable long-term sources of raw materials and natural resources if it were to continue its growth. As a result, it employed the *Chinese model* in Latin America.[194] This allowed Latin American countries to develop their natural resources and establish the required infrastructure necessary for monetizing their raw materials. It was a win-win. China obtained the long-term contracts for the natural resources it craved, while at the same time, Latin American countries were able to lock in future cash flow and profitability.

Attracting Political Support from Latin American Countries

China's agenda in Latin America is fairly straightforward: it wants to exercise its monetary influence in order for it to attain its geopolitical goals.

China's geopolitical goals include access to Latin America's natural resources, as well as the establishment of a political foothold. To accomplish this, it made loans and signed long-term natural resource contracts with the various countries it believed to be geopolitically important to its strategic objectives. For many countries, China's loans and industrial contracts provided economic prosperity, as well as political and social stability. The Chinese model allowed China to achieve political and social influence in a geographic area where it formerly had little involvement.

Why Is China Important to Latin America?

There are also a number of reasons why China is important to Latin America. These can be divided into several areas:[195]

- Latin America hopes for future access to Chinese markets.
- Latin America hopes for future investment by China.
- Latin America hopes to benefit from Chinese entities and infrastructure.
- Latin America hopes for China to be a counterweight to the United States, as well as other Western countries.
- Latin America views China as a role model for economic development.

Latin America's Hopes for Future Access to Chinese Markets

Latin American businesspeople are attracted to the sheer size of the Chinese market. With China's 1.3 billion people, the export potential for Latin American businesses is substantial. They want to manufacture and sell their products to an increasingly wealthy Chinese populace. That's currently happening on a small scale. But Latin Americans want China to increase the scope and size of their current trade with China.

Latin America's Hopes for Future Investment by China

China is Latin America's primary lender. In 2010 alone, $37 billion in loans were made by China throughout various Latin American countries. That was more than the World Bank, the Inter-American Bank, and the US Import-Export bank combined. Most of these investments have gone to four countries: Venezuela, Brazil, Argentina, and Ecuador, for mining, transport equipment, and infrastructure.[196]

In addition to providing loans to Latin American industries, China has also rapidly increased its trade with the various countries within Latin America. In 2000, for example, trade between China and Latin America was $10 billion. In 2011, it increased to $241 billion. This vast increase in trade has helped Latin America avoid the worst of the world financial and economic crisis. Particularly benefiting from Chinese loans were Venezuela and Ecuador, which had both been unable to access the world's capital markets since defaulting on previous loans.

Not only do the terms of China's loans make it difficult for other lenders to compete, they also make the recipient of the loan dependent on China. The reason for this is that repayment of these loans is guaranteed by the recipient's long-term commodity sales. This essentially means that the borrower is obligated to continue its natural resource exploration and development in order to be able to pay back the loan. Ecuador, for example, has debts to China of $17 billion and has therefore committed sales to the Chinese through 2019.[196]

The Benefit of Chinese Entities and Infrastructure in Latin America

As a requisite for obtaining many Chinese loans, Latin American countries are often contractually required to utilize Chinese corporations. In many cases, this is looked upon by the Chinese government as a way to employ a greater number of people, while ensuring that they have an up-to-date status on the project to which they've made a loan or investment. In addition, the Chinese believe that their labor force is highly skilled and, as a whole, more reliable than the labor available in many of the countries to which they're making loans. Depending on the circumstances, Chinese companies may contractually function as general contractors, operate machinery, conduct maintenance, or perform other tasks as specified in the contract. Some loans will also dictate that the entity receiving the loan will be a joint venture with a domestic company. In either case, the Chinese will exercise a great deal of operational influence.

In Ecuador, for example, according to R. Evan Ellis of the *National Defense University Press*, Chinese petroleum and service companies have assumed a prominent role in the country's petroleum industry. Chinese companies not only are a financial partner in Ecuadorian petroleum projects, but also operate petroleum facilities that account for almost 40 percent of non-state oil production. In addition, Chinese companies are constructing a $3 million project in Ecuador to provide access to future mining sectors and opening up previously untapped resources.[195] In Venezuela, Chinese companies are key factors in maintaining oil production in the country's mature oil fields, as well as extracting Venezuelan iron, gold, bauxite, and coal.

Besides mining, petroleum, and other industries related to natural resources, China provides Latin American countries with significant infrastructure in many unrelated areas. For example, in technology, Huawei and ZTE are playing a critical role in Latin American telecommunications. In logistics, China Overseas Shipping and Hutchinson Whampoa have an increasingly important role in Latin America's foreign transport[195] and trade.

China as a Counterweight to US and Other Western Institutions

The People's Republic of China is viewed by a number of countries in Latin America as a geopolitical alternative to the United States. The late president of Venezuela, Hugo Chavez, along with Rafael Correa, president of the Republic of Ecuador, and Evo Morales, president of Bolivia, have been substantial supporters of China's increased presence in Latin America. They've viewed China as a necessary counterweight to the United States and other Western institutions that they see as imposing their morality, politics, and agendas on Latin America.

China, for its part, sees itself as having to walk a fine line. It can't proclaim, or associate itself with, being anti-United States, as that would be counterproductive to its relationship with the West. Yet it nevertheless wants to differentiate itself and project its own influence in the region.

In many ways, its relationship with a number of Latin American countries is like looking at itself in the mirror, in that it somewhat resembles its own past relationship with the former Soviet Union and its satellites during the Cold War. Just as China turned to the former Soviet Union for arms that it was denied purchasing from the United States and its allies, Latin American countries have turned to China for hard-to-obtain items, especially the purchase of military weaponry, which they were denied purchasing from the West. For example, Bolivia turned to China to purchase K-8 combat aircraft after the United States blocked its ability to procure similar aircraft from the Czech Republic.[195]

China as a Role Model for Economic Development

Many Latin American countries look at China's combination of capitalism and authoritarianism as an ideal model to emulate. Many feel, according to R. Evan Ellis, that the US democratic model, with free markets and privatization, doesn't work well in a country with corruption, poverty, and inequality. China's model is more attractive to many, as it implies that you can achieve stellar economic growth without relinquishing political power.[195] For its part, China is marketing this concept in Latin America and is expanding its influence at a time when the United States and other Western countries are cutting back on aid and assistance programs in the region.

Marginalizing Taiwan

For the twelve nations in the Caribbean and Latin America that recognize Taiwan, China's approach can best be described as using a carrot and a stick. The stick: China makes investment funds less readily available in countries that recognize Taiwan. The carrot approach can best be illustrated in Costa Rica. When Costa Rica recognized China in 2007, at the expense of Taiwan, it received an aid package from China that included $83 million for a soccer stadium, the purchase of $300 million of Costa Rican government bonds, a $1 billion venture to expand the country's petroleum industry, various highway and public works projects, and access to China's domestic markets for Costa Rican products. Seeing how the carrot was better than the stick, Panama, Paraguay, and El Salvador have expressed an interest in changing their diplomatic posture.[195]

Chapter 12

Chinese Cyberespionage Is Common, Pervasive, and a Fact of Life

With computers involved in virtually every facet of our life, and with information constantly being transmitted over the Internet, it's perhaps natural that cyberespionage would be employed by individuals, businesses, and nation-states.

> Cyberespionage is defined as: *the intentional use of computers or digital communications activities in an effort to gain access to sensitive information about an adversary or competitor for the purpose of gaining an advantage or selling the sensitive information for monetary reward.*[197]

Protecting against cyberespionage isn't easy, and it's usually not simple. Instead, it's a multiphase approach that requires layers of protection against outside intruders, who are increasingly sophisticated and, in some cases, have the resources of a nation-state behind them. As a result, there's no magic bullet. There's no *one* thing you can do that makes you invulnerable to cyberespionage. The fact that there are so many different forms of cyberespionage means that defending against it will take a number of different approaches. But, *for the most part*, it can be done. We stated *for the most part* because defending against a nation-state often takes the sophistication and financial resources of a government. That's the nature of technology.

In order to prevent cyberespionage, you first have to understand what makes you vulnerable. You have to know how today's basic technology systems function. This includes the Internet. You don't have to have an engineering degree to accomplish this, but knowing how systems operate will show you where your potential vulnerabilities lie and enable you to better protect yourself.

In the past, the theft of trade secrets was typically the work of insiders, corporate moles, or disgruntled employees. But with the technological advances of the Internet, smartphones, and other electronic devices, proprietary information is mobile, and hackers only have to break into an employee's device in order to have access to corporate networks and a company's trade secrets.[198] Moreover, cyberespionage is global and continuous. Mike McConnell, a former director of national intelligence, stated that, "In looking at computer systems of consequence—in government, Congress, at the Department of Defense, aerospace, and companies with trade secrets—we've not examined one yet that has not been infected by an advanced persistent threat."[198]

The United States has two primary organizations tasked with protection against cyberespionage. The first is the US Cyber Command (CYBERCOM), which is headed by the director of the National Security Agency and is responsible for the protection of the Department of Defense networks. Protection for civilian networks is the responsibility of the second organization, the US Department of Homeland Security.[199]

Vulnerabilities of the Internet

Part of the problem in protecting against cyberespionage are the inherent vulnerabilities of the Internet. According to Richard A. Clarke, who served as national coordinator for Security, Infrastructure Protection, and Counterterrorism in the Clinton administration, and Robert K. Knake, an international affairs fellow at the Council on Foreign Relations, there are five vulnerabilities in the design of the Internet:[200]

- the Internet addressing system
- the routing among Internet service providers (ISPs)
- the fact that most information is sent in the clear, or unencrypted
- the ability to propagate intentionally malicious traffic
- the fact that it's one network, with a decentralized design

The Internet Addressing System

Internet service providers (ISPs) carry Internet traffic and are sometimes also referred to as carriers. But not all ISPs are the same. Some are national in scope and are known as *backbone providers,* or *Tier 1 ISPs.* AT&T is an example of such a backbone provider, whose fiber-optic cables run between big cities and from coast to coast. Smaller, local ISPs connect to these backbone providers and supply service to business and residential users. It's most likely that a local ISP will be the phone or cable company.

When you access information on your computer, you might go to your browser and type in the name of the company you're trying to access, such as Thornhill Capital. This request would then have to be translated into the number language that computers understand. To accomplish this, your browser uses the Domain Name System (DNS) to look up the proper digital address. This functions much like an information operator, in that you provide the name and the operator provides you with the correct number. The DNS is a frequent target in cyberespionage, as it wasn't designed with a high level of security in mind. Therefore, in cyberespionage, one might enter the DNS, change the information contained therein, and misdirect another party to a phony web page instead of Thornhill Capital's home page (www.thornhillcapital.net).

The process of sending information through a computer to an intended website is a multistep process, with which most end users are unfamiliar. When a user performs a task as simple as a search on his or her browser, the user's computer, for wireless connections, sends information by radio waves to his or her home or business router. The router then turns this radio wave into an electronic signal and sends it to a local ISP, which may be located some distance from the user. The local ISP will have a cable connecting it to a backbone provider's fiber-optic network. From there, the user's information request will go through one or more routers and through one or more Tier 1 companies until it arrives at an ISP and server for the website requested. Even though the process may take only a few seconds, the user's request went over radio waves, copper wires, and high-speed bundles of fiber-optic cables.[201] It also, more than likely, traveled several times the line-of-sight distance to the company's actual location. As a result, in cyberespionage, someone could attack the DNS and send a person requesting information to another digital address, where he or she would be requested to enter sensitive data, such as his or her account number and password.

The Routing among Internet Service Providers

Since the backbone provider does not connect directly to the Internet, the Border Gateway Protocol (BGP) was put in place to act much like a postal worker who routes mail. The postal worker sees your address on the envelope and now needs to get the letter to you. The BGP contains listings that, if they were not in digital form but in English, would say: "If you want to connect to Thornhill Capital, come to us."

The BGP is vulnerable to cyberespionage. According to the Internet Society, a nonprofit organization dedicated to developing Internet-related standards and policies, "there is no mechanism internal to the BGP that protects against attacks that modify, delete, forge, or replay data, any of which has the potential to disrupt overall network routing behavior."[202]

Most Information Is Sent in the Clear, or Unencrypted

Possibly the most effective method to achieve data security is through encryption, as one must have an access key or a password in order to decrypt a file. There are two primary types of encryption: asymmetric, or public-key encryption, and symmetric encryption.

Asymmetric encryption uses two keys: a public key that is known to everyone and a private key that is only known to the recipient. The sender of the message would encrypt the text with the public key, and the recipient would use their private key to decrypt the ciphertext. Although it's computationally easy to generate a public and private key pair, it's considered computationally infeasible for a properly generated private key to be determined from its corresponding public key, since both the public and the private key are mathematically linked. Therefore, a public key may be published without compromising security. The private, or recipient key, may not. This is a secure and relatively easy form of encryption.

Symmetric encryption uses the same cryptographic keys for both the encryption of plaintext and the decryption of ciphertext. The requirement that both parties have access to the same key is a drawback of symmetric encryption.

> Only a fraction of Internet traffic is encrypted. Therefore, a number of entities have access to your data, including mail-service providers and ISPs. One of the most common cyberespionage methods for obtaining access to your computer is through the use of either a *packet sniffer* or a *keystroke logger*.

The *packet sniffer* is essentially a wiretap device for the Internet and is usually installed on an operating system to steal other people's traffic. When you connect to the Internet, a standard Ethernet protocol tells your computer to ignore everything that isn't addressed to it so that someone can see only what's specifically addressed to him or her. What a packet sniffer does is look at all traffic; it may even trick the network into believing that it's the router for a certain user's computer. This information then goes to the sniffer, which copies it and sends the information on to its intended recipient.

In contrast, *keystroke loggers* work by hiding a piece of malicious code on your computer so that everything you type is sent to a designated location. In order for a keystroke logger to be installed on your computer, you would have to download it.[203] This usually happens when you download a file from someone you don't know or trust.

The Ability to Propagate Intentionally Malicious Traffic

Viruses, worms, and phishing scams are collectively called *malware*. Much like keystroke loggers, they come from opening attachments from unknown users or infected websites.

A *virus* will normally pass from user to user, causing some form of disruption, or as used in cyberespionage, it will give someone covert access to your system and allow him or her to copy information contained therein.

A *worm* is a malware program that replicates itself and spreads to other computers. It usually enters a computer due to a lack of security in one's computer system. It differs from a virus in that it doesn't need to attach itself to an existing program. A worm can change your computer system and install a back door, allowing the worm's creator access to your system.

Phishing scams, on the other hand, want to acquire sensitive information from you. In phishing, the cyberespionage attacker will create phony websites and false e-mail messages that seem to come from reputable institutions, such as a bank, a credit card company, a US government agency, and so on. Masquerading as a reputable entity, phishing e-mails direct you to a false website closely resembling the legitimate website.[204] This website will then attempt to have you enter sensitive financial, personal, or business information. This fake website may also be infected with other forms of malware.

The Internet Is One Network, with a Decentralized Design

When the Internet was designed, it was constructed with an emphasis on decentralization. The reason for this was that the original designers of the Internet wanted to ensure that it would not be controlled by the government. However, because of this decentralization and the fact that it was originally designed to be used for research purposes and the exchange of ideas by those who knew and trusted each other, it was never designed with a high degree of security in mind. No one envisioned that there would someday be billions of users. Nor did they envision that the Internet would become a critical part of our daily life. Because of this, some nation-states, businesses, and individuals will use the Internet as their gateway for cyberespionage. Richard A. Clarke and Robert K. Knake noted that "the Internet, much like the tribal areas of Pakistan or the tri-border region in South America, is not under the control of anyone and is therefore a place to which the lawless will gravitate."[205]

All Nations Conduct Cyberespionage

Every nation is involved, to one degree or another, in cyberespionage. Franz Stefan-Grady, a senior fellow at the EastWest Institute, a global think-and-do tank that devises innovative solutions to pressing security concerns, indicates that the West has fewer incentives to engage in cyberespionage than nations such as Russia and China. This is because, according to Stefan-Grady, the West is still home to the most innovative and technologically advanced companies in the world. The United States Armed Forces, in particular, has the most advanced military technologies in the world. Therefore, the West simply has fewer incentives to launch massive cyberespionage operations.[206]

It's difficult to prevent cyberespionage, given the West's current information infrastructure vulnerabilities. According to the Cyber Conflict Studies Association, the current cyber environment is unable to establish a credible deterrence and prevent the emergence of adversaries and conflicts in cyberspace.

> The barrier for those who want to engage in cyberespionage is fairly low, as cyber weapons are relatively cheap.[206] It's estimated that intellectual property espionage alone costs companies about a trillion dollars a year.[207]

The National Intelligence Estimate (NIE), an authoritative assessment produced by the National Intelligence Council, a group of sixteen US intelligence agencies, names China, Russia, Israel, and France as the four countries most engaged in cyberespionage for economic intelligence. The NIE states that cyberespionage by China is considerably more than that conducted by any other country.[208] According to Mike McConnell, China has long been the country with the most sophisticated and institutionalized cyberespionage program. He further notes that it's therefore not surprising that China prohibits anyone from entering the country with an encrypted device unless he or she has government permission.[198]

Unlike the West, China has long conducted censorship of the Internet. There are currently 546 million domestic Internet users in China, almost double the number of four years ago. Furthermore, China has implemented strict internal controls to prevent the free flow of information in or out of the country, especially if that information is political, involves human rights, or concerns religion. Within China, they refer to this control of the Internet as the *Great Firewall*. Some sites, such as Facebook and Twitter, have been completely blocked in China. Instead, China has its own version of Facebook and Twitter, known as RenRen and Weibo, respectively, providing a measure of government control that is not available in the West.

Internet cafes are also subject to government scrutiny, and some may even have a policeman stationed outside, in addition to the government tracking their patrons' usage. The reason for the government's control of social media, Internet cafés, and similar methods of interactive communication is that it's anxious to prevent the Internet from becoming a tool for promoting societal discontent or spreading information that is critical of the government or the Communist Party.[209] Therefore, some foreign websites are blocked within China when the government feels their content or use may cause controversy or lead to social unrest.

In China, Image and Harmony Are Everything

Two of the bigger concerns for the Chinese government are its domestic image and maintaining internal harmony. Therefore, the acquisition, control, and dissemination of information have always been a priority. Prior to the Internet, the government could simply control the flow of information disseminated by newspapers, pamphlets, and other written forms of communication. After all, it was, and still is, politically a communist country, where all media are directly or indirectly controlled by the government. The global ubiquity of the Internet has changed this, as information is now instantaneous and global.

China wants to keep its problems domestic, its shortcomings to itself, and its citizens in a world where they believe the Communist Party will protect and look after them better than any other form of leadership. To that end, the government doesn't want any criticism of its leaders, government policy, food scares, or pollution problems spread across the Internet. Instead, its priority is keeping its citizens complacent and remaining the sole governing authority in the country. If a problem does occur, the government prefers to handle it internally, outside of the media, and without international scrutiny. The present information age makes this difficult. Therefore, the government exercises tight control over the Internet.

Welcome to China—Give Us Your Data

Economic cyberespionage is of particular concern for businesspeople, government officials, and tourists visiting China. In addition to an active foreign cyberespionage program, China has an extremely sophisticated domestic program, which is focused on obtaining high-value data from the cell phones and computers of foreign visitors. According to Kenneth Lieberthal, a former senior White House official for Asia who is currently the director of the John L. Thornton China Center at the Brookings Institute, "I've been told that if you use an iPhone or Blackberry, everything on it—contracts, calendar, and e-mails—can be downloaded in a second. All it takes is someone sitting near you on a subway waiting for you to turn it on, and they've got it." Jody Westby, chief executive of Global Cyber Risk, a consulting firm, adds that "it's real easy for them (Chinese) to read everything that goes in and out of the country because the government owns all the networks."[210]

> We always assume that all data in our computers, as well as in our cell phones, are accessed and downloaded when we enter the country. If you don't want trade secrets, internal memos, or other sensitive data to be read by the government, don't take it into China. Many companies and government organizations mandate that *clean* computers and cell phones be used when in China.[210]

Moreover, we should note that this gathering of electronic information in this manner is probably not unique to China. We assume that a great many countries are doing exactly the same thing. China is just the most visible infringer trying to obtain your electronic data, but it isn't the only country. A great many governments, including those in the West, have this capability and employ it.

Buy Our Equipment—Give Us Your Data

The US government, in an appropriations bill signed into law in early 2013, requires that the US Department of Justice, US Department of Commerce, NASA, and National Science Foundation (NSF) perform a formal assessment as to the risk of cyberespionage before they purchase computer systems or IT equipment. Attached to this bill is a clause specifically aimed at China. It requires that, with the assistance of the FBI, "any such system being produced, manufactured, or assembled by one or more entities that are owned, directed, or subsidized by China [must be analyzed to determine if the purchase is] in the national interests of the United States."

The impetus for this bill was a report by the US House Intelligence Committee that found Chinese companies Huawei and ZTE posed a national security risk.[211] The fear is that these, and other Chinese companies such as Lenovo, could more easily conduct cyberespionage with their equipment integrated as part of the US infrastructure.

Just Give Us Your Data

In addition to the theft of trade secrets from laptop computers and cell phones, China's cyberespionage also seems to be directed at foreign companies and government agencies both within and outside the country.

Take, for example, the case of the US Chamber of Commerce in 2010. The US Chamber of Commerce only came to know that its servers in China were being hacked after the FBI told them. Following this revelation, it was discovered that the intruders had built at least a half-dozen back doors that allowed them to enter these servers at any time. In addition, the intruders installed mechanisms that sent data to an outside party every week or two.[212] They were also able to build tools that allowed them to search for keywords across a range of documents on the Chamber's network, including searches for financial and budget information. A subsequent investigation didn't determine whether the cyberespionage attack had taken the documents that turned up in the intruder searches, but these documents were accessible and able to be both read and copied.

In addition to a penetration of their computer system, the US Chamber of Commerce also discovered that a thermostat in a town house the Chamber owns on Capitol Hill was communicating with an Internet address in China, and in March 2010, that a printer used by Chamber executives spontaneously printed pages with Chinese characters.[212]

Most cyberespionage attacks are not discovered until years later, if at all. National cyberespionage programs, in particular, are extremely good at covering their tracks. The most common method of discovering that you've been the victim of cyberespionage is when a competitor comes out with a product exactly the same as yours, but at a much lower price.[198] This is especially true when this product comes from a foreign country that previously had little or no expertise in your product area.

According to Alan Paller, director of research for the SANS Institute, a provider of security training and certification, not all targets of cyberespionage are corporations or government agencies. China's People's Liberation Army (PLA) is responsible for both the military and economic security of the country. Therefore, it has an active industrial espionage program targeting economic and military targets of opportunity in an effort to give China an advantage in negotiating, or an outright economic or military windfall. As a result, the PLA's cyberespionage program frequently targets service providers, such as law firms, where security is usually weaker.

Jonathan Evans, director general of the British Security Service MI-5, has stated that information is as likely to be stolen from attorneys and international consultants as from a company's own computers. When you're in negotiations with a Chinese company in an area that the government feels is important to the country, especially in technology, the PLA will frequently conduct cyberespionage into the data on your computer system.[213] This provides valuable information to Chinese companies and gives them a substantial advantage at the negotiating table.

Given the likelihood that both the United States and China actively conduct cyberwarfare against each other, there's a fundamental difference in the use of the information each obtains. The Chinese government will take the cyberespionage information it's obtained from American industry and provide it to relevant Chinese state-owned companies, and even some who are not state-owned, provided that it's in their national interest. The US government, on the other hand, tends to retain this information within the government and isn't involved in sharing this information with US companies.[214]

Mandiant, a US cybersecurity company, according to *U.S. News & World Report*, has identified a unit of the PLA known as Unit 61398, which it says has intruded into at least 141 organizations and stolen terabytes of information over a seven-year period. Mandiant also indicates that nearly

90 percent of this unit's operations target English-speaking countries, primarily the United States.[214]

The Attack Process

Now that we know that business owners, government agencies, service providers, and even individuals are likely targets for cyberespionage, what's the attack process? How does it occur?

The attack process, according to Jason Andress and Steve Winterfeld in their book *Cyber Warfare*, normally has up to eight components:[215]

- reconnaissance
- scanning
- access
- escalate
- exfiltrate
- assault
- sustain
- obfuscation

In the *reconnaissance phase*, the entity conducting the cyberattack maps out and discovers information on the system environment without alerting the user. During this phase, an attacker may plant tools enabling him or her to remotely monitor the targeted system.

In the *scanning phase*, the attacker examines the system more closely to try to detect potential vulnerabilities. He or she will gather detailed information from the operating system, as well as from applications.

In the *access phase*, a variety of tools utilizing various methods can be employed by the attacker to gain system access. The attacker will first try to find user accounts within the system. Once these accounts are discovered, he or she will next try to gain access to these accounts by use of synchronized, cracked, or guessed passwords. In some instances, the attacker may even try to clone access cards in an effort to obtain access.

In the *escalate phase*, the attacker, who has already gained access to the targeted system, now needs to gain additional or different privileges. This is a process known as *privilege escalation*. This can be accomplished through taking advantage of misconfigurations, gaining access and being able to act as the system administrator, or gaining access to applications, such as those running backup systems.

In the *exfiltrate phase*, the attacker finds the data that is most valuable to him or her and then exfiltrates, or sends, that data to a location to which he or she has access. In some cases, he or she simply moves the data directly to his or her own system.

The *assault phase* is typically not used unless the attacker wants to sow chaos in the system environment. During a war, this phase would almost certainly be the focus of an attacker. However, this practice is usually not condoned by a nation-state, as discovery of such activities can lead to war.

The next phase in the attack process, the *sustain phase*, is one in which the attacker reconfigures the system in order to allow himself or herself future access. The attacker knows that computer systems are normally upgraded over a period of time as security patches, updated operating systems, and updated software are installed. Therefore, the attacker will more than likely reconfigure, or make other system changes, in order to allow himself or herself access in the future. Reconfiguration by the attacker most frequently takes the form of creating new accounts, opening services on additional ports, installing command and control software, and placing back doors in applications.

The final phase of the attack process is the *obfuscation phase*. To obfuscate means to confuse, bewilder, or stupefy. The attacker uses this phase to cover his or her tracks and erase any digital forensic evidence of the intrusion. In some situations, the attacker intentionally leaves traces of the intrusion, but alters these traces so that they point to another source. For example, one nation-state may leave an altered trace that points to another country as the source of the cyberespionage. In addition to being the final phase, obfuscation may sometimes take place before the recon phase.

Foreign Travelers Are Vulnerable

As we mentioned previously, foreign travelers are a target for cyberespionage, as they're usually the least protected against its employment. They're on someone else's home turf, where the rules of privacy and other international conventions are simply ignored. As such, nation-states have extremely sophisticated cyberespionage programs that are specifically tailored to the foreign traveler. Unless your company or government agency has an active program to counter or prevent cyberespionage intrusions when you're traveling, you're vulnerable to these government attacks.

Of particular focus are computers and cell phones containing sensitive business information. Most businesspeople who travel with their laptop and cell phone have antivirus software installed on their computer and a password that's alpha-numeric-character driven; they thus believe that they're insulated against a hacker, a virus, or other intrusion. They're wrong. They're not familiar with, and obviously not prepared for, the advanced methods of cyberespionage that make their computer and cell phone so vulnerable. Even for computers that never leave their home office or the boundaries of the United States, cyberespionage on business and government computers and cell phones is a fact of life. Individuals not associated with a business or the government tend to be less of a target. Cyberespionage tends to focus on those individuals, companies, and government agencies that can provide valuable economic, political, and business information.

The most common method for someone to gain access to your system in a foreign country is to use the web. This will allow an attacker to gain access to your IP address, or electronic tag, which allows other computers to send information to your computer. An attacker would then be able to find out the names of senior persons within your firm or government agency, and send them e-mails. This e-mail would have an attached document that appeared as if it came from you. When the document is opened, hidden codes contained within would create a back door and run a program that gives instructions on where to send the data. This data transfer does not show up on the system manager.[216] There's little defense against this type of attack since the e-mail has a valid e-mail address.[217] Moreover, these infected attachments are able to get through most firewalls and past antivirus tools.

Mitigating the Risk

Government agencies and some businesses have protocols for employees taking laptops and cell phones with them outside of the United States, and even outside of their domestic offices. Automatic security updates, such as Microsoft's updates to Windows or installed software programs, don't protect you against sophisticated cyberespionage attacks.[217] Cyberespionage by nation-states and sophisticated attackers employ a variety of methods to target computer systems.

Highly sophisticated cyberespionage intrusions are difficult to stop, and most of the time they go unnoticed. They're usually created by nation-states that have significant resources at their disposal and are willing to spend a great deal of money to create such programs. Consequently, in preventing cyberespionage, it almost always comes down to the economic benefit. The US government, which has deep pockets, has CYBERCOM to help protect against even the most sophisticated cyberespionage attacks. Companies, however, don't have this caliber of sophisticated technical resources available to them. Protecting against cyberespionage is expensive. As a result, most companies will assess whether the cost of protecting their information against various levels of cyberespionage is worth the economic benefit obtained. Most often, companies will expend resources to only protect against low- and medium-level cyberattacks, as they don't have the resources or the sophisticated knowledge of a government to protect against more sophisticated intrusions, particularly by nation-states.

Stopping low- and medium-level intrusions doesn't have to be expensive. The Australian Defense Signals Directorate (DSD) has come up with simple solutions that stop intrusions of low- and medium-sophistication cyberattacks at a relatively low cost.

The first method of stopping this type of intrusion is the creation of a *white listing*. This means that a computer can only run software that is on an approved programs list, the *white list*. Any program installed on your computer by an attacker would, therefore, not be on this list and would not be able to collect and send out data. However, the creation of a white list also necessitates the need for expedient updates, allowing new programs to be accepted by your computer.

Another method for limiting low- and medium-level cyberwarfare attacks is to limit a computer's administrative rights. This means your computer would operate as a simple user, rather than have the right to make changes. Cyberespionage attackers would consequently not have access to the powerful administrative rights features of a system administrator.[218] One downside to this approach is that not all programs are designed to run when a computer has normal versus administrative rights.

It's estimated that more than 150 countries have developed cyberattack capabilities, and many exercise these capabilities for their own economic and political benefit. Yet only recently did the US private sector begin to respond to these threats and enhance their cybersecurity. According to Dave Aitel, president of security firm Immunity Inc. and a former NSA computer scientist, companies are now realizing the true cost of outsourcing, as it's difficult to protect themselves against cyberspying when they don't control the security that controls the access to their data.[207] In addition, many countries have their telecommunications infrastructure structured to allow for heavy surveillance by the government.[219] China is one of these countries.

There are several methods to mitigate the risk of cyberespionage when you travel:[210, 220]

- Use disposable cell phones and loaner laptops stripped of sensitive data, and wipe these clean before you leave and when you return to the United States.
- Take sensitive data on thumb drives and use it on off-line computers.
- Disable Bluetooth and Wi-Fi on your electronic devices.
- Remove the battery from your phone to prevent your microphone from being turned on remotely.
- Copy and paste your password from a USB thumb drive, as nation-states are very good at installing key-logging software on your laptop.
- Connect to the Internet through an encrypted, password-protected channel.
- Don't assume an Internet café is safe, as these frequently have key-loggers as well as spyware installed that can steal data and passwords.

Cyberespionage is a global concern. Although China seems to be the most active perpetrator of cyberespionage, it's not alone, as nearly every developed nation is thought to conduct cyberespionage in one form or another. Cyberattacks are costly to businesses and to national economies.

Protection against these attacks requires an enhanced level of technical sophistication that many companies don't currently employ.

When traveling to a country where you know you're likely to be the target of a cyberespionage attack, such as China and Russia, it's best to bring a computer and cell phone with a minimal amount of information residing in memory. If you don't want your information copied, don't bring a computer and cell phone loaded with sensitive corporate data. This is the easiest and safest way of protecting information when traveling.

Businesses with economically valuable data on their electronic devices, or in sensitive business negotiations with a company in a foreign country, especially China and Russia, should consider hiring a cybersecurity specialist. This is particularly true when the outcome of your negotiations could impact a nation-state. Regarding cyberespionage, always assume you're under attack. Be aggressive in protecting sensitive data.

CHAPTER 13

Take Control, Negotiate, and Win

Most Westerners have a difficult time understanding the Chinese negotiating style and how to successfully consummate a business transaction in China. That's understandable, as we've previously mentioned, given that the West has only been interacting with a non-isolationist China for the past thirty-five years. Similarly, the Chinese were just as unprepared and were largely unfamiliar with the Western mind-set. As a result, there was no common ground between parties in early negotiation sessions, except for a desire by both sides to make money from their mutual interaction. Over time, both sides have learned a great deal more about the other. But surprisingly, while the Chinese now seem to better understand our mind-set and have adjusted their negotiation practices accordingly, most Westerners haven't followed suit.

On the contrary, most Westerners seem to be focused on keeping their negotiating style unchanged in a "we know what we're doing" or "if it worked successfully in other industrialized countries, then it'll also work in China" attitude. This philosophy has been an obituary for many companies who tried to forge a successful business venture in China.

Understanding how to negotiate with Chinese businesspeople has assumed paramount importance for most businesses that want to take advantage of China's immense growth. In the West, negotiations tend to be individualistic, impersonal, and aggressive in trying *to get the order*. While we want a mutually profitable business relationship with our Chinese counterpart, our primary focus is on signing the contract and then filling the order. It's transactional. After all, that's how business is conducted in the United States, and it's how we believe other countries conduct theirs. Consequently, we're on business autopilot when we enter a negotiating session. We'll usually prepare for a meeting by putting together a computer presentation, prepare ourselves for questions the other side may ask, and take with us supporting documentation and visual aids that will help support our dialogue. Even the most mundane items, from the number of business handouts we take to the wearing of a *power* business suit, will be included in our planning for the meeting.

When most Westerners arrive at their meeting, they expect to sit down with their Chinese counterpart and, after exchanging a few pleasantries, get down to business and make their presentation. After all, they reason, that's why we're all here. Following their presentation, they expect the other side to ask insightful questions. By most Western standards, they've been successful when their Chinese counterpart nominally agrees with what's been presented and indicates he or she wants to move forward. This is how we expect to conduct business and how we judge a business meeting and negotiating session to be successful. It therefore comes as a surprise when we're just about to begin our presentation, and our Chinese counterpart begins to inquire about whether we've seen the maple trees changing color on Xiangshan Mountain outside Beijing, or had an opportunity to go to the Longxi Hotspring Resort and bathe in their mineral pools, or other matters equally outside the scope of business. We then think, *What's wrong with this guy—doesn't he want to talk business? Isn't he interested in what we have to say?*

Exchanging pleasantries, to some degree, is an expected part of negotiating sessions. Most businesspeople expect it. It's an icebreaker. But when it continues for an extended period of time, most Westerners get impatient. They want to move on. They believe it's eating up a substantial amount of time that would be more efficiently spent consummating a deal. Westerners tend to label this type of interaction inefficient, unfocused, and unproductive, even to the point of believing that their counterpart wants to avoid the intended purpose of the meeting. *What a colossal waste of time* is a mantra muttered by more than a few foreigners experiencing this type of behavior.

What many Westerners fail to understand is that this discussion *is* part of the negotiating process. In fact, it's an important part. In China, relationships and trust are extremely important components for transacting business. Without an understanding of the other party, typical Chinese businesspeople will have a difficult time consummating the transaction. They want to get to know who they're dealing with, and until they find out, you're likely going to be spending an inordinate amount of time negotiating in an infinite circle. Therefore, when negotiations go down a seemingly endless highway with no end in sight, Westerners are generally quick to blame this inaction and failure to consummate the transaction on the Chinese being insincere or unfocused. "After all," most reason, "we came prepared to do business, to sign a contract, and to move forward. We have the best product and the best pricing. What's their problem?"

> Most Westerners set themselves up for failure by not understanding how negotiations are conducted in China. To succeed, they must understand that relationships and trust are the foundations for negotiations and business relationships. Without these foundations, you might, in some circumstances, consummate a transaction, but the chances are small that the transaction would ultimately be successful to term.

Although this makes sense to just about everyone we speak with at conferences and seminars, a majority of Western businesspeople still have a bias and a narrow comfort zone. They treat negotiations in China much as they would treat negotiations, for example, in Germany or Britain, when in fact, it would be more appropriate to analogize China as the moon and Germany and Britain as planet earth.

Characteristics of American Negotiators

Before we fully understand how to negotiate with the Chinese, it's necessary to understand how we, as Americans, negotiate. What are our prejudices, preferences, and expectations? In addition, we should understand that the American style of negotiating is not going to be the gold-plated and standard form of negotiations. Each country has its own style, which is influenced by its culture, history, geography, and other factors that comprise people's prejudices and expectations in the negotiating process.

Listed below are what we consider to be American characteristics in the negotiation process:

- businesslike
- view negotiations as joint problem solving
- negotiate according to their own set of values
- preference for directness and bluntness
- ambivalence
- legalistic
- judgmental
- use of inducements
- impatience
- negotiating style affected by regional differences
- respect achievements, rather than individuals' pedigrees
- have a bottom line

Businesslike

Americans are purpose-driven. They have an agenda, and they have an objective. They tend to be positive and unemotional as they pursue a well-planned course of action designed to help them attain their goals. They don't shoot from the hip, but like to chart a path and stick to it. Yet they retain the flexibility to change direction, if necessary, in order to accomplish their objectives. In maintaining their businesslike approach, they tend to be very focused on the endgame. Therefore, they're less prone to rhetoric and making grand statements that sound good but are of little consequence. They tend to stay away from small talk and discussions that stray from their focused objective and, instead, outline a course of action that they expect to modify as necessary in getting the other side to accept their premises and viewpoints. Since they tend to be objective rather than subjective, Americans usually provide the other side with the data necessary to support their positions. While doing this, they maintain an eye on the goal line and what actions are required in order for them to accomplish their objectives.[221] American businesspeople tend to be well-prepared, pragmatic, calm, persistent, and goal-oriented.

View Negotiations as Joint Problem Solving

Americans generally perceive that *we're both in the boat together* and therefore need to jointly navigate around various obstacles in order to simultaneously reach the shore on the other side. They believe this leads to a *win-win* scenario.[222] Therefore, Americans generally don't *skip over an issue* and come back to it later. Instead, they try to jointly resolve issues as they occur. They also try not to dictate terms, as this generally leads to a lack of compromise and increases the difficulty in attaining their goals. And although Americans are competitive by nature, they generally put this trait behind them as they try to quickly solve issues that can derail the negotiating process or prevent them from moving forward.

Negotiate according to Their Own Set of Values

American negotiators tend, at times, to be moralistic and act according to their inherent sense of values. In negotiating according to their internal beliefs, they can be idealistic and passionately express these beliefs. Therefore, an American's moral values frequently set the framework for their negotiating style and demeanor. Whether or not the other side shares these values will carry little weight on the American side. They'll still try to win the other side over by having them accept their core beliefs. This process, however, sometimes meets with resistance when the other side also has a firm set of values to which they adhere. In this event, the evangelism expressed by both sides will have to be placed on the back burner as they jointly try to resolve the issues and move forward.

Preference for Directness and Bluntness

Americans dislike vagary. They also like to get to the point. They're direct and expect the other side to reciprocate and be just as frank and straightforward. If they aren't, Americans feel they'll never reach their goal, or it will take them substantially longer to get there. Some non-American negotiators may find this directness to be rude and prefer a more subtle *easing into it* approach in negotiations. American bluntness and directness most often express themselves when the other side is evasive or ambiguous.[222] In this event, Americans believe the direct approach will help get everyone back on track and focused on the issues in front of them.

Most Americans are aware that directness and bluntness can cross the line into rudeness and arrogance. When they do, they can derail the negotiating process, cause animosity on both sides, and lead to confrontation. This is obviously counterproductive.[223] Therefore, in negotiating with those who may have sensitivities to directness and bluntness, we advocate *toning it down,* to make the other side feel they have a voice in the process and that they're not being steamrolled.

Ambivalent

Ambivalence is a state of having simultaneous, conflicting feelings. When we say Americans tend to be ambivalent, we mean that, on the one hand, Americans want to sit down and work out the issues in a businesslike manner, which hopefully will lead to an agreement.[224] On the other hand, they usually have a flip side or another set of values, which may directly conflict with their businesslike approach.

Sometimes this ambivalence is due to the attitude, temperament, and moralistic outlook of the other side not being aligned with their view of the world and their projected course of action. The end result of this state of ambivalence is that, even as these traits coexist within their personality and one side is often kept in check, one or more of these traits will sometimes escape and manifest itself in the negotiating process. For example, they may be businesslike, but they're also impatient and pushy in getting the other side to move forward. They may be cordial, but also blunt. They may also give a concise opinion, but then go on to lecture the other side on the merits of a specific position. In other words, Americans frequently use both sides of the coin in the negotiating process.

Legalistic

Americans tend to follow the letter of the law. They like contracts that are binding and that memorialize exactly what's been negotiated.[225]

They don't like to be told, "We'll work it out if that happens" or "We'll have a gentlemen's agreement between us." That doesn't work. Instead, an American's attorneys will usually draw up long and involved contracts that try to cover every eventuality. No vagaries; no guesswork. They want a concise written agreement between parties at the end of the negotiating process so that both sides can strictly adhere to its terms. Of course, some countries, such as China, where enforcement action against an infringing party is difficult, may adhere to the contract only when it's to their benefit. When it's not, they seem to say, "Come and get us." This is in contrast to the Western world, where most parties feel bound by the terms of the contract.

Although American companies are sometimes criticized for long and involved contracts, such contracts are actually worth their weight in gold when they cover an eventuality that was never expected to occur and where both parties now don't have to go to court to resolve the issue.

Judgmental

America is a country of individualists. As such, Americans tend to demonstrate more personal initiative, form their own opinions, and largely draw their own conclusions. In other words, they're judgmental. These judgments, especially in the form of initial impressions, can form the basis for prejudices in the negotiation process.

For example, if an American has antipathy toward someone, that prejudice may manifest itself in believing that the negotiating partner is not being truthful, or that he or she is unwilling to compromise even knowing that what's being said is true. Being judgmental clouds the objectivity of the negotiating process and very often leads to faulty decisions based on inaccurate assessments. Consequently it's best to set aside individualistic tendencies and wipe the slate clean of biases and antipathy before commencing the negotiating process.

Use of Inducements

In the negotiating process, Americans tend to favor inducements over compromise. Compromise makes Americans uneasy. A compromise generally means that, in order to close the transaction, you have to give up something of value. Many Americans feel that compromise is a sign of weakness, and America is not a nation that likes weak negotiators. Inducements, on the other hand, are different. They provide something of value to the other side.[226] Inducements fit well with an American's businesslike approach in negotiating. It's a quid pro quo. For whatever the reason, American negotiators favor inducements over compromise.

Impatient

American negotiators are generally known to have less patience than many of their foreign counterparts. They want instant gratification and, therefore, tend to negotiate quickly. They tend to break down the important issues as they see them, negotiate each separately, and are usually unwilling to revisit issues that have been previously discussed. They're monochronic, meaning that they successfully complete one task before going on to the next. But not everyone is monochronic. Some are polychronic, meaning that they're more interested in social interaction rather than the completion of the task. As such, they might work on a task for a period of time, and then, when they feel the urge, will simply move on to another task before the previous task is complete. This tends to extend the negotiating process and cause a great deal of stress for Americans.

Americans generally tend to want to conclude negotiations on their first visit. If negotiations can't be concluded during their visit, they'll quickly follow up with e-mails and phone calls, moving forward based on the relationship they established during their visit. Americans want the total focus of the meeting to be on resolving issues. As a result, they don't like anything that interferes with the negotiation process, such as interruptions and distractions.[227] If interruptions and distractions occur, they will generally provoke a quick response.

If negotiations take too long, Americans will consider alternatives that save time.[228] Americans are a monochronic nation that's impatient and wants a quick resolution to the issues before them.

Negotiating Style Affected by Regional Differences

Americans negotiate differently based on regional differences and cultural backgrounds. Negotiators from the western portion of the United States tend to be more open-minded, leisurely in their negotiating style, and more naive than negotiators who reside in other areas of the country. Those who are from the Midwest tend to be more risk-adverse and formal, and follow tradition. Negotiators who reside in the Northeast tend to be more tolerant, especially if they're from big cities. Those who reside in the southern portions of the United States tend to be more competitive and aggressive, and think more narrowly than other negotiators.[222]

Respect Achievements, Rather Than Individuals' Pedigrees

In many areas of the world, a great deal of importance is placed on one's family background and the schools one attended. Some feel that a person who's attended a prestigious center of learning and has a storied family name will be better equipped to be successful in business. Americans, on the other hand, take a different position. Americans are individualistic and give their respect to those who have demonstrated achievements, irrespective of their family name or school. Therefore, American negotiators sometimes differ substantially from their counterparts in other areas of the world. If an American negotiator has a demonstrated record of achievements, then we generally consider him or her to be the right person for the job, but he or she might not enjoy the same measure of respect from his or her negotiating counterpart.

Have a Bottom Line

Americans believe in negotiations as a means of achieving their goals, but also have a bottom line where they'll take a firm position and go no further.[222] Generally that position is a price change of between 20 percent and 30 percent from the other side's initial offer. If the price change is outside of that range, an American negotiator will usually feel that the other side is acting in bad faith.

Both sides want to achieve a win-win and consummate a transaction that provides value to each party. However, there are economic realities that sometimes make a win-win scenario difficult to attain. Consequently it's better to field price expectations early in the negotiating process, so that you don't get to the end only to find out that you don't have a deal.

Understand the Culture First

A foreigner wishing to negotiate in China should first start by understanding their culture. There are four cultural threads that bind Chinese people together and show through in Chinese negotiations, according to John L. Graham, a professor of international business at the Graduate School of Management at the University of California, Irvine, and N. Mark Lam, an attorney at Graham and Lam specializing in East-West negotiations.[229] These four threads are

- agrarianism,
- morality,
- language, and
- wariness of foreigners.

Agrarianism

Two-thirds of the Chinese populace live in rural areas, where there's a communal rather than an individualistic relationship between parties. In these areas, harmony, loyalty, and obedience are highly valued among members of the commune. These agrarian values are held in high esteem by Chinese businesspeople. Many believe that these values are part of their cultural heritage and, as such, should be practiced in both their business and their everyday life.

Morality

Morality in China and in the West often differ. As a result, when a foreigner and a Chinese negotiator sit across the table from one another, their views of what constitutes moral and immoral behavior often vary. We therefore advise *stepping into his or her* shoes and using what insights you've gained on China to understand his or her moralistic point of view.

> The Chinese believe that everyone outside of China are outsiders and that it's acceptable to take advantage of them. This moralistic view is a cultural thread that binds Chinese people together. As an example, you may be provided data during a negotiating session, and you expect that data to be accurate. But in fact, there's a high likelihood that they may not be. If the data do turn out to be inaccurate, it would be considered deceitful by Western standards and an immoral act. In China, the act of providing false data can best be summed up by the Latin words *caveat emptor*, or *let the buyer beware*. It may not be considered immoral by your Chinese counterpart, just good business.

The reason for this is that the Chinese expect the people they're negotiating with to look out for themselves and independently verify the data that have been presented. If they don't, then they're naive, negligent, and also at fault.

Language

Language is the third cultural thread that binds Chinese people together. Chinese is an ideogram language, where words are graphic symbols rather than a sequence of letters. This leads to the Chinese thought process of seeing the entire picture, rather than the individual details. In other words, Chinese businesspeople are less likely to get involved with the minutia. Instead, they're more likely to step back and look at the entire landscape of the transaction.

Wariness of Foreigners

The Chinese have an inherent wariness of foreigners due the country's long history of conflict with other nationalities. The Chinese don't trust foreigners and, more to the point, anyone outside of their family. It's a cultural thread that runs through every Chinese person. As close as you may think you are to the Chinese negotiator or other Chinese participants, don't ever expect them to think of you in any way other than as a foreigner. You'll never be on equal ground, and they'll always be wary of your intentions and motives.

Characteristics of Chinese Negotiators

After discussing an American negotiator's biases and preferences, we've listed below what we consider the biases and preferences of a Chinese negotiator:

- relationship-driven
- motivated to save face
- belief in a defined hierarchy
- belief in a defined consensus
- interpersonal harmony is paramount
- frugality
- reciprocity

Relationship-Driven

Chinese business is driven by relationships. There's no cold calling in China. It simply wouldn't work. The Chinese don't trust someone they don't have a relationship with. If you want to approach a Chinese company to propose a transaction, for example, then you'll need an introduction in order to make that happen.[230] That introduction will have to be from someone who has guanxi, or a trusted relationship, with the company. If that type of relationship doesn't exist, then there's not going to be a transaction.

The Chinese side of the negotiation table will have a working relationship among themselves and will all be insiders, whereas, as we've said, you'll be an outsider in the negotiating process. What this means is that, from the start, your Chinese counterpart will take what you're saying *with a grain of salt* because what you say may or may not be true. However, when Chinese people hear the same thing you're saying from a person they trust, then they tend to believe it. That's not to say that you can't have a relationship, even as a foreigner and outsider, with your Chinese counterpart. You can. But it will take time to build up the level of trust necessary for them to take you at your word. Even then, they'll be wary.

Motivated to Save Face

Face is extremely important in China. In America, the concept of face would be akin to prestige, honor, and dignity all rolled into one.[231] Face is a measure of an individual's worth in Chinese society. Consequently, when negotiating with your Chinese counterpart, it's important that your actions don't cause your counterpart to lose face.

Even if your action is inadvertent, it can still have a profound negative effect. For example, in a meeting, you try to get your point across that your company has a better product than your Chinese counterpart's company, as his or her company's product has a markedly higher failure rate due to design deficiencies. What you want to achieve from the meeting is to combine your superior product with your counterpart's cheaper in-country manufacturing capabilities, native sales force, and extensive client list. In your negotiating style, you let the company know that their product has failed, your product is the best on the market, and they're lucky to have you here to discuss a joint venture.

If that supposition were presented in the United States, it would be quickly evaluated, and the other side might very well come back with a comment of their own, such as, "That's not true" or "I agree with you, and that's why we're here to discuss a joint venture." In either case, they'd take what you said as informational, make their own evaluation as to the validity of your remarks, and formulate their own opinion. They'd then move on. In China, that's more than likely not going to be the case. Instead, the remark about the quality of your counterpart's product will almost certainly cause a loss of face for your Chinese counterpart among his or her staff. Even though your intent was to demonstrate that putting your product in the hands of both companies would enable you both to jointly dominate the market, the fact that you've caused your counterpart to lose face because he or she knowingly sold an inferior product would more than likely doom your potential venture.

Another example would be that you catch your counterpart making an error, or a number of errors, in a discussion or in his or her presentation, perhaps citing incorrect data. You correct him or her repeatedly in front of the group, trying to impress those present with your encyclopedic knowledge of the subject matter. This will cause your counterpart to lose face, as you're demonstrating to everyone present that he or she is uninformed and unknowledgeable in his or her profession. The negotiations would then very likely come to an end.

Maintaining your counterpart's face in the negotiation process is important. Therefore, take an opportunity to praise him or her in front of the staff and tell how appreciative you are of his or her efforts. Giving your counterpart face will substantially help the progress of the negotiations.

Belief in a Defined Hierarchy

As we previously mentioned, the Chinese believe in adherence to a hierarchical relationship. As a result, Western negotiators notice that their Chinese counterpart is almost always older than the rest of the staff and that he or she also holds a corporate position that's hierarchically superior to other members of the team. While this is almost always the rule with Chinese negotiators, it doesn't necessarily hold true in the West, where negotiators are generally selected on the basis of their negotiating skills and industry knowledge rather than age.

Belief in a Defined Consensus

Chinese and Western negotiating teams vocalize their opinions differently. A Chinese negotiator's staff, for example, will offer him or her their guarded opinions privately during the course of the negotiations so that no one from the other side can hear what's being said. This allows the Chinese negotiator to accept or reject what's been told to him or her, and since he or she is the sole spokesperson for the group, publicly maintain the team's unified position in the negotiating process. In contrast, a Western team member may at times *chime in* with a *free flow of ideas* and offer advice to the group in support of the Western negotiator's position and his or her corporate objectives. In negotiating sessions, the Chinese tend to be more formal than many of their foreign counterparts, who have a tendency toward informality.

Interpersonal Harmony Is Paramount

Tough love doesn't work in China. The Chinese normally won't enter into a business relationship where both parties don't get along and have mutual respect for one another. In Confucian teaching, respect and harmony are the glue that binds a relationship. As a result, politeness is essential.[232] If you believe that brusque behavior and rudeness can be overcome by the potential monetary rewards of the transaction, you're wrong. No matter how much the Chinese want to make money, they'll almost never consummate a transaction or stay in a long-term relationship where there's a lack of harmony. The Chinese mind-set is that a lack of harmony will eventually lead to disputes and to a harmful and unprofitable business relationship. Getting mad, throwing a tantrum, and similar forms of behavior are guaranteed ends to the negotiations and a ride to the airport.

Frugality

The Chinese are frugal and cost-conscious. Negotiating pricing with your Chinese counterpart is one of the most difficult tasks you'll have and will, more than likely, become the most time-consuming portion of your negotiations. The Chinese have an advantage over Americans in this respect. The reason for this is that most Americans tend to be impatient and want to get a transaction closed as quickly as possible. Consequently they tend to make concessions due to their impatience and desire to close the deal quickly. The Chinese, on the other hand, aren't in any hurry. They want to make sure they haven't given away any more than they have to. They're more interested in maximizing their monetary benefits than in a quick resolution of negotiations.[233] The Chinese will look at a transaction from every conceivable angle, get inputs from their staff, and try to form a consensus opinion in an effort to make the best financial transaction possible. It's very common for the Chinese to extend negotiations to the point of frustration on the part of foreigners in an effort to obtain monetary concessions that would otherwise be difficult to negotiate on their own merit.

Reciprocity

Foreign negotiators who haven't previously negotiated with someone from China aren't generally familiar with China's *rules of the road*. As a result, they make assumptions based on past negotiating experiences in other countries, which may or may not have relevance in China. Learning China's rules of the road will allow you to become more successful in your negotiating efforts.

One of the most important rules of the road in Chinese negotiations is reciprocity. Reciprocity is simple: "You do me a favor, and I'll return that favor. I may not return it immediately, but the favor you extended to me will eventually be reciprocated."[234]

So often in negotiations, we hear of companies making concession after concession to the Chinese side of the table without asking for a concession in return. They should. Your Chinese counterpart will expect there to be some form of reciprocity. But in order for that to occur, you'll have to point that out. If you feel you're being polite by not asking for a reciprocal concession and this will give you better negotiating power on more important issues, you're wrong. By your not asking for a reciprocal concession, your Chinese counterpart will know that you're inexperienced in negotiating Chinese transactions. This will probably make it more difficult in the future for you to negotiate and receive concessions, since your counterpart knows you're not familiar with the reciprocity process.

Foreigners generally don't have a clue about reciprocity. But once you understand a favor for a favor, negotiating with your Chinese counterpart will get a little easier.

The Negotiating Process

Once the negotiating process begins, your Chinese counterpart may employ a variety of tactics in order to attain his or her business goals. According to Carolyn Blackman, director of the Asian Studies Unit at the University of Ballarat and vice president of the Australia-China Chamber of Commerce and Industry, one or more of the following strategies might be employed by your Chinese counterpart in the negotiating process:[235]

- using false authority
- exerting time pressure
- psychological pressure
- left-field issues
- using competitors
- changing negotiators and locations
- pushing to find the bottom line
- reopening closed issues

Using False Authority

Whenever we travel to another country to conduct business, we don't always know what to expect. Each country has different customs, different laws, and a slightly different outlook on life. What's particularly difficult to understand in a foreign country are the local and national laws, as they're not always in sync and often are seemingly in conflict with one another. That's especially true in China. Without a professional guide, such as a local attorney, to take you through this tangled morass, you have every possibility of violating one or more laws in the process of transacting business. Chinese negotiators know this and exploit it. As a result, when you're negotiating with your Chinese counterpart, he or she may cite a number of Chinese laws that you would be in violation of if he or she adopted your proposal. The only legal way to accomplish your goal, he or she may tell you, is to structure the transaction his or her way. Of course, that's probably not true.

Using false authority is a common ploy on the part of a Chinese negotiator to try to get you to do something his or her way, indicating that any other path would be illegal. Let me give you an example using

188

what happened to us several years ago in Nanjing. We were meeting with a company that wanted to negotiate a joint venture with one of our clients. That company was a consumer products manufacturing company that wanted to export its products outside China. Our client was a US consumer products company that wanted to manufacture and sell its products in China. It seemed, on the face of it, to be a good match and one where we could negotiate a win-win for both sides.

At the beginning of our negotiation, the CEO, who was the chief negotiator for his company, told us that the local government required that all joint ventures in the city be majority-owned by the Chinese joint venture partner. As *proof* of this, he had a government official and an attorney with him who assured us that, although this was not the situation nationally, it was the policy of the local government in Nanjing. As if on cue, the attorney gave us a set of joint venture documents, in both Chinese and English, which established the joint venture with the majority ownership by the Chinese side.

The next day, our US attorney referred us to an attorney in Nanjing who refuted the need for Chinese majority ownership in a joint venture. The other attorney, obviously a friend of the CEO, had tried to make everything easy for us and prepared documents that would give our client a minority interest in the newly established joint venture. Those documents could obviously be modified according to other points that would be negotiated, but it still wouldn't change the fact that the Chinese joint venture partner owned a majority of the company. The company's attorney had obviously counted on the fact that we would not want to incur legal expenses when they had given us *the only* Chinese legal opinion possible and drawn up the necessary documents accordingly. We believe he assumed, since it was local law and nothing could be done about it, that we would take his document and sign it, with some modest changes. In the United States, we find this hard to believe, as using our own attorney in a business transaction is second nature. For the Chinese, it's not.

Using false authority is a tactic that's commonly employed with foreigners, and Chinese businesspeople will have no compunction in citing a nonexistent authority as a way to attain their business goals.

Westerners normally have respect for authority. We abide by the law. A Chinese negotiator knows this and counts on it. Consequently, on many occasions, Chinese corporate executives, and even government officials, have tried to give us *Chinese law* as a justification for the course of action they're proposing. "No other course is possible," they tell us. "It's the law!"

The best defense is, of course, knowledge. A domestic Chinese attorney from a reputable law firm, not the company's, is essential for anyone in situations such as this. We've also found that many Western law firms now have offices in China with well-trained multilingual staffs. They'd more than likely be excellent at guiding you through the intricacies of Chinese business law and addressing potential issues of false authority.

Exerting Time Pressure

As we've mentioned, most Chinese believe foreigners have very little patience and a penchant for acting quickly and decisively. They also believe we have a *shoot-from-the-hip* individualistic mentality or, better described, we're cowboys entering their world of exactness. The Chinese decision-making process, in contrast, is team-oriented, hierarchical, and process-oriented. Even though there may be a team approach in arriving at a decision, the staff's decision is only a recommendation to the person in authority. Chinese decisions are always made at the top of the corporate hierarchy, normally after getting staff consensus. It may, therefore, take some time before an actual decision is made. Chinese leaders, whether they're in government or in industry, always look before they leap. They're plodders and planners who will not make a decision until they believe they know the outcome and it meets their objectives.

A foreign company, in contrast, frequently allows employees to exercise a specified level of decision making and empowers these employees to carry out those decisions in an expeditious manner. As slow as we might believe our bureaucracy is, it's turbocharged when compared to the Chinese style of decision making—the US Congress being the obvious exception.

The average Chinese also believes that group decisions are usually superior to those that are individualistic, and that foreigners tend to act rashly and make mistakes in their rush to consummate a transaction. They feel it may take them longer to arrive at a decision, but that decision is usually correct. They're not rushing, but they know we're in a rush. As a result, they often create artificial time lines for foreigners in an effort to try to get them to act more expeditiously than they otherwise would.

As an example, we were in Beijing speaking with a company that was trying to get us to invest in their automotive repair business. During our conversation, the CEO of the company told us that there was a unique opportunity to expand by purchasing some repair centers directly from a large Chinese conglomerate that was looking to exit that business. The conglomerate wanted to focus on consumer goods, rather than the automotive sector. If we acted quickly, he added, we could buy these centers before the company solicited potential buyers. Integrating these centers into his company would, he assured us, substantially increase profit margins and earnings. In addition, the CEO went on to explain, the senior official who ran the conglomerate's automotive repair centers was a close friend of his. We were only getting to see this deal early because of him.

On the face of it, this type of transaction was not unusual for a multifaceted business. Companies divest themselves of noncore assets all the time. Furthermore, most divesting companies call other companies in the same line of business and ask if they would be interested buyers. This saves them quite a bit of time and possibly a fee if they were to use an outside firm for the sale of the asset. This all made sense up to this point. What made this transaction unusual was that the CEO went on to add that his friend could only give us a week, an unusually short period of time, to consummate the transaction before the company solicited bids from other interested parties. When this happened, we became suspicious and decided to tell the CEO that our due diligence process alone would take substantially longer than one week and that we would have to pass. Three days later, the CEO told us he had worked a deal out with his friend to extend the deadline, but we would have to put up good faith money. We walked away from the transaction.

The first lesson to be learned from this is to realize that time pressure in China is usually a one-way street. It's applied to foreigners to get them to act quickly and without much thought, because foreigners are accustomed to time pressure. Time constraints are common in Western society, and the Chinese know it. While a Chinese businessperson might very well walk away from a transaction that was under time constraints, a Westerner might look upon it as a challenge.

When time pressure is placed on you, the best course of action, which we've successfully used many times, is to say you just have to think about it and don't care about time lines, whatever the consequences. This usually makes your Chinese counterpart angry, but it also conveys an important message to him or her: you're not going to be rushed into last-minute decisions, and if a decision is required, then you need enough time to study the matter to make an informed decision. We've found that the Chinese have very little defense against this tactic if the time line they're presenting doesn't exist.

Indeed, after trying to convince you of the seriousness of the situation and the absurdness of your inaction, they'll almost always start to soften their position and become much easier to negotiate with as the deadline approaches or passes. They'll probably now tell you, as in the above example, that a friend is doing them a one-time favor and will extend, or eliminate, the time line. Of course, there are legitimate time lines that have to be respected in business transactions, but for the most part, we find that many Chinese businesspeople try to create artificial time lines when money is involved. They'll push to try to get you to make a monetary decision in a short period of time based on little information. Our advice: take a step back, perform your due diligence, and make an informed decision within your time frame. Take enough time in your decision making, and the tables will eventually be turned, as the Chinese won't walk away from someone with money. In the end, they usually compromise.

Psychological Pressure

Both sides in the negotiating process understandably feel that consummating a transaction is all-important and that they'd rather not settle on a compromise if at all possible. Instead, they'd like to sway the other side to their position. In order to accomplish this, your Chinese counterpart will likely employ psychological pressure. This can take many forms. For example, we were at a hotel restaurant adjacent to the Nanjing airport with the CEO of a company from Anhui province. During this meeting, the CEO let it be known that he was in discussions with several of our competitors, and if we didn't substantially improve our contract, he would sign with one of them. This point was made very forcefully and in a voice that boomed throughout the restaurant. After his short tirade, the CEO quickly glanced over to his staff, who were seated around him at the table, and gave a short nod of satisfaction.

We felt that the attitude we saw was more a show for his staff than a line he'd drawn in the sand. But his message was clear: sign the contract as is, or I'll bring it to one of your competitors and you'll have wasted your time and money. We were about to respond when, ignoring us, he turned his chair to the side and stared out the window of the restaurant. Clearly this was meant to demonstrate his distaste for the contract we'd presented to him. The CEO expected us to now negotiate a compromise and draw up a new contract. However, we felt that we'd already negotiated to the point where there was nothing more to give.

We're of the belief that, when you've given up all there is to give, then simply walk away from the contract or the negotiation. In this instance, we believed that the contract he had in front of him was as good as he was likely to receive from anyone. Moreover, there was no evidence that anyone but us had conducted the extensive due diligence necessary to complete this transaction. Instead of suggesting a compromise, as he probably expected, we both just stared back at him, wondering if this were a person we really wanted to work with. After a few seconds of our speechless stare, the CEO made an angry comment in Chinese, got up from the table, and exited the restaurant. He was followed in close formation by his staff. We believe that at this point he expected us to follow him out of the restaurant and ask him to return so we could come to a compromise.

When we didn't, it wasn't five minutes later when one of his staff walked back into the restaurant and asked if we could compromise on a couple of almost insignificant points in the contract. If we could make those pen-and-ink changes, she promised, she would bring him back into the restaurant to sign the contract. Not ten minutes later, everyone was shaking hands.

During negotiations the other side may try to intimidate you and tell you that, if you don't agree to their terms, you'll lose their business or they won't sign the contract. Our advice is to determine your bottom line ahead of the meeting and don't negotiate below it. Don't negotiate on the basis that you'll make it up on the next contract. You won't. The Chinese view every contract as a stand-alone that exists on its own merits. If they'll make money from the agreement, they'll almost certainly sign the contract.

Left-Field Issues

Left-field issues are sometimes brought up in negotiations. These are issues that have little or no relevance. The Chinese use left-field issues to test your resolve and outlook on what's being discussed and to wear you down by taking a lot of your time and energy in resolving issues that have little or no bearing on what you're negotiating. Their expectation is that, by forcing you to argue the mundane and wearing you down, you'll more easily concede important issues because you're tired and just want to get the next issue out of the way.[236] This tactic normally ends once the Chinese feel that they've sufficiently accomplished their goal and no more is to be gained by bringing up left-field issues.

When we see a left-field issue come up in our business negotiations, we try to apply time pressure on our Chinese counterpart. Although the Chinese are very methodical and don't usually succumb to time pressure, they may if they believe you're going to walk away for a period of time and the delay will end up costing them money, or perhaps even the deal.

We initiate this time pressure by first apologizing and telling the Chinese negotiator that our time is very short and it doesn't appear that, with these new issues, we'll finish our discussions. We then tell them that we'll resume the meeting at a later date, when we have more time to study the issues they brought up as well as the issues still remaining. This usually gets their attention. If they really want to negotiate a deal, they won't want us to leave. If, however, they tell us that a later date is acceptable, this usually indicates that they aren't that committed to the transaction and feel that a delay is therefore not that important. Either way, this is the most effective way to address left-field issues.

Using Competitors

The Chinese business landscape is extremely competitive. If you work with a Chinese company, don't expect an exclusive, long-term contract unless you've worked with that company for quite some time. A Chinese company is always trying to decrease its costs and will usually go out to at least three companies for a bid. They do this for a number of reasons. One is to try to obtain the lowest cost. They'll negotiate between bidders, letting each know they're in competition with the others in an effort to try to push their costs as low as possible. Another reason for going out to multiple bidders is to try to obtain more favorable terms and other nonmonetary concessions.[237]

Business loyalty in China, other than when guanxi is involved, is transitory. Loyalty exists only as long as your counterpart is making money, and then only for the term of the contract. Be prepared to start from square one if the contract is again up for bid. It's likely at that time the Chinese company will regard everyone as equal going forward and will again try to ask for the maximum amount of monetary and nonmonetary concessions in the negotiating process. In China, it's all about the profit.

Our *strong* advice is to leave something for the end. By that, we mean never execute a contract where you've given your best terms up front. If you do that, it'll work against you. No matter how thin your margins or how many up-front concessions you make, it won't be good enough.[238] The person reviewing the contract will always believe that you've left an indeterminate amount of profit in the contract for yourself, and he or she will still want a part of that. Consequently he or she will try to negotiate better terms, as he or she doesn't want to leave anything on the table. Therefore, you'll need one or more toughly given concessions at the end of the negotiating session for your counterpart to feel that he or she received the best contract possible.

Changing Negotiators and Locations

In the negotiating process, the Chinese side will usually have a well-scripted game plan. They'll know who the key decision maker is in your organization, what authority that person has to make a deal, who's more likely to make compromises on your team, who they can anger and get to make impulsive decisions or statements, which team member will not take a definitive stand or make a decision, and other information that will enable them to better anticipate the direction negotiations will take in various scenarios. They will be very well-prepared.

If, however, the negotiations do not proceed according to their game plan and their negotiating objectives are not being accomplished, then look for the Chinese negotiator to be removed and replaced by someone else. Whether the Chinese negotiator claims personal illness, that a family member has become ill, or provides another excuse that allows him or her to terminate the negotiation process and keep face, he or she will withdraw and let another person take over and try to obtain better results.[239] When this happens, the new Chinese negotiator will look at this as a new opportunity to hit the reset button and treat the former negotiating sessions as if they never occurred.

Changing venues is also sometimes done when a location just doesn't feel right to your Chinese counterpart. Very often, this is a subjective feeling. Our position, when faced with a venue change, is not to grant it. Usually a refusal to change venues is not a deal breaker. If your Chinese counterpart feels ill at ease in your current venue, then this will probably work to your advantage.

We believe you only have four options when a new negotiator is introduced into the process. The first is to accept the new negotiator, realizing that each side now understands the other's negotiating strategies. The second is to terminate negotiations and walk away. The third option is to tell your negotiating counterpart that waiting until his or her family illness, or whatever the excuse is, is over will not be a problem and you can simply continue negotiations after he or she returns. Obviously this puts the other side on the defensive, and you may be waiting till retirement age for your counterpart to return. But this will demonstrate two good traits to the other side: your patience and your resolve. Both of these will work in your favor, even if another negotiator is brought in; he or she will be unsure of using strategies such as *time pressure* in future negotiating sessions.

The fourth option is to tell the new negotiator that you're not going over the same ground again and refuse to discuss any point where agreement has already been reached. Obviously you would only employ this option if you feel that what you've so far achieved meets your objectives. This option will, more than likely, not be acceptable to your new Chinese negotiator, as the reason he or she has replaced the previous negotiator is that the negotiated terms to date were unsatisfactory and failed to achieve their designated goals. Consequently, option one is normally employed when a new negotiator is brought in.

Pushing to Find the Bottom Line

No one wants to overpay for goods or services. We all want to get the lowest price possible. The Chinese are no exception. The problem is, as we've said earlier, how do you convince them that there's no more to give? That's no easy task, given their inherent distrust of foreigners.

As we've previous mentioned, we never start by giving our Chinese counterpart *our best and final price*, nor our final contract terms. It simply doesn't work. It's very un-Chinese. In typical Chinese negotiating style, your counterpart will feel the need to keep negotiating until he or she believes the best pricing possible has been achieved and he or she has received a satisfactory number of other concessions. Therefore, in your negotiations, build in room for one or more rounds of price concessions. Once you've arrived at a price point you feel you can't go below, stop price negotiations and show a total lack of flexibility. If you show any flexibility, then your counterpart will keep trying to chip away at the price.[240] With no flexibility, he or she will believe that there are no more concessions to be given, and he or she will usually end price discussions at that point. The same is true for other concessions.

One way to convince the person you're negotiating with that you've reached the limit of your ability to lower the price further is to provide him or her documentation that will verify what you've been saying. Since you're an outsider and the Chinese expect to be cheated and lied to by all outsiders, whether domestic or foreign, documentation can substantially help. It can help verify your cost of goods and labor and establish the reasonableness of your profit margins. Of course, a great many companies understandably don't want to share this information. But when a company does, it usually helps to establish that you've reached your bottom line.

Reopening Closed Issues

In many ways, negotiations with a Chinese company are like entering an endless turnabout where, after a time, you feel that you're constantly going over the same issues time and again. Issues you thought were previously addressed are reopened, and nothing ever seems to be final. The Chinese will keep you in this circle, going over previously resolved issues, until they believe you've reached your limit on concessions or your level of patience is at an end and you want to terminate negotiations. At that point, they're likely to drop any further demands and accept what's in front of them.[241] You'll then be able to exit the turnabout so that negotiations can be concluded and the contract signed.

One of the reasons we frequently see the reopening of closed issues is the Chinese negotiator, or one of his or her superiors, is not satisfied with the outcome of what's previously been negotiated. They feel they should have done a better job in obtaining concessions. Therefore, they now want to try their hand at negotiating these issues again. They'll take you into the turnabout and readdress the same issues, hoping to attain a more satisfactory result.

Another reason for reopening issues is that unforeseen circumstances on your counterpart's side necessitates recrafting previously negotiated issues. Whether it's a change in government policy or another situation that requires a renegotiation to what's previously been agreed to, your counterpart will again take you back into the turnabout. This doesn't happen frequently, but enough so that it's not an uncommon occurrence. Therefore, the only time we're sure we've exited the turnabout is when both sets of signatures are on the contract.

The Chinese don't like to leave anything on the table, and that's why it's never a good idea to give them your *best and final* contract up front during early meetings. They *always* want to negotiate to ensure they've received every concession possible. Even if what they propose is acceptable to you, even if you keep agreeing to their demands, the circular process never seems to end. Reciprocity will help. It's important. *If you give a concession, get a concession.* That's the way they would negotiate domestically, and that's the way you should negotiate. If you give ground grudgingly and concessions are also demanded in return, it will be easier to get out of the turnabout when you draw your line in the sand. Unless you draw a line in the sand and show a lack of inflexibility, they'll continue to try to push for concessions until they feel there are no more to be had. If both sides expect to make money from the contract, we rarely, in our experience, see a Chinese company walk away. They're in this to make money. Unless they have someone that will provide them with a better contract, they'll sign yours quickly after you've shown inflexibility on further concessions and after you've drawn a line in the sand.

If you feel that you're going to end negotiations by making one last concession, then you're wrong. Making a concession is tantamount to reopening negotiations and informing the Chinese that you haven't given them your best and final offer and there's still room to negotiate further. If you want to end negotiations, end them. Get out of the turnabout. Be inflexible. The Chinese, at that point, will either accept or walk. If the deal is good, they'll rarely leave and will quickly sign the agreement.

CHAPTER 14

Putting It All Together and Prospering in Modern-Day China

Four decades ago, no businessperson would have given China a second thought. At that time, it was all about Japan, the United States, and Europe. Today it's a different world, and we don't believe that any country or union of countries will be able to match the sustained growth of China. If we were twenty years in the future and looking back in time, we'd undoubtedly see unparalleled business opportunities and prosperity for all those who had the foresight to become involved in modern-day China.

There are those who will say that China will eventually collapse under the weight of communism, corruption, environmental issues, nonperforming bank loans, and subsidies, as well as other domestic and international issues that we've discussed. But those harbingers of doom are wrong and living in denial. China will become the world's number-one economy, importer, and exporter. Period. It will establish its currency as one of the world's standards, it will become more politically sophisticated, and it will maintain its economic leadership position for decades to come.

The business opportunities available in China have seldom been seen in other economically developing nations.

"China will only continue to grow robustly," according to Peter Navarro, professor of economics and public policy at the University of California, Irvine, "if it makes the transition from an export-dependent economy to one driven by domestic consumption and investment, coupled with key reforms, including better health care and pension systems and allowing the yuan to strengthen."[242]

The government is listening. It's enabling the spending power of domestic consumers by targeting a 13 percent annual increase in the minimum wage through 2015, along with a projected increase in household income of 7 percent per year. It's hoped that this will help increase domestic consumption.

China is transitioning from a country that's historically purchased few foreign goods to one with an increasing appetite for foreign products. It's become a nation of consumers. This offers enormous opportunities at many different levels for those that can provide the desired products and services we've previously mentioned. As examples, in business the Chinese government needs advanced technologies and skills to remediate its environmental problems before they erode national growth and more seriously impact the health of its people. In law, Chinese companies are investing and making acquisitions globally that require the assistance of knowledgeable law firms with requisite skills. In industry, China is transitioning from a nation of cheap labor to one with value-added technology and skills. This requires industry partnering with international businesses, increased technical expertise and skills, and investment capital.

China is rapidly assimilating itself into the international community. According to the *New York Times*, no major state can modernize without integrating into the globalized capitalist system. If a country wants to be a world power, then it has no choice but to join the WTO and work with multilateral economic institutions. Internationalized economies need continued access to global capital.[243]

China recognizes this and has steadily increased its foreign direct investment. It's also making global acquisitions, particularly in natural resources and technology, and is taking investment positions in companies that prove catalytic to its domestic industries.

As we've discussed, the issue that most companies have is not the lack of business opportunities, but rather an understanding of how to take advantage of those opportunities and prosper in modern-day China, a unique business environment when compared to other Westernized countries. This uniqueness frequently causes problems for many companies, as they try to apply the same techniques in China that have proved successful in other parts of the world. As a result, they often fail. But when these companies understand and adapt to this uniqueness, they invariably prosper and attain a level of growth they seldom expected.

Some companies come to China more out of desperation than from a need to continue their already successful growth at home or abroad. They perceive China's vast consumer market as a way for their company to financially survive. In this situation, trying to enter the Chinese marketplace may be significantly more difficult. Chinese companies can smell desperation and will make demands that would not otherwise be made of a more financially stable company.[244] For example, in exchange for doing business, they may ask for a technology transfer, a greater percentage of the profits, an equity position in the company, and anything else they feel they can get away with because of the company's desperate circumstances. Everything will be on the negotiating table if they know the company needs to be successful in the Chinese marketplace in order to survive.

> As China's economic prominence is transforming global economies, it's also created a new structural dynamic. Stephen King, chief global economist at HSBC, wrote in a report released in January 2013 that "We are moving away from the U.S.- or Europe-led world to a world led by China."[245]

The *old* world, represented by France, Italy, and other European countries, along with the United States, are relatively small exporters to China and export only about 0.7 percent of their GDP to China annually. The United Kingdom is even lower, at 0.4 percent of its GDP.[245] With such a small amount of Western, or old-world, exports as a percentage of GDP going to China, there's an enormous potential for substantial sales of consumer and industrial products. China requires these products in order to sustain its economic growth, which offers significant opportunities for foreign companies willing to address these needs.

Foreign businesses are not only taking advantage of China's growth by selling goods and investing in domestic business opportunities, but they're also seeking investment capital. China's investments outside its borders are growing rapidly. In 2008, for example, China invested $1 billion in European Union countries and a similar amount in the United States. In 2012, Chinese investments surged to $10 billion and $6.7 billion respectively, according to the Rhodium Group, an economic research firm. The Rhodium Group estimates that China's foreign direct investment could reach as much as $1 trillion to $2 trillion by 2020.[246]

For anyone who wants to take advantage of what will soon become the largest economy in the world, now is the time to become involved. By 2030, according to the United States National Intelligence Council, Asia will surpass Europe and North America in population size, GDP, military spending, and technological investment.[247] As a result, most experts expect China's rapid growth to continue for at least another fifteen to twenty years. There's not going to be an implosion, crash, or collapse. Although China's economic growth will not be steady during the next two decades and will slow down at times, it will continue to be dynamic as it lifts China to the number-one position in world economies.

Take advantage of this growth. In our lifetime, we may never see another country transform into the economic superpower of modern-day China. If you aren't currently doing business in China, it's not too late. Start! Take advantage of this robust economy and prosper in modern-day China.

ENDNOTES

1. Author Unknown. "How Economies Grow," *China Global Trade*, http://www.chinaglobaltrade.com/article/how-us-china-economic-growth-develops.

2. Author Unknown. "China's 2011 GDP growth slows to 9.2%," *Chinadaily*, http://www.chinadaily.com.cn/business/2012-01/17/content_14460323_2.htm.

3. Author Unknown. "Report predicts 7.7% growth for China's 2012 GDP," *People's Daily Online*, http://english.peopledaily.com.cn/102774/8047591.html.

4. Madigan, Kathleen. "Economists Trim 2013 GDP Growth Forecasts," *The Wall Street Journal,* http://blogs.wsj.com/economics/2013/08/16/economists-trim-2013-gdp-growth-forecasts/.

5. Perkowski, Jack. "Major Trends in China: The Next 10 Years," *Forbes*, http://www.forbes.com/sites/jackperkowski/2012/11/27/major-trends-in-china-the-next-10-years/.

6. Lin, Yifu Justin. *Demystifying the Chinese Economy* (Cambridge: Cambridge University Press, 2012), 4.

7. Lin, Yifu Justin. *Demystifying the Chinese Economy* (Cambridge: Cambridge University Press, 2012), 8.

8. Author Unknown. "China's to be World's Biggest Economy by 2025," *The Telegraph*, http://www.telegraph.co.uk/

finance/china-business/9655058/China-to-be-worlds-biggest-economy-by-2025.html.

9. Author Unknown. "China Still Has 10 Year Advantages in Manufacturing," *China Labour Market*, http://www.china.org.cn/opinion/2013-02/25/content_28049447.htm http://chinalabourmarket.com/china-still-has-10-year-advantages-in-manufacturing.html.

10. Zheng, Yangpeng. "High-end Manufacturing Holds the Key," *Chinadaily*, http://usa.chinadaily.com.cn/weekly/2013-03/01/content_16265887_4.htm.

11. Vivek Wadhwa. "Technology Advances to End China's Manufacturing Dominance, Open up New Possibilities for India," *The Economic Times*, http://articles.economictimes.indiatimes.com/2012-10-22/news/34653778_1_indian-companies-vivek-wadhwa-technology.

12. Wang, Helen H. "China to Become the World's Largest Importer by 2014," *Forbes*, http://www.forbes.com/sites/helenwang/2012/01/11/china-to-become-the-worlds-largest-importer-by-2014/.

13. Atsmon, Yuval; Ding, Jennifer; Dixit, Vinay; St. Maurice, Ian; Suessmuth-Dyckerhoff, Claudia. "The coming of age: China's new class of wealthy consumers," *Insights China*, McKinsey & Company, https://solutions.mckinsey.com/insightschina/_SiteNote/WWW/GetFile.aspx?uri=/insightschina/default/en-us/aboutus/news/Files/wp2055036759/Insights%20China_v9_060ba3e4-ef85-43b3-b9a9-0f583012a10b.pdf.

14. Author Unknown. "What is a Lower Tier City?" *China Normal*, http://www.chinanormal.com/cities.

15. Barry. "What Makes a City Tier in China?" *The China Sourcing Blog*, http://www.chinasourcingblog.org/2011/07/what-makes-a-city-tier-in-chin.html.

16. Lui, Vincent; Kuo, Youchi. "Affluent Hold Keys to Corporate Success," *Chinadaily*, http://europe.chinadaily.com.cn/epaper/2012-12/14/content_16016726.htm.

17. Author Unknown. "Ivy funds—The World Covered," *Ivy Funds*, http://theworldcovered.ivyfunds.com/home/u-s-companies-customize-services-for-china%E2%80%99s-high-end-buyers/.

18. Indvik, Lauren. "Ecomerce in China: How the World's Biggest Market Buys Online," *mashable*, http://mashable.com/2012/05/20/ecommerce-china/.

19. Author Unknown. "Selling in China," *The Boston Consulting Group*, http://knowledge.wharton.upenn.edu/papers/download/BCGChinaReport3.pdf.

20. Allen, Arika M.; Gosling, Paul; Powell, Grant D.; Yang, Claire. "The human touch behind Asia Inc.'s global push," *accenture*, http://www.accenture.com/us-en/outlook/pages/outlook-journal-2007-chinese-consumers.aspx.

21. Teo, Lay Lim; Piotroski, Susan A.; Nunes, Paul F.; Wang, Sophie X. "Why Winning the Wallets of China's Consumers is Harder than You Think," *The European Business Review*, http://www.europeanbusinessreview.com/?p=1429.

22. Author Unknown. "Micro-Segmentation," *MZI Global*, http://www.mziglobal.com/en/micro-segmentation.

23. Long, Xinming. "Foreign Companies in China: Expansion Plans by Foreign Companies in China—Part 2," *bearcanada*, http://www.bearcanada.com/china/expansionplans02.html.

24. Author Unknown. "The Alibaba Phenomenon," *The Economist*, http://www.economist.com/news/leaders/21573981-chinas-e-commerce-giant-could-generate-enormous-wealthprovided-countrys-rulers-leave-it.

25. Author Unknown. "China and Subsidies," *American Manufacturing. org*, http://americanmanufacturing.org/category/issues/china/ china-and-subsidies.

26. Author Unknown. "subsidy," *Merriam-Webster*, http://www. merriam-webster.com/dictionary/subsidy.

27. Navarro, Peter. "The Economics of the China Price," *China Perspectives*, http://chinaperspectives.revues.org/3063.

28. Haley, Usha C. V.; Haley, George T. "How Chinese Subsidies Changed the World," *Harvard Business Review*, http://blogs.hbr.org/ cs/2013/04/how_chinese_subsidies_changed.html.

29. Author Unknown. "Fact Sheet: WTO Case Challenging Chinese Subsidies," *USTR.gov*, http://www.ustr.gov/about-us/press-office/ fact-sheets/2012/september/wto-case-challenging-chinese-subsidies.

30. Author Unknown. "China's economy—Perverse advantage," *The Economist*, http://www.economist.com/news/finance-and-economics/21576680-new-book-lays-out-scale-chinas-industrial-subsidies-perverse-advantage.

31. Haley, Usha C. V.; Haley, George T. *Subsidies to Chinese Industry: State capitalism, Business Strategy, and Trade Policy* (Oxford: Oxford University Press, 2013), 30–32.

32. Author Unknown. "SOE Reform in China," *UK Essays*, http://www. ukessays.com/essays/politics/soe-reform-in-china.php.

33. Author Unknown. "China Unemployment," *Economy Watch*, http:// www.economywatch.com/unemployment/countries/china.html

34. Author Unknown. "Chinese Subsidies Under Scrutiny," *The New York Times*, Global Business with Reuters, http://www.nytimes. com/2013/04/28/business/global/chinese-subsidies-under-scrutiny. html?_r=0

35. Stearns, Jonathan. "EU Drops Threat of Anti-Subsidy Tariffs on Chinese Bicycles," *Bloomberg*, http://www.bloomberg.com/ news/2013-05-23/eu-drops-threat-of-anti-subsidy-tariffs-on-chinese-bicycles.html.

36. Rovnick, Naomi. "Most Big Chinese Companies Get Some Kind of State Subsidy," *Quartz*, http://qz.com/72354/ most-big-chinese-companies-get-some-kind-of-state-subsidies/.

37. Author Unknown. "China Graduates Face Tough Job Market As Youth Unemployment Rises," *BBC News Business*, http://www.bbc.co.uk/news/business-22564249.

38. Pettis, Elizabrth L. "Challenging Chinese Currency Manipulation as a Subsidy under the WTO Subsidies and Countervailing Measures Agreement," *SelectedWorks*, http://works.bepress.com/ cgi/viewcontent.cgi?article=1000&context=elizabeth_pettis&sei-redir=1&referer=http%3A%2F%2Fwww.google.com%2Furl%3 Fsa%3Dt%26rct%3Dj%26q%3Dchinese%2520subsidize%252 0their%2520currency%26source%3Dweb%26cd%3D9%26ve d%3D0CF4QFjAI%26url%3Dhttp%253A%252F%252Fworks. bepress.com%252Fcgi%252Fviewcontent.cgi%253Farticle%253 D1000%2526context%253Delizabeth_pettis%26ei%3DfLqnUZ jnOIeo9gTD0oGgAg%26usg%3DAFQjCNG7_hY-bcfMLEsf_ t6mM3vAxRt25w#search=%22chinese%20subsidize%20their%20 currency%22.

39. Magnus, John R.; Brightbill, Timothy C. "China's Currency Regime is Legitimately Challengeable as a Subsidy under ASCM Rules," *VoxEU.org*, http://www.voxeu.org/article/ china-s-currency-regime-legitimately-challengeable-subsidy.

40. Author Unknown. "China Says U.S. Subsidies Violate Trade Rules," *China Digital Times*, http://chinadigitaltimes.net/2012/05/ china-says-u-s-renewable-subsidies-violate-trade-rules/.

41. Prestowitz, Clyde. "Down with Subsidies," *Foreign Policy*, http://prestowitz.foreignpolicy.com/posts/2013/05/16/ down_with_subsidies.

42. Author Unknown. "Moving to China," *Expat Info Desk*, http:// www.expatinfodesk.com/expat-guide/deciding-on-the-right-country/ top-expatriate-destinations/china/.

43. Author Unknown. "Individualism and Collectivism: Reconsidering Old Assumptions," *FreePatentsOnline.com*, http://www. freepatentsonline.com/article/Journal-International-Business- Research/208956140.html.

44. Tang, Jie; Routledge, Anthony Ward. *Changing Face of Chinese Management* (Working in Asia)—an imprint of the Taylor & Francis Group, 2003, page 11.

45. Refkin, Alan; Cray, Scott. *Doing the China Tango* (Bloomington: iUniverse, 2012), xviii–xix.

46. Williamson, Andrew. *Living and Working in China* (Oxford: How To Books Ltd, 2005), 41–43.

47. Author Unknown. "Understanding China: The influence of Confucianism in Chinese society (II of II)," *pepegins.com*, http:// pepegins.com/2012/02/08/understanding-the-china-the-influence- of-confucianism-in-chinese-society-ii-of-ii/.

48. Williamson, Andrew. *Living and Working in China* (Oxford: How To Books Ltd, 2005), 23–24.

49. Zhao, Yun. "How Many Languages are Spoken in China Today?" *China History Forum*, http://www.chinahistoryforum.com/index. php?/topic/28491-how-many-languages-are-spoken-in-china-today/.

50. Author Unknown. "How many dialects are there in China?" *Yahoo! Answers*, http://answers.yahoo.com/question/index?qid=2007070409 2243AArFZcV.

51. Zhao, Yinan. "Foreigners without Permit May Lose Rights in China," *The China Post*, http://www.chinapost.com.tw/business/asia-china/2012/08/14/350932/p2/Foreigners-without.htm

52. Wang, Tiffany. "The Decline of the Expat: Foreigners in China Proliferate, But Become Less Special," *Tea Leaf Nation*, http://www.tealeafnation.com/2013/02/the-decline-of-the-expat-foreigners-in-china-proliferate-but-become-less-special/.

53. Author Unknown. "Finding Job for Expats in China," *Chinadaily*, http://www.chinadaily.com.cn/business/2012-06-05/content_15474947.htm.

54. Author Unknown. "6 Tips on How to Find a Decent Expat Job in China," *Vings Stuff*, http://www.vingsstuff.co.uk/2011/06/6-tips-on-how-to-find-a-decent-expat-job-in-china/.

55. Author Unknown. "How to Network and Find a Job in Shanghai," *City Weekend*, http://www.cityweekend.com.cn/shanghai/articles/blogs-shanghai/expat-affairs/how-to-network-and-find-a-job-in-shanghai/.

56. Freeke, Lois. "Expat Job Search: 11 Deadly Sins," *Shanghai Expat*, http://www.shanghaiexpat.com/article/expat-job-search-11-deadly-sins-why-you-wont-get-interview-quick-fixes-12899.html.

57. Author Unknown. "The Expat Job Market in Beijing," *InterNations*, http://www.internations.org/beijing-expats/guide/working-in-beijing-15418/the-expat-job-market-in-beijing-2.

58. Gu, Xiaolei. "Obtaining a Z Visa, Work Permit and Residence Permit in China," *China Briefing*, http://www.china-briefing.com/news/2012/05/17/obtaining-a-z-visa-work-permit-and-residence-permit-in-china.html.

59. Harris, Dan. "How to Change Your China Employer AND You're your Work Permit," *China Law Blog*, http://www.chinalawblog.com/2011/12/

how_to_change_your_china_employer_and_keep_your_work_visa.
html.

60. Zheng, Xin. "Agencies Help Foreigners Evade Rules to Land
Jobs," *Chinadaily,* http://usa.chinadaily.com.cn/china/2012-09/06/
content_15737017.htm.

61. Logan, Tim. "Stranded in China: Debt Dispute Leaves Missouri
Businessman in Limbo," *St.Louis Post-dispatch,* http://www.
stltoday.com/business/local/stranded-in-china-debt-dispute-leaves-
missouri-businessman-in-limbo/article_ad02e834-b71b-11e1-9b6a-
0019bb30f31a.html.

62. Wang, Huazhong. "Foreigners OKed to Handle State Secrets,"
Chinadaily, http://usa.chinadaily.com.cn/china/2012-05/16/
content_15313601.htm.

63. Bamberg, Jeneil. "Will China Enforce Its Constitution?"
Nextgen, http://ewinextgen.tumblr.com/post/43657898997/
will-china-enforce-its-constitution.

64. Lo, Vai Io; Tian, Xiaowen Tian. *Law and Investment in China*
(London: Routledge's Taylor & Francis Group, 2005), 6–10.

65. Zhang, Bill H. "Litigation and Arbitration in China," *HG.org,
Global Legal Resources,* http://www.hg.org/article.asp?id=7820.

66. Author Unknown. "China's Political System," *China.org.cn,* http://
www.china.org.cn/english/Political/28842.htm.

67. Lo, Vai Io; Tian, Xiaowen Tian. *Law and Investment in China*
(London: Routledge's Taylor & Francis Group, 2005), 17–18.

68. Chow, Daniel C. K. *The Legal System of the People's Republic of
China in a Nutshell* (United States: West Group, 2003), 225–239.

69. Author Unknown. "Difference among Mediation, Arbitration and Litigation in China," *China Lawyer Blog*, http://www.chinalawblog.org/law-topics/litigation-lawyer/154-china-arbitration-litigation.

70. Wigley, Richard W.; Xu, Jing. "Evidence Collection and Alternatives to Discovery in P.R.C. Litigation," *China Law Insight*, http://www.chinalawinsight.com/2011/04/articles/dispute-resolution/evidence-collection-and-alternatives-to-discovery-in-prc-litigation/.

71. Bennett, Steven C. "Litigation in China: Ten Things You Must Know," *The Metropolitan Corporate Counsel*, http://www.metrocorpcounsel.com/articles/10466/litigation-china-ten-things-you-must-know.

72. Roos, Maarten. "China: Monetary Costs to Litigation in China," *Mondaq*, http://www.mondaq.com/x/122480/Monetary+Costs+to+Litigation+in+China.

73. Author Unknown. "Enforcing China Court Decisions: Help Is On the Way?" *China Hear Say*, http://www.chinahearsay.com/enforcing-china-court-decisions-help-is-on-the-way/.

74. Peerenboom, Randy; Zhang, Dacai. "Preservation of Assets in China: Law and Reality," *China Law And Practice*, http://www.chinalawandpractice.com/Article/1694743/Channel/9930/Preservation-of-Assets-in-China-Law-and-Reality.html.

75. Rabinovitch, Simon. "Chinese Groups Turn to Law in Disputes," *The Financial Times*, http://www.ft.com/intl/cms/s/0/e4e57188-e455-11e1-affe-00144feab49a.html?ftcamp=published_links%2Frss%2Fhome_asia%2Ffeed%2F%2Fproduct&ftcamp=crm/email/2012813/nbe/AsiaMorningHeadlines/product#axzz243GgH8VP.

76. Author Unknown. "How to Protect Your Intellectual Property," *Bullfax.com*, http://www.bullfax.com/?q=node-how-protect-your-intellectual-property.

77. Locke, Gary. "Ambassador's Roundtable on Intellectual Property Protection," *Embassy of the United States-Beijing, China*, US Department of State, http://beijing.usembassy-china.org. cn/20120412roundtable-on-intellectual-property-protection.html.

78. Kremers, Nancy. "Protecting Your Intellectual Property Rights (IPR) in China," *US Patent and Trademark Office*, http://www. stopfakes.gov/sites/default/files/Protecting%20IPR%20in%20 China%20Slides.pdf.

79. Slater, Derek. "Intellectual Property Protection: The Basics," *csoonline*, http://www.csoonline.com/article/204600/ intellectual-property-protection-the-basics.

80. Author Unknown. "Protecting Your Intellectual Property Rights (IPR) in China—A Practical Guide for U.S. Companies," *US Department of Commerce International Trade Administration*, http://www.mac.doc.gov/china/docs/businessguides/ intellectualpropertyrights.htm.

81. Author Unknown. "IP Contracts," *The US-China Business Council*, https://www.uschina.org/info/ipr/ip-contacts.html.

82. Author Unknown. "Roadmap for Intellectual Property Protection in China," *European Union Patent Office*, http://www.turkpatent. gov.tr/dosyalar/basvuru/yayin/trademark_protection_in_china.pdf.

83. Author Unknown. "China's Patent Application Jump 20% in 2012," *China Patent Information Center*, http://www.cnpat.com.cn/ EnNews.aspx?NewsId=3611.

84. Ho, Wai-Ling Esther. "SIPO Becomes Largest Patent Office in the World," *Wilkinson & Grist*, http://www.lexology.com/library/detail. aspx?g=39927053-3bde-4a80-8bdb-16a168939e9e.

85. Author Unknown. "China to Become World's Largest Patent Filing Country," *chinaipsummit.com*, http://chinaipsummit.com/2012/ press_1202/20.html.

86. Author Unknown. "National Copyright Administration," *The US-China Business Council*, https://www.uschina.org/public/china/govstructure/nca.html.

87. Author Unknown. "General Administration of Customs," *Yangtze Business Services*, http://www.yangtzebusinessservices.com/government-body-profiles-general-administration-of-customs-.

88. Author Unknown. "China to Boost Crackdown on IPR Infringement in 2013," *China.org.cn*, http://www.china.org.cn/china/2012-12/29/content_27545568.htm.

89. Ong, Ryan. "Tacking Intellectual Property Infringement in China," *China Business Review*, http://www.chinabusinessreview.com/tackling-intellectual-property-infringement-in-china/.

90. Author Unknown. "Intellectual Property in China Still Murky," *The Economist*, http://www.economist.com/node/21553040.

91. Author Unknown. "Our Partner Agencies," *iprcenter.gov*, http://www.ice.gov/iprcenter/.

92. Author Unknown. "Our Partner Agencies," *iprcenter.gov*, http://www.iprcenter.gov/.

93. Author Unknown. "Computer Crime & Intellectual Property Section," *US Department of Justice*, http://www.justice.gov/criminal/cybercrime/.

94. Author Unknown. "What's New on STOPfakes," *STOPfakes.gov*, www.stopfakes.gov.

95. Author Unknown. "Stopfakes.Gov—Small Business and Intellectual Property from the USPTO," *In House Blog*, http://www.inhouseblog.com/stopfakesgov_-_/.

96. Author Unknown. "Intellectual Property Rights in China," *Embassy of the United States-Beijing, China,* US Department of State, http://beijing.usembassy-china.org.cn/ipr.html.

97. Author Unknown. "IPR Enforcement," *US Customs and Border Protection,* https://apps.cbp.gov/e-recordations/.

98. Author Unknown. "A Case of Corporate and National Defamation: AMSC v. Sinovel, hot air in legal and media exercises," *Hidden Harmonies China Blog,* http://blog.hiddenharmonies.org/2012/12/a-case-of-corporate-and-national-defamation-amsc-v-sinovel-hot-air-in-legal-and-media-exercises/.

99. Downing, Louise; Doom, Justin. "American Superconductor Says China Will Review Sinovel Suit," *Bloomberg,* http://www.bloomberg.com/news/2013-01-11/amsc-says-china-s-supreme-court-will-review-suit-with-sinovel.html.

100. Kwang, Kevin. "China Sees Rising Intellectual Property Tussles," *ZDNet,* http://www.zdnet.com/china-sees-rising-intellectual-property-tussles-2062304161/.

101. Yang, Jia Lynn. "Chinese Firms Put Intellectual Property Lawsuits to Work," *The Washington Post,* http://www.washingtonpost.com/business/economy/chinese-firms-put-intellectual-property-lawsuits-to-work/2012/08/30/12d9a418-f1c3-11e1-adc6-87dfa8eff430_story.html.

102. Martina, Michael. "Geithner Slams China's Intellectual Property Policies," *Reuters,* http://www.reuters.com/article/2011/09/23/us-china-geithner-idUSTRE78M15G20110923.

103. Harris, Dan. "Protecting Your Intellectual Property In China, Part II," *China Law Blog,* http://www.chinalawblog.com/2011/06/protecting_your_intellectual_property_in_china_part_ii.html.

104. Yu, Peter K. "The U.S.-China Dispute Over TRIPS Enforcement," *Drake University Law School,* http://www.law.drake.edu/academics/ip/docs/ipResearch-op5.pdf

105. Author Unknown. "Intellectual Property Theft: Get Real," *National Crime Prevention Council,* http://www.ncpc.org/topics/intellectual-property-theft/trends-globalization-and-digitalization-usher-in-a-new-era-of-intellectual-property-theftc.

106. Author Unknown. "Finding and Keeping Good Employees in China," *China Primer,* http://www.chinaprimer.com/human-resources-china-hr/recruiting-in-china-good-employees.html.

107. Chu, Kathy. "China Factories Try Karaoke, Speed Dating to Keep Workers," *The Wall Street Journal,* http://online.wsj.com/article/SB10001424127887323798104578452634075519230.html.

108. Chu, Kathy. "China Manufacturers Survive by Moving to Asian Neighbors," *The Wall Street Journal,* http://online.wsj.com/article/SB10001424127887323798104578453073103566416.html.

109. Bradsher, Keith. "Wary of China, Companies Head to Cambodia," *New York Times,* Global Business, http://www.nytimes.com/2013/04/09/business/global/wary-of-events-in-china-foreign-investors-head-to-cambodia.html?pagewanted=all&_r=0.

110. Young, Laura W. "Hiring and Managing Employees in China," *The Law Offices of Wang & Wang,* http://www.wangandwang.com/news-articles/articles/hiring-managing-employees-china/.

111. Sy, Gregory. "Terminating Employees in China: Some Practical Considerations," *China Window,* http://www.china-window.com/china_business/doing_business_in_china/terminating-mployees.shtml.

112. Author Unknown. "Guide to China workplace laws and regulations," *Kingfisher,* http://files.the-group.net/library/kgf/responsibility/pdfs/cr_13.pdf.

113. Livermore, Adam. "Mandatory Social Welfare Benefits for Chinese Employees," *China Briefing*, http://www.china-briefing.com/news/2012/02/21/mandatory-social-welfare-benefits-for-chinese-employees.html.

114. Gross, Ames; Dyson, Patricia. "The End of China's Iron Rice Bowl," *Pacific Bridge Recruiting*, http://www.pacificbridge.com/publications/the-end-of-chinas-iron-rice-bowl/.

115. Brown, Mayer. "PRC Labour Law—Bitesize: How many days bereavement leave is an employee entitled to in the PRC?" *Mayer Brown JSM Newsletter*, http://www.mayerbrown.com/publications/BPRC-Labour-Law—BitesizeB-How-many-days-bereavement-leave-is-an-employee-entitled-to-in-the-PRC-02-18-2010/.

116. Abrams, Stan. "Here's What Henry Blodget Doesn't Understand About Overtime At Foxconn," *Business Insider*, http://articles.businessinsider.com/2012-04-03/home/31278877_1_chen-yamei-foxconn-work-week.

117. Brown, Ronald C. *Understanding Labor and Employment Law in China* (Cambridge: Cambridge University Press, 2010), 37.

118. Brown, Ronad C. *East Asian Labor and Employment Law* (Cambridge: Cambridge University Press, 2012), 420.

119. Brown, Ronald C. *Understanding Labor and Employment Law in China* (Cambridge: Cambridge University Press, 2010), 38–39.

120. Rein, Shaun. "How to Deal with Corruption in China," *Forbes*, http://www.forbes.com/2009/10/07/china-corruption-bribes-leadership-managing-rein.html.

121. Hays, Jeffrey. "Corruption and Perks in China: Fires, Guanxi. Parties, Mistresses and Expensive Cars," *Yahoo! Facts and Details*, http://factsanddetails.com/china.php?itemid=304.

122. Refkin, Alan; Cray, Scott. *Doing the China Tango* (Bloomington: iUniverse, 2012), 23.

123. Carlson, Benjamin. "Are Anti-corruption Campaigns Causing China's Economy to Slow?" *Global Post,* http://www.globalpost. com/dispatch/news/regions/asia-pacific/china/130415/ anti-corruption-slowing-economy.

124. Coonan, Clifford. "Communist Officials Sidestep Xi's Anti-corruption Efforts," *The Irish Times*, http:// www.irishtimes.com/news/world/asia-pacific/ communist-officials-sidestep-xi-s-anti-corruption-efforts-1.1380894.

125. Chow, Daniel. "China Under the Foreign Corrupt Practices Act," *Wisconsin Law Review,* http://wisconsinlawreview.org/wp-content/ files/12-Chow.pdf.

126. Author Unknown. "Foreign Corrupt Practices Act," *US Department of Justice*, http://www.justice.gov/criminal/fraud/fcpa/.

127. Author Unknown. "FCPA: Building a Proactive Compliance Approach," *The Wall Street Journal*, http:// deloitte.wsj.com/riskandcompliance/2013/04/01/ foreign-corrupt-practices-act-proactive-compliance-advised-test/.

128. Marks, Robert B. *China: Its Environment and History* (Maryland: Rowman & Littlefield Publishers, Inc., 2012), 312–314.

129. Wong, Edward. "Air Pollution Linked to 1.2 Million Premature Deaths in China," *New York Times*, Asia Pacific, http://www. nytimes.com/2013/04/02/world/asia/air-pollution-linked-to-1-2- million-deaths-in-china.html.

130. Lallanilla, Marc. "China's Top 6 Environmental Concerns," *Livescience*, http://www.livescience.com/27862-china- environmental-problems.html.

131. Author Unknown. "China's Pollution Facts," *China Smog,* http://chinasmog.wordpress.com/china-pollution-facts/.

132. Zhang, Yiqian. "Chinese, US Air Quality Index Not the Same," *The Global Times,* http://www.globaltimes.cn/content/755525.shtml.

133. Author Unknown. "China to Impose Limits on Six Industries to Tackle Air Pollution," *Bloomberg,* http://www.bloomberg.com/news/2013-02-20/china-to-impose-limits-on-six-industries-to-tackle-air-pollution.html.

134. Author Unknown. "The Real Story Behind China's Energy Policy and What America Can Learn From It," *United States Senate Committee on Environment and Public Works,* http://www.inhofe.senate.gov/download/?id=e0a37b82-fc70-48ff-b1fb-3293ca76dd39&download=1.

135. Solidiance. "The Importance of Renewable Energy in China," *Ecology Global Network,* http://www.ecology.com/2013/03/07/renewable-energy-in-china/.

136. Tan, Monica. "8 Must-know Facts about China's Air Pollution," *Greenpeace,* http://www.greenpeace.org/eastasia/news/blog/8-must-know-facts-about-chinas-air-pollution-/blog/43862/.

137. Wang, Xiao. "Alternative Energy to Improve China's Air Quality," *CRI,* http://english.cri.cn/7146/2013/03/16/2361s754026.htm.

138. Wong, Edward. "In China, Breathing Becomes a Childhood Risk," *New York Times,* Asia Pacific, http://www.nytimes.com/2013/04/23/world/asia/pollution-is-radically-changing-childhood-in-chinas-cities.html?pagewanted=all.

139. Watt, Louise. "China Pollution: Cars Cause Major Air Problems in Chinese Cities," *The Huffington Post,* http://www.huffingtonpost.com/2013/01/31/china-pollution-cars-air-problems-cities_n_2589294.html.

140. Hays, Jeffrey. "Water Pollution in China," *Yahoo! Facts and Details*, http://factsanddetails.com/china.php?itemid=391.

141. Gu, Yongqiang. "In China, Water You Wouldn't Dare Swim in, Let Alone Drink," *TIME*, http://world.time.com/2013/03/06/in-china-water-you-wouldnt-dare-swim-in-let-alone-drink/.

142. Author Unknown. "Desertification," *Oxford Dictionaries*, http://oxforddictionaries.com/us/definition/american_english/desertification.

143. Tudela, Rita Alvarez. "Fighting Desertification in China," *Aljazeera*, http://www.aljazeera.com/indepth/features/2012/12/2012126123056457256.html.

144. Klok, Chris; Zhang, Tiehan. "Biodiversity and its Conservation in China," *Alterra, Wageningen*, http://webdocs.alterra.wur.nl/pdffiles/alterraRapporten/AlterraRapport1733.pdf.

145. Liu, Jianguo; Ouyang, Zhiyun; Pimm, Stuart L.; Raven, Peter H.; Wang, Xiaoke; Miao, Hong; Han, Nianyong. "Protecting China's Biodiversity," *Science,* http://www.nicholas.duke.edu/people/faculty/pimm/publications/pimmreprints/181_Liu_et_al_2003_Science.pdf.

146. Cooper, Marta. "Pollution: Farms Worse than Factories in China," *Shanghaiist*, http://shanghaiist.com/2010/02/10/chinas_first_national_consensus_on.php.

147. Author Unknown. "Majority of China's Arable Land Heavily Polluted," *ChinaGaze,* http://www.chinagaze.com/2013/04/23/majority-of-chinas-arable-land-heavily-polluted/.

148. Yu, Dawei. "Chinese waste: the burning issue," *chinadialogue,* http://www.chinadialogue.net/article/show/single/en/4739-Chinese-waste-the-burning-issue.

149. Handley, Meg. "China Leads the Renewable Energy World," *U.S. News & World Report,* http://www.usnews.com/news/articles/2013/04/17/china-leads-the-renewable-energy-world.

150. Cockerham, Sean. "Who's the world leader in clean energy? China," *McClatchy Newspapers,* http://www.mcclatchydc.com/2013/04/17/188706/whos-the-world-leader-in-clean.html#.UZ3oao3D_s0.

151. Schwab, Charles. "China is Ground Zero for a Green Energy Revolution," *The Slant Investor Place,* http://slant.investorplace.com/2013/03/china-is-ground-zero-for-a-green-energy-revolution/.

152. Solidiance. "Wind Power in China," *Ecology Global Network,* http://www.ecology.com/2013/03/21/wind-power-in-china/.

153. Wong, Edward. "2 Major Pollutants Increase in Beijing," *New York Times,* Asia Pacific, http://www.nytimes.com/2013/04/04/world/asia/two-major-air-pollutants-increase-in-china.html.

154. Author Unknown. "China Struggles with Choking Air Pollution," *The News-Herald,* http://www.news-herald.com/articles/2013/05/10/news/af7cd421-8dae-4d2c-bfcb-23ce596835b6.txt?viewmode=3.

155. Walter, Carl E.; Howie, Fraser J. T. *Red Capitalism* (Singapore: John Wiley & Sons, 2012), 27–28.

156. Bharatwaj, Shanthi. "Bank of America Sells China Construction Bank Stake for $6.6B," *The Street,* http://www.thestreet.com/story/11309329/1/bank-of-america-sells-china-construction-bank-stake-for-66b.html.

157. Tudor, Alison. "Banks Find Promise Unfulfilled in China Forays," *The Wall Street Journal,* http://online.wsj.com/article/SB10001424127887324442304578236224087592996.html.

158. Ho, Prudence; Lee, Yvonne; Baer, Justin. "Goldman Sachs Selling ICBC Stake," *The Wall Street Journal*, http://online.wsj.com/article/ SB10001424127887324787004578494632098998150.html.

159. Perl, Stephen M. *Doing Business with China, The Secrets of Dancing with the Dragon* (ChinaMart USA Book Publishing Inc., 2012), 134.

160. Kuhn, Robert Lawrence. *How China's Leaders Think* (Singapore: John Wiley & Sons, 2011), 253.

161. Author Unknown. "China's Policy Banks," *Caijing*, http://english. caijing.com.cn/2009-09-09/110243991.html.

162. Author Unknown. "China Development Bank's overseas investments: An assessment of environmental and social policies and practices," *Friends of the Earth*, http://libcloud.s3.amazonaws. com/93/2b/2/2245/China_Development_Banks_overseas_ investments_-_An_assessment_of_environmental_and_social_ policies_and_practices.pdf.

163. Author Unknown. "China Development Bank Steps up Leading to Private Firms," *Economy Watch*, http://www.economywatch.com/ in-the-news/china-development-bank-steps-up-lending-to-private- firms.05-09.html.

164. Jacques, Martin. *When China Rules the World* (London: Penguin Books, 2012), 481.

165. Devereux, Charlie. "China Bankrolling Chavez's Re-Election Bid With Oil Loans," *Bloomberg*, http://www.bloomberg.com/ news/2012-09-25/china-bankrolling-chavez-s-re-election-bid-with- oil-loans.html.

166. Downs, Erica S. "Inside China, Inc: China Development Bank's Cross-Border Energy Deals," *Brookings*, http://www.brookings.edu/ research/papers/2011/03/21-china-energy-downs.

167. Sanderson, Henry; Forsythe, Michael. *China's Superbank* (Singapore: John Wiley & Sons, 2013), 157.

168. Hochberg, Fred P. *How the US Can Lead the World in Exports: Retooling Our Export Finance Strategy for the 21st Century* (Remarks at the Center for American Progress, Washington, DC, June 15, 2011).

169. Author Unknown. "Bank Capital to Assets Ratio (%)," *The World Bank*, http://data.worldbank.org/indicator/FB.BNK.CAPA.ZS.

170. Author Unknown. "China's Banks: Storing up Trouble," *The Economist*, http://www.economist.com/node/21554234.

171. Chee, Harold; West, Chris. *Myths about doing business in China* (Great Britain: Palgrave Macmillan, 2007), 24.

172. Mcmahon, Dinny; Wei, Lingling. "Back in Fashion: China's Bad Debt," *The Wall Street Journal*, http://online.wsj.com/article/SB1000 14241278873239261045782764704966660166.html.

173. Martin, Michael F. "China's Banking System: Issues for Congress," *Congressional Research Service*, http://www.fas.org/sgp/crs/row/R42380.pdf.

174. Rabinovitch, Simon; Anderlini, Jamil. "China Blocks MasterCard Processing Renminbi Transactions," *The Financial Times*, http://www.ft.com/intl/cms/s/0/ce3973f4-cb6c-11e2-8ff3-00144feab7de.html?ftcamp=published_links%2Frss%2Fworld_asia-pacific_ch ina%2Ffeed%2F%2Fproduct&ftcamp=crm/email/201363/nbe/ChinaBusiness/product#axzz2V8lwoOt5.

175. McConnell, Tristan. "Seeking Proof of China's Ancient Trade with Africa," *GlobalPost*, http://www.globalpost.com/dispatch/kenya/100910/seeking-proof-chinas-ancient-trade-africa?page=0,1.

176. Guerrero, Dorothy-Grace; Manji, Firoze. *China's New Role in Africa and the South: A Search for a New Perspective* (Cape Town: Fahamu, 2008), 91–95.

177. Rotberg, Robert I. *China into Africa: Trade, Aid, and Influence* (Cambridge: World Peace Foundation, 2008), 1–4.

178. Carmody, Padraig. *The New Scramble for Africa* (Cambridge: Polity Press, 2011), 2–10.

179. Brautigam, Deborah. *The Dragon's Gift: The Real Story of China in Africa* (Oxford: Oxford University Press, 2011), 1–3.

180. Wang, Jian-Ye; Bio-Tchané, Abdoulaye. "Africa's Burgeoning Ties with China," *International Monetary Fund,* http://www.imf.org/external/pubs/ft/fandd/2008/03/wang.htm.

181. Douglas, Kate. "Africa becoming an increasingly important trading partner for BRICS countries," *How we made it in Africa,* http://www.howwemadeitinafrica.com/africa-becoming-an-increasingly-important-trading-partner-for-brics-countries/24312/.

182. Wang, Yi. *Australia-China Relations post 1949* (Burlington: Ashgate Publishing Company, 2012).

183. Yang, Bai. "China: Australia's largest trading partner," *CCTV.com English,* http://english.cntv.cn/program/china24/20130409/107022.shtml.

184. He, Fan. "Australia's China Challenge," *Financial Review,* http://www.afr.com/p/lifestyle/review/australia_china_challenge_mfKFhXBmoPloDIURjy33yN.

185. Author Unknown. "Why China is so Important to Australia & Our Stockmarket," *Stewart Partners,* http://www.stewartpartners.com.au/why-china-is-so-important-to-australia-our-stockmarket.

186. Inglis, Hilary. "Why China is Important to Australia," *ipac,* http://www.ipac.com.au/blog/why-china-is-important-to-australia.

187. Cheng, Sara. "China—A Gold Mine for Consumer Goods Exporters?" *Australian Business Consulting & Solutions,* http://www.

australianbusiness.com.au/international-trade/export-markets/china/
china-a-gold-mine-for-consumer-goods-exporters-.

188. Curran, Enda. "Australia Gets Closer to China," *The Wall Street Journal*, http://online.wsj.com/article/SB100014241278873247666045784601723206863626.html.

189. He, Fan. "Australia's China Challenge," *Financial Review*, http://www.afr.com/p/lifestyle/review/australia_china_challenge_mfKFhXBmoPloDIURjy33yN.

190. McInnes, Eileen. "Australians Attitudes Hold Back China Ties," *Asia Times*, http://www.atimes.com/atimes/China/CHIN-02-030513.html.

191. Author Unknown. "Why China Means Business," *Shell Australia*, http://www.shell.com.au/products-services/solutions-for-businesses/inmotion/library/inmotion3/china.html.

192. Author Unknown. "Australian to Cater to China's Rising Food Demand," *SINA English*, http://english.sina.com/business/2013/0526/593832.html.

193. Jiang, Shixue. "Latin American Studies in China," *Institute of Latin American Studies*, Chinese Academy of Social Sciences, http://blog.china.com.cn/jiangshixue/art/848640.html.

194. Roett, Riordan; Paz, Guadalupe. *China's Expansion into the Western Hemisphere* (Washington, DC: Brookings Institution Press, 2008), 52–57.

195. Ellis, R. Evan. "Chinese Soft Power in Latin America: A Case Study," *National Defense University Press*, http://www.ndu.edu/press/chinese-soft-power-latin-america.html.

196. Watts, Jonathan. "China's Exploitation of Latin American Natural Resources Raises Concern," *EurActiv*, http://www.euractiv.com/development-policy/chinas-exploitation-latin-americ-news-518799.

197. Coleman, Kevin G. "Cyber Espionage Targets Sensitive Data," *SIP Trunking*, http://sip-trunking.tmcnet.com/topics/security/articles/47927-cyber-espionage-targets-sensitive-data.htm.

198. Perlroth, Nicole. "Traveling Light in a Time of Digital Thievery," *The New York Times,* http://www.nytimes.com/2012/02/11/technology/electronic-security-a-worry-in-an-age-of-digital-espionage.html?pagewanted=all.

199. Andress, Jason; Winterfeld, Steve. *Cyber Warfare: techniques, tactics, and Tools for Security Practitioners* (Waltham: Elsevier, 2011), 69–70.

200. Clarke, Richard A.; Knake, Robert K. *Cyber War: The Next Threat to National Security and What to Do About It* (New York: Harper-Collins Publishers, 2010), 74.

201. Clarke, Richard A.; Knake, Robert K. *Cyber War: The Next Threat to National Security and What to Do About It* (New York: Harper-Collins Publishers, 2010), 75–77.

202. Clarke, Richard A.; Knake, Robert K. *Cyber War: The Next Threat to National Security and What to Do About It* (New York: Harper-Collins Publishers, 2010), 77–79.

203. Clarke, Richard A.; Knake, Robert K. *Cyber War: The Next Threat to National Security and What to Do About It* (New York: Harper-Collins Publishers, 2010), 79–80.

204. Clarke, Richard A.; Knake, Robert K. *Cyber War: The Next Threat to National Security and What to Do About It* (New York: Harper-Collins Publishers, 2010), 81.

205. Clarke, Richard A.; Knake, Robert K. *Cyber War: The Next Threat to National Security and What to Do About It* (New York: Harper-Collins Publishers, 2010), 82–84.

206. Gady, Franz-Stefan. "Cyber Espionage: Reducing Tensions Between China and the US," *China-US Focus*, http://www.chinausfocus.

com/peace-security/cyber-espionage-reducing-tensions-between-china-and-the-united-states/.

207. Author Unknown. "China's Cyber Threat A High-Stakes Spy Game," *NPR*, http://www.npr.org/2011/11/27/142828055/chinas-cyber-threat-a-high-stakes-spy-game.

208. Nakashima, Ellen. "U.S. Said to be Target of Massive Cyber-espionage Campaign," *The Washington Post*, http://articles.washingtonpost.com/2013-02-10/world/37026024_1_cyber-espionage-national-counterintelligence-executive-trade-secrets.

209. Young, Jeffrey R. "In China's Internet Cafes, Content-Blocking Is Largely Effective," *The Chronicle of Higher Education,* http://chronicle.com/blogs/college20/in-chinas-internet-cafes-content-blocking-is-largely-effective/26872.

210. Nakashima, Ellen; Wan, William. "In China, Business Travelers Take Extreme Precautions to Avoid Cyber-espionage," *The Washington Post*, http://www.washingtonpost.com/world/national-security/in-china-business-travelers-take-extreme-precautions-to-avoid-cyber-espionage/2011/09/20/gIQAM6cR0K_story.html.

211. D'Orazio, Dante. "US Congress Restricts Government Purchase of Chinese Computer Equipment, Citing Cyber-espionage Concerns," *The Verge*, http://www.theverge.com/2013/3/27/4154442/us-congress-restricts-purchase-of-chinese-computer-equipment-fearing-cyber-espionage.

212. Gorman, Siobhan. "China Hackers Hit U.S. Chamber," *The Wall Street Journal*, http://online.wsj.com/article/SB10001424052970204058404577110541568535300.html.

213. Savitz, Eric. "Conversations on Cybersecurity: The Trouble with China, Part 1," *Forbes*, http://www.forbes.com/sites/ciocentral/2012/01/31/conversations-on-cybersecurity-the-trouble-with-china-part-1/.

214. Healey, Jason. "How the U.S. Should Respond to Chinese Cyberespionage," *U.S. News & World Report*, http://www.usnews.com/opinion/blogs/world-report/2013/02/19/how-the-us-should-respond-to-chinese-cyberespionage.

215. Andress, Jason; Winterfeld, Steve. *Cyber Warfare: techniques, tactics, and Tools for Security Practitioners* (Waltham: Elsevier, 2011), 170–177.

216. Savitz, Eric. "Conversations on Cybersecurity: The Trouble with China, Part 2," *Forbes*, http://www.forbes.com/sites/ciocentral/2012/02/05/conversations-on-cybersecurity-the-trouble-with-china-part-2/2/.

217. Savitz, Eric. "Conversations on Cybersecurity Part 3: Why You aren't Protected," *Forbes*, http://www.forbes.com/sites/ciocentral/2012/02/12/conversations-on-cybersecurity-part-3-why-you-arent-protected/.

218. Savitz, Eric. "Conversations on Cybersecurity, Part 4: Effective Protection," *Forbes*, http://www.forbes.com/sites/ciocentral/2012/03/05/conversations-on-cybersecurity-part-4-effective-protection/2/.

219. Goldman, David. "China vs. U.S.: The Cyber Cold War is Raging," *CNNMoney*, http://money.cnn.com/2011/07/28/technology/government_hackers/index.htm.

220. Schneier, Bruce. "Computer Security When Traveling to China," *Schneier on Security*, http://www.schneier.com/blog/archives/2012/02/computer_securi_2.html.

221. Solomon, Richard H.; Quinney, Nigel. *American negotiating Behavior: Wheeler-Dealers, legal Eagles, Bullies, and Preachers* (Washington, DC: United States Institute of Peace, 2010), 21–27.

222. Author Unknown. "Negotiating with Americans," *Tunghai University,* http://www.slideshare.net/Laoshi_Steve/ negotiating-with-americans-sav-lecture.

223. Solomon, Richard H.; Quinney, Nigel. *American negotiating Behavior: Wheeler-Dealers, legal Eagles, Bullies, and Preachers* (Washington, DC: United States Institute of Peace, 2010), 81–83.

224. Pierannunzi, Meaghan. "American Negotiating Behavior: Questions and Answers," *United States Institute of Peace Press,* http://www.usip.org/american-negotiating-behavior/ american-negotiating-behavior-questions-and-answers.

225. Solomon, Richard H.; Quinney, Nigel. *American negotiating Behavior: Wheeler-Dealers, legal Eagles, Bullies, and Preachers* (Washington, DC: United States Institute of Peace, 2010), 29–32.

226. Solomon, Richard H.; Quinney, Nigel. *American negotiating Behavior: Wheeler-Dealers, legal Eagles, Bullies, and Preachers* (Washington, DC: United States Institute of Peace, 2010), 55–57.

227. Solomon, Richard H.; Quinney, Nigel. *American negotiating Behavior: Wheeler-Dealers, legal Eagles, Bullies, and Preachers* (Washington, DC: United States Institute of Peace, 2010), 74–75.

228. Author Unknown. "What is Wrong with Punctuality," *Positive Acorn,* http://positiveacorn.com/tag/polychromic.

229. Graham, John L.; Lam, N. Mark. "The Chinese Negotiation," *Harvard Business Review,* http://www.globalnegotiationbook.com/ John-Graham-research/negotiation-v1.pdf.

230. Requejo, William Hernandez; Graham, John L. *Global Negotiation: The New Rules* (New York: Palgrave Macmillan, 2008), 220.

231. Requejo, William Hernandez; Graham, John L. *Global Negotiation: The New Rules* (New York: Palgrave Macmillan, 2008), 221.

232. Requejo, William Hernandez; Graham, John L. *Global Negotiation: The New Rules* (New York: Palgrave Macmillan, 2008), 223.

233. Requejo, William Hernandez; Graham, John L. *Global Negotiation: The New Rules* (New York: Palgrave Macmillan, 2008), 226.

234. Requejo, William Hernandez; Graham, John L. *Global Negotiation: The New Rules* (New York: Palgrave Macmillan, 2008), 227.

235. Blackman, Carolyn. *Negotiating China* (Crows Nest, NSW: Allen & Unwin Pty Ltd, 1997), 76–93.

236. Blackman, Carolyn. *Negotiating China* (Crows Nest, NSW: Allen & Unwin Pty Ltd, 1997), 78–79.

237. Blackman, Carolyn. *Negotiating China* (Crows Nest, NSW: Allen & Unwin Pty Ltd, 1997), 81–82.

238. Blackman, Carolyn. *Negotiating China* (Crows Nest, NSW: Allen & Unwin Pty Ltd, 1997), 77–78.

239. Blackman, Carolyn. *Negotiating China* (Crows Nest, NSW: Allen & Unwin Pty Ltd, 1997), 82–83.

240. Blackman, Carolyn. *Negotiating China* (Crows Nest, NSW: Allen & Unwin Pty Ltd, 1997), 83.

241. Blackman, Carolyn. *Negotiating China* (Crows Nest, NSW: Allen & Unwin Pty Ltd, 1997), 83–84.

242. Lim-Loges, Lelia. "Can China Continue to Grow?" *The Korn/Ferry Institute*, http://www.kornferryinstitute.com/briefings-magazine/can-china-continue-grow.

243. Ikenberry, G. John. "The Rise of China and the Future of the West," *The New York Times,* http://www.nytimes.com/cfr/world/20080101faessay_v87n1_ikenberry.html?pagewanted=all&_r=0.

244. McGregor, James. *One Billion Customers* (New York: Free Press, a division of Simon & Schuster, Inc., 2005), 188.

245. Keck, Zachary. "China Powers Two World Economy," *The Diplomat*, http://thediplomat.com/pacific-money/2013/01/12/china-powers-two-world-economy/.

246. Araujo, Heriberto; Cardenal, Juan Pablo. "China's Economic Empire, *The New York Times*, http://www.nytimes.com/2013/06/02/opinion/sunday/chinas-economic-empire.html?pagewanted=all&_r=0.

247. Zalan, Kira. "The Rise of China and the Global Future of the U.S.," *US News & World Report*, http://www.usnews.com/opinion/articles/2013/01/03/the-rise-of-china-and-the-global-future-of-the-us.

BIBLIOGRAPHY

Abrams, Stan. "Here's What Henry Blodget Doesn't Understand About Overtime At Foxconn," *Business Insider*, http://articles.businessinsider.com/2012-04-03/home/31278877_1_chen-yamei-foxconn-work-week.

Allen, Arika M.; Gosling, Paul; Powell, Grant D.; Yang, Claire. "The human touch behind Asia Inc.'s global push," *accenture*, http://www.accenture.com/us-en/outlook/pages/outlook-journal-2007-chinese-consumers.aspx.

Andress, Jason; Winterfeld, Steve. *Cyber Warfare: techniques, tactics, and Tools for Security Practitioners* (Waltham: Elsevier, 2011), 69–70.

Andress, Jason; Winterfeld, Steve. *Cyber Warfare: techniques, tactics, and Tools for Security Practitioners* (Waltham: Elsevier, 2011), 170–177.

Araujo, Heriberto; Cardenal, Juan Pablo. "China's Economic Empire," *The New York Times*, http://www.nytimes.com/2013/06/02/opinion/sunday/chinas-economic-empire.html?pagewanted=all&_r=0.

Atsmon, Yuval; Ding, Jennifer; Dixit, Vinay; St. Maurice, Ian; Suessmuth-Dyckerhoff, Claudia. "The coming of age: China's new class of wealthy consumers," *Insights China*, McKinsey & Company, https://solutions.mckinsey.com/insightschina/_SiteNote/WWW/GetFile.aspx?uri=/insightschina/default/en-us/aboutus/news/Files/wp2055036759/Insights%20China_v9_060ba3e4-ef85-43b3-b9a9-0f583012a10b.pdf.

Author Unknown. "Selling in China," *The Boston Consulting Group*, http://knowledge.wharton.upenn.edu/papers/download/BCGChinaReport3.pdf.

Author Unknown. "Finding and Keeping Good Employees in China," *China Primer*, http://www.chinaprimer.com/human-resources-china-hr/recruiting-in-china-good-employees.html.

Author Unknown. "Why China Means Business," *Shell Australia*, http://www.shell.com.au/products-services/solutions-for-businesses/inmotion/library/inmotion3/china.html.

Author Unknown. "China's to be World's Biggest Economy by 2025," *The Telegraph*, http://www.telegraph.co.uk/finance/china-business/9655058/China-to-be-worlds-biggest-economy-by-2025.html.

Author Unknown. "subsidy," *Merriam-Webster*, http://www.merriam-webster.com/dictionary/subsidy.

Author Unknown. "6 Tips on How to Find a Decent Expat Job in China," *Vings Stuff*, http://www.vingsstuff.co.uk/2011/06/6-tips-on-how-to-find-a-decent-expat-job-in-china/.

Author Unknown. "A Case of Corporate and National Defamation: AMSC v. Sinovel, hot air in legal and media exercises," *Hidden Harmonies China Blog*, http://blog.hiddenharmonies.org/2012/12/a-case-of-corporate-and-national-defamation-amsc-v-sinovel-hot-air-in-legal-and-media-exercises/.

Author Unknown. "Australian to Cater to China's Rising Food Demand," *SINA English*, http://english.sina.com/business/2013/0526/593832.html.

Author Unknown. "Bank Capital to Assets Ratio (%)," *The World Bank*, http://data.worldbank.org/indicator/FB.BNK.CAPA.ZS.

Author Unknown. "China and Subsidies," *American Manufacturing. org*, http://americanmanufacturing.org/category/issues/china/ china-and-subsidies.

Author Unknown. "China Development Bank Steps up Leading to Private Firms," *Economy Watch*, http://www.economywatch.com/in-the-news/china-development-bank-steps-up-lending-to-private-firms.05-09. html.

Author Unknown. "China Development Bank's overseas investments: An assessment of environmental and social policies and practices," *Friends of the Earth*, http://libcloud.s3.amazonaws.com/93/2b/2/2245/ China_Development_Banks_overseas_investments_-_An_assessment_ of_environmental_and_social_policies_and_practices.pdf.

Author Unknown. "China Graduates Face Tough Job Market As Youth Unemployment Rises," *BBC News Business*, http://www.bbc.co.uk/news/ business-22564249.

Author Unknown. "China Says U.S. Subsidies Violate Trade Rules," *China Digital Times*, http://chinadigitaltimes.net/2012/05/ china-says-u-s-renewable-subsidies-violate-trade-rules/.

Author Unknown. "China Still Has 10 Year Advantages in Manufacturing," *China Labour Market*, http://www.china.org.cn/ opinion/2013-02-25/content_28049447.htm http://chinalabourmarket. com/china-still-has-10-year-advantages-in-manufacturing.html.

Author Unknown. "China Struggles with Choking Air Pollution," *The News-Herald*, http://www.news-herald.com/articles/2013/05/10/news/ af7cd421-8dae-4d2c-bfcb-23ce596835b6.txt?viewmode=3.

Author Unknown. "China to Become World's Largest Patent Filing Country," *chinaipsummint.com*, http://chinaipsummit.com/2012/ press_1202/20.html.

Author Unknown. "China to Boost Crackdown on IPR Infringement in 2013," *China.org.cn*, http://www.china.org.cn/china/2012-12/29/content_27545568.htm.

Author Unknown. "China to Impose Limits on Six Industries to Tackle Air Pollution," *Bloomberg*, http://www.bloomberg.com/news/2013-02-20/china-to-impose-limits-on-six-industries-to-tackle-air-pollution.html.

Author Unknown. "China Unemployment," *Economy Watch*, http://www.economywatch.com/unemployment/countries/china.html.

Author Unknown. "China's 2011 GDP growth slows to 9.2%," *Chinadaily*, http://www.chinadaily.com.cn/business/2012-01/17/content_14460323_2.htm.

Author Unknown. "China's Banks: Storing up Trouble," *The Economist*, http://www.economist.com/node/21554234.

Author Unknown. "China's economy—Perverse advantage," *The Economist*, http://www.economist.com/news/finance-and-economics/21576680-new-book-lays-out-scale-chinas-industrial-subsidies-perverse-advantage.

Author Unknown. "China's Patent Application Jump 20% in 2012," *China Patent Information Center*, http://www.cnpat.com.cn/EnNews.aspx?NewsId=3611.

Author Unknown. "China's Policy Banks," *Caijing*, http://english.caijing.com.cn/2009-09-09/110243991.html.

Author Unknown. "China's Political System," *China.org.cn*, http://www.china.org.cn/english/Political/28842.htm.

Author Unknown. "China's Pollution Facts," *China Smog*, http://chinasmog.wordpress.com/china-pollution-facts/.

Author Unknown. "China's Cyber Threat A High-Stakes Spy Game," *NPR*, http://www.npr.org/2011/11/27/142828055/chinas-cyber-threat-a-high-stakes-spy-game.

Author Unknown. "Chinese Subsidies Under Scrutiny," *The New York Times*, Global Business with Reuters, http://www.nytimes.com/2013/04/28/business/global/chinese-subsidies-under-scrutiny.html?_r=0.

Author Unknown. "Computer Crime & Intellectual Property Section," *US Department of Justice,* http://www.justice.gov/criminal/cybercrime/.

Author Unknown. "Desertification," *Oxford Dictionaries*, http://oxforddictionaries.com/us/definition/american_english/desertification.

Author Unknown. "Difference among Mediation, Arbitration and Litigation in China," *China Lawyer Blog*, http://www.chinalawblog.org/law-topics/litigation-lawyer/154-china-arbitration-litigation.

Author Unknown. "Enforcing China Court Decisions: Help Is On the Way?" *China Hear Say*, http://www.chinahearsay.com/enforcing-china-court-decisions-help-is-on-the-way/.

Author Unknown. "Fact Sheet: WTO Case Challenging Chinese Subsidies," *USTR.gov*, http://www.ustr.gov/about-us/press-office/fact-sheets/2012/september/wto-case-challenging-chinese-subsidies.

Author Unknown. "FCPA: Building a Proactive Compliance Approach," *The Wall Street Journal*, http://deloitte.wsj.com/riskandcompliance/2013/04/01/foreign-corrupt-practices-act-proactive-compliance-advised-test/.

Author Unknown. "Finding Job for Expats in China," *Chinadaily*, http://www.chinadaily.com.cn/business/2012-06-05/content_15474947.htm.

Author Unknown. "Foreign Corrupt Practices Act," *US Department of Justice*, http://www.justice.gov/criminal/fraud/fcpa/.

Author Unknown. "General Administration of Customs," *Yangtze Business Services*, http://www.yangtzebusinessservices.com/ government-body-profiles-general-administration-of-customs-.

Author Unknown. "Guide to China workplace laws and regulations," *Kingfisher*, http://files.the-group.net/library/kgf/responsibility/pdfs/cr_13. pdf.

Author Unknown. "How Economies Grow," *China Global Trade*, http://www.chinaglobaltrade.com/article/ how-us-china-economic-growth-develops.

Author Unknown. "How many dialects are there in China?" *Yahoo! Answers*, http://answers.yahoo.com/question/index?qid=2007070409224 3AArFZcV.

Author Unknown. "How to Network and Find a Job in Shanghai," *City Weekend*, http://www.cityweekend. com.cn/shanghai/articles/blogs-shanghai/expat-affairs/ how-to-network-and-find-a-job-in-shanghai/.

Author Unknown. "How to Protect Your Intellectual Property," *Bullfax.com*, http://www.bullfax. com/?q=node-how-protect-your-intellectual-property.

Author Unknown. "Individualism and Collectivism: Reconsidering Old Assumptions," *FreePatentsOnline.com*, http://www.freepatentsonline. com/article/Journal-International-Business-Research/208956140.html.

Author Unknown. "Intellectual Property in China Still Murky," *The Economist*, http://www.economist.com/node/21553040.

Author Unknown. "Intellectual Property Rights in China," *Embassy of the United States-Beijing, China*, US Department of State, http://beijing. usembassy-china.org.cn/ipr.html.

Author Unknown. "Intellectual Property Theft: Get Real," *National Crime Prevention Council*, http://www.ncpc.org/topics/

intellectual-property-theft/trends-globalization-and-digitalization-usher-in-a-new-era-of-intellectual-property-theftc.

Author Unknown. "IP Contracts," *The US-China Business Council,* https://www.uschina.org/info/ipr/ip-contacts.html.

Author Unknown. "IPR Enforcement," *US Customs and Border Protection,* https://apps.cbp.gov/e-recordations/.

Author Unknown. "Ivy funds—The World Covered," *Ivy Funds,* http://theworldcovered.ivyfunds.com/home/u-s-companies-customize-services-for-china%E2%80%99s-high-end-buyers/.

Author Unknown. "Majority of China's Arable Land Heavily Polluted," *ChinaGaze,* http://www.chinagaze.com/2013/04/23/majority-of-chinas-arable-land-heavily-polluted/.

Author Unknown. "Micro-Segmentation," *MZI Global,* http://www.mziglobal.com/en/micro-segmentation.

Author Unknown. "Moving to China," *Expat Info Desk,* http://www.expatinfodesk.com/expat-guide/deciding-on-the-right-country/top-expatriate-destinations/china/.

Author Unknown. "National Copyright Administration," *The US-China Business Council,* https://www.uschina.org/public/china/govstructure/nca.html.

Author Unknown. "Negotiating with Americans," *Tunghai University,* http://www.slideshare.net/Laoshi_Steve/negotiating-with-americans-sav-lecture.

Author Unknown. "Our Partner Agencies," *iprcenter.gov,* http://www.ice.gov/iprcenter/.

Author Unknown. "Our Partner Agencies," *iprcenter.gov,* http://www. iprcenter.gov/.

Author Unknown. "Protecting Your Intellectual Property Rights (IPR) in China—A Practical Guide for U.S. Companies," *US Department of Commerce International Trade Administration,* http://www.mac.doc.gov/ china/docs/businessguides/intellectualpropertyrights.htm.

Author Unknown. "Report predicts 7.7% growth for China's 2012 GDP," *People's Daily Online,* http://english.peopledaily.com. cn/102774/8047591.html.

Author Unknown. "Roadmap for Intellectual Property Protection in China," *European Union Patent Office,* http://www.turkpatent.gov.tr/ dosyalar/basvuru/yayin/trademark_protection_in_china.pdf.

Author Unknown. "SOE Reform in China," *UK Essays,* http://www. ukessays.com/essays/politics/soe-reform-in-china.php.

Author Unknown. "Stopfakes.Gov—Small Business and Intellectual Property from the USPTO," *In House Blog,* http://www.inhouseblog. com/stopfakesgov_-_/.

Author Unknown. "The Alibaba Phenomenon," *The Economist,* http:// www.economist.com/news/leaders/21573981-chinas-e-commerce-giant-could-generate-enormous-wealthprovided-countrys-rulers-leave-it.

Author Unknown. "The Expat Job Market in Beijing," *InterNations,* http://www.internations.org/beijing-expats/guide/ working-in-beijing-15418/the-expat-job-market-in-beijing-2.

Author Unknown. "The Real Story Behind China's Energy Policy and What America Can Learn From It," *United States Senate Committee on Environment and Public Works,* http://www.inhofe.senate.gov/ download/?id=e0a37b82-fc70-48ff-b1fb-3293ca76dd39&download=1.

Author Unknown. "Understanding China: The influence of Confucianism in Chinese society (II of II)," *pepegins.com,* http://

pepegins.com/2012/02/08/understanding-the-china-the-influence-of-confucianism-in-chinese-society-ii-of-ii/.

Author Unknown. "What is a Lower Tier City?" *China Normal*, http://www.chinanormal.com/cities.

Author Unknown. "What is Wrong with Punctuality," *Positive Acorn*, http://positiveacorn.com/tag/polychromic.

Author Unknown. "What's New on STOPfakes," *STOPfakes.gov*, www.stopfakes.gov.

Author Unknown. "Why China is so Important to Australia & Our Stockmarket," *Stewart Partners*, http://www.stewartpartners.com.au/why-china-is-so-important-to-australia-our-stockmarket.

Bamberg, Jeneil. "Will China Enforce Its Constitution?" *Nextgen*, http://ewinextgen.tumblr.com/post/43657898997/will-china-enforce-its-constitution.

Barry. "What Makes a City Tier in China?" *The China Sourcing Blog*, http://www.chinasourcingblog.org/2011/07/what-makes-a-city-tier-in-chin.html.

Bennett, Steven C. "Litigation in China: Ten Things You Must Know," *The Metropolitan Corporate Counsel*, http://www.metrocorpcounsel.com/articles/10466/litigation-china-ten-things-you-must-know.

Bharatwaj, Shanthi. "Bank of America Sells China Construction Bank Stake for $6.6B," *The Street*, http://www.thestreet.com/story/11309329/1/bank-of-america-sells-china-construction-bank-stake-for-66b.html.

Blackman, Carolyn. *Negotiating China* (Crows Nest, NSW: Allen & Unwin Pty Ltd, 1997).

Bradsher, Keith. "Wary of China, Companies Head to Cambodia," *New York Times*, Global Business, http://www.nytimes.com/2013/04/09/

business/global/wary-of-events-in-china-foreign-investors-head-to-cambodia.html?pagewanted=all&_r=0.

Brautigam, Deborah. *The Dragon's Gift: The Real Story of China in Africa* (Oxford: Oxford University Press, 2011).

Brown, Mayer. "PRC Labour Law—Bitesize: How many days bereavement leave is an employee entitled to in the PRC?" *Mayer Brown JSM Newsletter,* http://www.mayerbrown.com/publications/BPRC-Labour-Law-BitesizeB-How-many-days-bereavement-leave-is-an-employee-entitled-to-in-the-PRC-02-18-2010/.

Brown, Ronad C. *East Asian Labor and Employment Law* (Cambridge: Cambridge University Press, 2012).

Brown, Ronald C. *Understanding Labor and Employment Law in China* (Cambridge: Cambridge University Press, 2010).

Carlson, Benjamin. "Are Anti-corruption Campaigns Causing China's Economy to Slow?" *Global Post,* http://www.globalpost.com/dispatch/news/regions/asia-pacific/china/130415/anti-corruption-slowing-economy.

Carmody, Padraig. *The New Scramble for Africa* (Cambridge: Polity Press, 2011).

Chee, Harold; West, Chris. *Myths about doing business in China* (Great Britain: Palgrave Macmillan, 2007).

Cheng, Sara. "China—A Gold Mine for Consumer Goods Exporters?" *Australian Business Consulting & Solutions,* http://www.australianbusiness.com.au/international-trade/export-markets/china/china-a-gold-mine-for-consumer-goods-exporters-.

Chow, Daniel C. K. *The Legal System of the People's Republic of China in a Nutshell* (United States: West Group, 2003).

Chow, Daniel. "China Under the Foreign Corrupt Practices Act," *Wisconsin Law Review,* http://wisconsinlawreview.org/wp-content/files/12-Chow.pdf.

Chu, Kathy. "China Factories Try Karaoke, Speed Dating to Keep Workers," *The Wall Street Journal,* http://online.wsj.com/article/SB10001 42412788732379810457845263407551 9230.html.

Chu, Kathy. "China Manufacturers Survive by Moving to Asian Neighbors," *The Wall Street Journal,* http://online.wsj.com/article/SB100 01424127887323798104578453073103566416.html.

Clarke, Richard A.; Knake, Robert K. *Cyber War: The Next Threat to National Security and What to Do About It* (New York: Harper-Collins Publishers, 2010).

Cockerham, Sean. "Who's the world leader in clean energy? China," *McClatchy Newspapers,* http://www.mcclatchydc.com/2013/04/17/188706/whos-the-world-leader-in-clean.html#.UZ3oao3D_s0.

Coleman, Kevin G. "Cyber Espionage Targets Sensitive Data," *SIP Trunking,* http://sip-trunking.tmcnet.com/topics/security/articles/47927-cyber-espionage-targets-sensitive-data.htm.

Coonan, Clifford. "Communist Officials Sidestep Xi's Anti-corruption Efforts," *The Irish Times,* http://www.irishtimes.com/news/world/asia-pacific/communist-officials-sidestep-xi-s-anti-corruption-efforts-1.1380894.

Cooper, Marta. "Pollution: Farms Worse than Factories in China," *Shanghaiist,* http://shanghaiist.com/2010/02/10/chinas_first_national_consensus_on.php.

Curran, Enda. "Australia Gets Closer to China," *The Wall Street Journal,* http://online.wsj.com/article/SB10001424127887324766604578460172320683626.html.

D'Orazio, Dante. "US Congress Restricts Government Purchase of Chinese Computer Equipment, Citing Cyber-espionage Concerns," *The Verge*, http://www.theverge.com/2013/3/27/4154442/us-congress-restricts-purchase-of-chinese-computer-equipment-fearing-cyber-espionage.

Devereux, Charlie. "China Bankrolling Chavez's Re-Election Bid With Oil Loans," *Bloomberg*, http://www.bloomberg.com/news/2012-09-25/china-bankrolling-chavez-s-re-election-bid-with-oil-loans.html.

Douglas, Kate. "Africa becoming an increasingly important trading partner for BRICS countries," *How we made it in Africa*, http://www.howwemadeitinafrica.com/africa-becoming-an-increasingly-important-trading-partner-for-brics-countries/24312/.

Downing, Louise; Doom, Justin. "American Superconductor Says China Will Review Sinovel Suit," *Bloomberg*, http://www.bloomberg.com/news/2013-01-11/amsc-says-china-s-supreme-court-will-review-suit-with-sinovel.html.

Downs, Erica S. "Inside China, Inc: China Development Bank's Cross-Border Energy Deals," *Brookings*, http://www.brookings.edu/research/papers/2011/03/21-china-energy-downs.

Ellis, R. Evan. "Chinese Soft Power in Latin America: A Case Study," *National Defense University Press*, http://www.ndu.edu/press/chinese-soft-power-latin-america.html.

Freeke, Lois. "Expat Job Search: 11 Deadly Sins," *Shanghai Expat*, http://www.shanghaiexpat.com/article/expat-job-search-11-deadly-sins-why-you-wont-get-interview-quick-fixes-12899.html.

Gady, Franz-Stefan. "Cyber Espionage: Reducing Tensions Between China and the US," *China-US Focus*, http://www.chinausfocus.com/peace-security/cyber-espionage-reducing-tensions-between-china-and-the-united-states/.

Goldman, David. "China vs. U.S.: The Cyber Cold War is Raging," *CNNMoney*, http://money.cnn.com/2011/07/28/technology/government_hackers/index.htm.

Gorman, Siobhan. "China Hackers Hit U.S. Chamber," *The Wall Street Journal*, http://online.wsj.com/article/SB10001424052970204058404577110541568535300.html.

Graham, John L.; Lam, N. Mark. "The Chinese Negotiation," *Harvard Business Review*, http://www.globalnegotiationbook.com/John-Graham-research/negotiation-v1.pdf.

Gross, Ames; Dyson, Patricia. "The End of China's Iron Rice Bowl," *Pacific Bridge Recruiting*, http://www.pacificbridge.com/publications/the-end-of-chinas-iron-rice-bowl/.

Gu, Xiaolei. "Obtaining a Z Visa, Work Permit and Residence Permit in China," *China Briefing*, http://www.china-briefing.com/news/2012/05/17/obtaining-a-z-visa-work-permit-and-residence-permit-in-china.html.

Gu, Yongqiang. "In China, Water You Wouldn't Dare Swim in, Let Alone Drink," *TIME*, http://world.time.com/2013/03/06/in-china-water-you-wouldnt-dare-swim-in-let-alone-drink/.

Guerrero, Dorothy-Grace; Manji, Firoze. *China's New Role in Africa and the South: A Search for a New Perspective* (Cape Town: Fahamu, 2008).

Haley, Usha C. V.; Haley, George T. "How Chinese Subsidies Changed the World," *Harvard Business Review*, http://blogs.hbr.org/cs/2013/04/how_chinese_subsidies_changed.html.

Haley, Usha C. V.; Haley, George T. *Subsidies to Chinese Industry: State capitalism, Business Strategy, and Trade Policy* (Oxford: Oxford University Press, 2013).

Handley, Meg. "China Leads the Renewable Energy World," *U.S. News & World Report*, http://www.usnews.com/news/articles/2013/04/17/china-leads-the-renewable-energy-world.

Harris, Dan. "How to Change Your China Employer AND You're your Work Permit," *China Law Blog*, http://www.chinalawblog.com/2011/12/how_to_change_your_china_employer_and_keep_your_work_visa.html.

Harris, Dan. "Protecting Your Intellectual Property In China, Part II," *China Law Blog*, http://www.chinalawblog.com/2011/06/protecting_your_intellectual_property_in_china_part_ii.html.

Hays, Jeffrey. "Corruption and Perks in China: Fires, Guanxi. Parties, Mistresses and Expensive Cars," *Yahoo! Facts and Details*, http://factsanddetails.com/china.php?itemid=304.

Hays, Jeffrey. "Water Pollution in China," *Yahoo! Facts and Details*, http://factsanddetails.com/china.php?itemid=391.

He, Fan. "Australia's China Challenge," *Financial Review*, http://www.afr.com/p/lifestyle/review/australia_china_challenge_mfKFhXBmoPloDIURjy33yN.

He, Fan. "Australia's China Challenge," *Financial Review*, http://www.afr.com/p/lifestyle/review/australia_china_challenge_mfKFhXBmoPloDIURjy33yN.

Healey, Jason. "How the U.S. Should Respond to Chinese Cyberespionage," *U.S. News & World Report*, http://www.usnews.com/opinion/blogs/world-report/2013/02/19/how-the-us-should-respond-to-chinese-cyberespionage.

Ho, Prudence; Lee, Yvonne; Baer, Justin. "Goldman Sachs Selling ICBC Stake," *The Wall Street Journal*, http://online.wsj.com/article/SB10001424127887324787004578494632098998150.html.

Ho, Wai-Ling Esther. "SIPO Becomes Largest Patent Office in the World," *Wilkinson & Grist*, http://www.lexology.com/library/detail. aspx?g=39927053-3bde-4a80-8bdb-16a168939e9e.

Hochberg, Fred P. *How the US Can Lead the World in Exports: Retooling Our Export Finance Strategy for the 21st Century* (Remarks at the Center for American Progress, Washington, DC, June 15, 2011).

Ikenberry, G. John. "The Rise of China and the Future of the West," *The New York Times*, http://www.nytimes.com/cfr/world/20080101faessay_v87n1_ikenberry.html?pagewanted=all&_r=0.

Indvik, Lauren. "Ecomerce in China: How the World's Biggest Market Buys Online," *mashable*, http://mashable.com/2012/05/20/ecommerce-china/.

Inglis, Hilary. "Why China is Important to Australia," *ipac*, http://www.ipac.com.au/blog/why-china-is-important-to-australia.

Jacques, Martin. *When China Rules the World* (London: Penguin Books, 2012).

Jiang, Shixue. "Latin American Studies in China," *Institute of Latin American Studies*, Chinese Academy of Social Sciences, http://blog.china.com.cn/jiangshixue/art/848640.html.

Keck, Zachary. "China Powers Two World Economy," *The Diplomat*, http://thediplomat.com/pacific-money/2013/01/12/china-powers-two-world-economy/.

Klok, Chris; Zhang, Tiehan. "Biodiversity and its Conservation in China," *Alterra, Wageningen*, http://webdocs.alterra.wur.nl/pdffiles/alterraRapporten/AlterraRapport1733.pdf.

Kremers, Nancy. "Protecting Your Intellectual Property Rights (IPR) in China," *US Patent and Trademark Office*, http://www.stopfakes.gov/sites/default/files/Protecting%20IPR%20in%20China%20Slides.pdf.

Kuhn, Robert Lawrence. *How China's Leaders Think* (Singapore: John Wiley & Sons, 2011).

Kwang, Kevin. "China Sees Rising Intellectual Property Tussles," *ZDNet*, http://www.zdnet.com/china-sees-rising-intellectual-property-tussles-2062304161/.

Lallanilla, Marc. "China's Top 6 Environmental Concerns," *Livescience*, http://www.livescience.com/27862-china-environmental-problems.html.

Lim-Loges, Lelia. "Can China Continue to Grow?" *The Korn/Ferry Institute*, http://www.kornferryinstitute.com/briefings-magazine/can-china-continue-grow.

Lin, Yifu Justin. *Demystifying the Chinese Economy* (Cambridge: Cambridge University Press, 2012).

Liu, Jianguo; Ouyang, Zhiyun; Pimm, Stuart L.; Raven, Peter H.; Wang, Xiaoke; Miao, Hong; Han, Nianyong. "Protecting China's Biodiversity," *Science*, http://www.nicholas.duke.edu/people/faculty/pimm/publications/pimmreprints/181_Liu_et_al_2003_Science.pdf.

Livermore, Adam. "Mandatory Social Welfare Benefits for Chinese Employees," *China Briefing*, http://www.china-briefing.com/news/2012/02/21/mandatory-social-welfare-benefits-for-chinese-employees.html.

Lo, Vai Io; Tian, Xiaowen Tian. *Law and Investment in China* (London: Routledge's Taylor & Francis Group, 2005).

Locke, Gary. "Ambassador's Roundtable on Intellectual Property Protection," *Embassy of the United States-Beijing, China*, US Department of State, http://beijing.usembassy-china.org.cn/20120412roundtable-on-intellectual-property-protection.html.

Logan, Tim. "Stranded in China: Debt Dispute Leaves Missouri Businessman in Limbo," *St.Louis Post-dispatch*, http://www.stltoday.com/business/local/

stranded-in-china-debt-dispute-leaves-missouri-businessman-in-limbo/
article_ad02e834-b71b-11e1-9b6a-0019bb30f31a.html.

Long, Xinming. "Foreign Companies in China: Expansion Plans
by Foreign Companies in China—Part 2," *bearcanada*, http://www.
bearcanada.com/china/expansionplans02.html.

Lui, Vincent; Kuo, Youchi. "Affluent Hold Keys to Corporate Success,"
Chinadaily, http://europe.chinadaily.com.cn/epaper/2012-12/14/
content_16016726.htm.

Madigan, Kathleen. "Economists Trim 2013 GDP Growth Forecasts,"
The Wall Street Journal, http://blogs.wsj.com/economics/2013/08/16/
economists-trim-2013-gdp-growth-forecasts/.

Magnus, John R.; Brightbill, Timothy C. "China's Currency
Regime is Legitimately Challengeable as a Subsidy under
ASCM Rules," *VoxEU.org*, http://www.voxeu.org/article/
china-s-currency-regime-legitimately-challengeable-subsidy.

Marks, Robert B. *China: Its Environment and History* (Maryland:
Rowman & Littlefield Publishers, Inc., 2012).

Martin, Michael F. "China's Banking System: Issues for Congress,"
Congressional Research Service, http://www.fas.org/sgp/crs/row/R42380.
pdf.

Martina, Michael. "Geithner Slams China's Intellectual Property
Policies," *Reuters*, http://www.reuters.com/article/2011/09/23/
us-china-geithner-idUSTRE78M15G20110923.

McConnell, Tristan. "Seeking Proof of China's Ancient Trade with
Africa," *GlobalPost*, http://www.globalpost.com/dispatch/kenya/100910/
seeking-proof-chinas-ancient-trade-africa?page=0,1.

McGregor, James. *One Billion Customers* (New York: Free Press, a
division of Simon & Schuster, Inc., 2005).

McInnes, Eileen. "Australians Attitudes Hold Back China Ties," *Asia Times*, http://www.atimes.com/atimes/China/CHIN-02-030513.html.

Mcmahon, Dinny; Wei, Lingling. "Back in Fashion: China's Bad Debt," *The Wall Street Journal*, http://online.wsj.com/article/SB1000142412788 7323926104578276470496660166.html.

Nakashima, Ellen. "U.S. Said to be Target of Massive Cyber-espionage Campaign," *The Washington Post*, http://articles.washingtonpost. com/2013-02-10/world/37026024_1_cyber-espionage-national-counterintelligence-executive-trade-secrets.

Nakashima, Ellen; Wan, William. "In China, Business Travelers Take Extreme Precautions to Avoid Cyber-espionage," *The Washington Post*, http://www.washingtonpost.com/world/national-security/in-china-business-travelers-take-extreme-precautions-to-avoid-cyber-espionage/2011/09/20/gIQAM6cR0K_story.html.

Navarro, Peter. "The Economics of the China Price," *China Perspectives*, http://chinaperspectives.revues.org/3063.

Ong, Ryan. "Tacking Intellectual Property Infringement in China," *China Business Review*, http://www.chinabusinessreview.com/ tackling-intellectual-property-infringement-in-china/.

Peerenboom, Randy; Zhang, Dacai. "Preservation of Assets in China: Law and Reality," *China Law And Practice*, http://www. chinalawandpractice.com/Article/1694743/Channel/9930/Preservation-of-Assets-in-China-Law-and-Reality.html.

Perkowski, Jack. "Major Trends in China: The Next 10 Years," *Forbes*, http://www.forbes.com/sites/jackperkowski/2012/11/27/ major-trends-in-china-the-next-10-years/.

Perl, Stephen M. *Doing Business with China, The Secrets of Dancing with the Dragon* (ChinaMart USA Book Publishing Inc., 2012).

Perlroth, Nicole. "Traveling Light in a Time of Digital Thievery," *The New York Times,* http://www.nytimes.com/2012/02/11/technology/electronic-security-a-worry-in-an-age-of-digital-espionage.html?pagewanted=all.

Pettis, Elizabrth L. "Challenging Chinese Currency Manipulation as a Subsidy under the WTO Subsidies and Countervailing Measures Agreement," *SelectedWorks,* http://works.bepress.com/cgi/viewcontent.cgi?article=1000&context=elizabeth_pettis&sei-redir=1&referer=http%3A%2F%2Fwww.google.com%2Furl%3Fsa%3Dt%26rct%3Dj%26q%3Dchinese%2520subsidize%2520their%2520currency%26source%3Dweb%26cd%3D9%26ved%3D0CF4QFjAI%26url%3Dhttp%253A%252F%252Fworks.bepress.com%252Fcgi%252Fviewcontent.cgi%253Farticle%253D1000%2526context%253Delizabeth_pettis%26ei%3DfLqnUZjnOIeo9gTD0oGgAg%26usg%3DAFQjCNG7_hY-bcfMLEsf_t6mM3vAxRt25w#search=%22chinese%20subsidize%20their%20currency%22.

Pierannunzi, Meaghan. "American Negotiating Behavior: Questions and Answers," *United States Institute of Peace Press,* http://www.usip.org/american-negotiating-behavior/american-negotiating-behavior-questions-and-answers.

Prestowitz, Clyde. "Down with Subsidies," *Foreign Policy,* http://prestowitz.foreignpolicy.com/posts/2013/05/16/down_with_subsidies.

Rabinovitch, Simon. "Chinese Groups Turn to Law in Disputes," *The Financial Times,* http://www.ft.com/intl/cms/s/0/e4e57188-e455-11e1-affe-00144feab49a.html?ftcamp=published_links%2Frss%2Fhome_asia%2Ffeed%2F%2Fproduct&ftcamp=crm/email/2012813/nbe/AsiaMorningHeadlines/product#axzz243GgH8VP.

Rabinovitch, Simon; Anderlini, Jamil. "China Blocks MasterCard Processing Renminbi Transactions," *The Financial Times,* http://www.ft.com/intl/cms/s/0/ce3973f4-cb6c-11e2-8ff3-00144feab7de.html?ftcamp=published_links%2Frss%2Fworld_asia-pacific_china%2F feed%2F%2Fproduct&ftcamp=crm/email/201363/nbe/ChinaBusiness/product#axzz2V8lwoOt5.

Refkin, Alan; Cray, Scott. *Doing the China Tango* (Bloomington: iUniverse, 2012).

Rein, Shaun. "How to Deal with Corruption in China," *Forbes*, http://www.forbes.com/2009/10/07/china-corruption-bribes-leadership-managing-rein.html.

Requejo, William Hernandez; Graham, John L. *Global Negotiation: The New Rules* (New York: Palgrave Macmillan, 2008).

Roett, Riordan; Paz, Guadalupe. *China's Expansion into the Western Hemisphere* (Washington, DC: Brookings Institution Press, 2008).

Roos, Maarten. "China: Monetary Costs to Litigation in China," *Mondaq*, http://www.mondaq.com/x/122480/Monetary+Costs+to+Litig ation+in+China.

Rotberg, Robert I. *China into Africa: Trade, Aid, and Influence* (Cambridge: World Peace Foundation, 2008).

Rovnick, Naomi. "Most Big Chinese Companies Get Some Kind of State Subsidy," *Quartz*, http://qz.com/72354/most-big-chinese-companies-get-some-kind-of-state-subsidies/.

Sanderson, Henry; Forsythe, Michael. *China's Superbank* (Singapore: John Wiley & Sons, 2013).

Savitz, Eric. "Conversations on Cybersecurity: The Trouble with China, Part 1," *Forbes*, http://www.forbes.com/sites/ciocentral/2012/01/31/conversations-on-cybersecurity-the-trouble-with-china-part-1/.

Savitz, Eric. "Conversations on Cybersecurity: The Trouble with China, Part 2," *Forbes*, http://www.forbes.com/sites/ciocentral/2012/02/05/conversations-on-cybersecurity-the-trouble-with-china-part-2/2/.

Savitz, Eric. "Conversations on Cybersecurity Part 3: Why You aren't Protected," *Forbes*, http://www.forbes.com/sites/ciocentral/2012/02/12/conversations-on-cybersecurity-part-3-why-you-arent-protected/.

Savitz, Eric. "Conversations on Cybersecurity, Part 4: Effective Protection," *Forbes*, http://www.forbes.com/sites/ciocentral/2012/03/05/conversations-on-cybersecurity-part-4-effective-protection/2/.

Schneier, Bruce. "Computer Security When Traveling to China," *Schneier on Security*, http://www.schneier.com/blog/archives/2012/02/computer_securi_2.html.

Schwab, Charles. "China is Ground Zero for a Green Energy Revolution," *The Slant Investor Place*, http://slant.investorplace.com/2013/03/china-is-ground-zero-for-a-green-energy-revolution/.

Slater, Derek. "Intellectual Property Protection: The Basics," *csoonline*, http://www.csoonline.com/article/204600/intellectual-property-protection-the-basics.

Solidiance. "The Importance of Renewable Energy in China," *Ecology Global Network*, http://www.ecology.com/2013/03/07/renewable-energy-in-china/.

Solidiance. "Wind Power in China," *Ecology Global Network*, http://www.ecology.com/2013/03/21/wind-power-in-china/.

Solomon, Richard H.; Quinney, Nigel. *American negotiating Behavior: Wheeler-Dealers, legal Eagles, Bullies, and Preachers* (Washington, DC: United States Institute of Peace, 2010).

Stearns, Jonathan. "EU Drops Threat of Anti-Subsidy Tariffs on Chinese Bicycles," *Bloomberg*, http://www.bloomberg.com/news/2013-05-23/eu-drops-threat-of-anti-subsidy-tariffs-on-chinese-bicycles.html.

Sy, Gregory. "Terminating Employees in China: Some Practical Considerations," *China Window*, http://www.china-window.com/china_business/doing_business_in_china/terminating-mployees.shtml.

Tan, Monica. "8 Must-know Facts about China's Air Pollution," *Greenpeace*, http://www.greenpeace.org/eastasia/news/blog/8-must-know-facts-about-chinas-air-pollution-/blog/43862/.

Tang, Jie; Routledge, Anthony Ward. *Changing Face of Chinese Management* (Working in Asia)—an imprint of the Taylor & Francis Group, 2003.

Teo, Lay Lim; Piotroski, Susan A.; Nunes, Paul F.; Wang, Sophie X. "Why Winning the Wallets of China's Consumers is Harder than You Think," *The European Business Review*, http://www.europeanbusinessreview.com/?p=1429.

Tudela, Rita Alvarez. "Fighting Desertification in China," *Aljazeera*, http://www.aljazeera.com/indepth/features/2012/12/2012126123056457256.html.

Tudor, Alison. "Banks Find Promise Unfulfilled in China Forays," *The Wall Street Journal*, http://online.wsj.com/article/SB10001424127887324442304578236224087592996.html.

Wadhwa, Vivek. "Technology Advances to End China's Manufacturing Dominance, Open up New Possibilities for India," *The Economic Times*, http://articles.economictimes.indiatimes.com/2012-10-22/news/34653778_1_indian-companies-vivek-wadhwa-technology.

Walter, Carl E.; Howie, Fraser J. T. *Red Capitalism* (Singapore: John Wiley & Sons, 2012).

Wang, Huazhong. "Foreigners OKed to Handle State Secrets," *Chinadaily*, http://usa.chinadaily.com.cn/china/2012-05/16/content_15313601.htm.

Wang, Helen H. "China to Become the World's Largest Importer by 2014," *Forbes*, http://www.forbes.com/sites/helenwang/2012/01/11/china-to-become-the-worlds-largest-importer-by-2014/.

Wang, Jian-Ye; Bio-Tchané, Abdoulaye. "Africa's Burgeoning Ties with China," *International Monetary Fund,* http://www.imf.org/external/pubs/ft/fandd/2008/03/wang.htm.

Wang, Tiffany. "The Decline of the Expat: Foreigners in China Proliferate, But Become Less Special," *Tea Leaf Nation,* http://www.tealeafnation.com/2013/02/the-decline-of-the-expat-foreigners-in-china-proliferate-but-become-less-special/.

Wang, Xiao. "Alternative Energy to Improve China's Air Quality," *CRI,* http://english.cri.cn/7146/2013/03/16/2361s754026.htm.

Wang, Yi. *Australia-China Relations post 1949* (Burlington: Ashgate Publishing Company, 2012).

Watt, Louise. "China Pollution: Cars Cause Major Air Problems in Chinese Cities," *The Huffington Post,* http://www.huffingtonpost.com/2013/01/31/china-pollution-cars-air-problems-cities_n_2589294.html.

Watts, Jonathan. "China's Exploitation of Latin American Natural Resources Raises Concern," *EurActiv,* http://www.euractiv.com/development-policy/chinas-exploitation-latin-americ-news-518799.

Wigley, Richard W.; Xu, Jing. "Evidence Collection and Alternatives to Discovery in P.R.C. Litigation," *China Law Insight,* http://www.chinalawinsight.com/2011/04/articles/dispute-resolution/evidence-collection-and-alternatives-to-discovery-in-prc-litigation/.

Williamson, Andrew. *Living and Working in China* (Oxford: How To Books Ltd, 2005).

Wong, Edward. "2 Major Pollutants Increase in Beijing," *New York Times,* Asia Pacific, http://www.nytimes.com/2013/04/04/world/asia/two-major-air-pollutants-increase-in-china.html.

Wong, Edward. "Air Pollution Linked to 1.2 Million Premature Deaths in China," *New York Times*, Asia Pacific, http://www.nytimes.

com/2013/04/02/world/asia/air-pollution-linked-to-1-2-million-deaths-in-china.html.

Wong, Edward. "In China, Breathing Becomes a Childhood Risk," *New York Times,* Asia Pacific, http://www.nytimes.com/2013/04/23/world/asia/pollution-is-radically-changing-childhood-in-chinas-cities.html?pagewanted=all.

Yang, Bai. "China: Australia's largest trading partner," *CCTV.com English,* http://english.cntv.cn/program/china24/20130409/107022.shtml.

Yang, Jia Lynn. "Chinese Firms Put Intellectual Property Lawsuits to Work," *The Washington Post,* http://www.washingtonpost.com/business/economy/chinese-firms-put-intellectual-property-lawsuits-to-work/2012/08/30/12d9a418-f1c3-11e1-adc6-87dfa8eff430_story.html.

Young, Jeffrey R. "In China's Internet Cafes, Content-Blocking Is Largely Effective," *The Chronicle of Higher Education,* http://chronicle.com/blogs/college20/in-chinas-internet-cafes-content-blocking-is-largely-effective/26872.

Young, Laura W. "Hiring and Managing Employees in China," *The Law Offices of Wang & Wang,* http://www.wangandwang.com/news-articles/articles/hiring-managing-employees-china/.

Yu, Dawei. "Chinese waste: the burning issue," *chinadialogue,* http://www.chinadialogue.net/article/show/single/en/4739-Chinese-waste-the-burning-issue.

Yu, Peter K. "The U.S.-China Dispute Over TRIPS Enforcement," *Drake University Law School,* http://www.law.drake.edu/academics/ip/docs/ipResearch-op5.pdf.

Zalan, Kira. "The Rise of China and the Global Future of the U.S.," *U.S. News & World Report,* http://www.usnews.com/opinion/articles/2013/01/03/the-rise-of-china-and-the-global-future-of-the-us.

Zhang, Bill H. "Litigation and Arbitration in China," *HG.org, Global Legal Resources*, http://www.hg.org/article.asp?id=7820.

Zhang, Xiaojun Joseph. "News Analysis: China, Australia to Expand Exchanges of Students, Academics," *Xinhua Net*, http://news.xinhuanet.com/english/indepth/2012-12/03/c_132016258.htm.

Zhang, Yiqian. "Chinese, US Air Quality Index Not the Same," *The Global Times*, http://www.globaltimes.cn/content/755525.shtml.

Zhao, Yinan. "Foreigners without Permit May Lose Rights in China," *The China Post*, http://www.chinapost.com.tw/business/asia-china/2012/08/14/350932/p2/Foreigners-without.htm.

Zhao, Yun. "How Many Languages are Spoken in China Today?" *China History Forum*, http://www.chinahistoryforum.com/index.php?/topic/28491-how-many-languages-are-spoken-in-china-today/.

Zheng, Xin. "Agencies Help Foreigners Evade Rules to Land Jobs," *Chinadaily*, http://usa.chinadaily.com.cn/china/2012-09-06/content_15737017.htm.

Zheng, Yangpeng. "High-end Manufacturing Holds the Key," *Chinadaily*, http://usa.chinadaily.com.cn/weekly/2013-03-01/content_16265887_4.htm.

INDEX

Beijing Environmental Monitoring
 Center 113
Beijing Intermediate Court 61
Beijing Municipal Bureau of Labor
 and Social Security 42
Beijing Public Security Bureau 43
Benin 142
Bennett, Steven C. 59
Bereavement leave 94
Berlin 17
Best Talent 41
BGP (Border Gateway Protocol) 158
Bicycles 30
Biodiversity 112, 118
Blackberry 163
Blackman, Carolyn 188
Blakemore, Art 2
Bloomberg 105, 132
BMW 20, 101
BNP Paribas 128
BOC (Bank of China) 126, 128
Boeing 10
Bolivia 152, 153
Bonus 86
Border Gateway Protocol (BGP) 158
Boston Consulting Group 14, 16,
 21, 22
BP Statistical Review of World
 Energy 113
Bradsher, Keith 87
Brands 15, 19
 foreign/multinational 15
Brazil 7, 9, 22, 133, 143, 145,
 147, 151
BRICS 145
Brisbane 146
Britain 13, 20, 21, 148, 174, 202
British Security Service 165

British Virgin Islands 147
Brookings Institute 163
Brooks Brothers Group 86
Brown, Ronald 98
Browser 157
Burberry Group 86
Burkina 142

C

C&A 20
CaixaBank 128
Cameroon 142
Canada 138
Capitalism 38, 153, 201
Capital Trade Incorporated 23
Carbon dioxide 123
Caribbean 153
Carnegie Endowment for
 International Peace in
 Washington 102
Carrefour 10
Caterpillar 10, 34
Cayman Islands 147
CCB (China Construction Bank)
 126, 128, 129
CCIPS (US Department of Justice's
 Computer Crime and
 Intellectual Property Section)
 76, 77
CDB (China Development Bank)
 130, 131, 132, 133, 134
Cell phones 22, 163, 164, 168,
 170, 171
Center for International Industry
 Competitiveness 27
Certificate
 expert 43

Geithner, Timothy 81

General Administration of Customs (GAC) 69, 72

Germany 7, 14, 19, 20, 21, 80, 115, 148, 174

Glass 25

Global Cyber Risk 163

Global Manufacturing Competitiveness Index 8

GlobalPost 107

Gobi desert 117

Gold 152

Golden Rule 37

Goldman Sachs 127

Government
  local 24, 30, 43, 61, 62, 63, 68, 70, 71, 78, 103, 107, 129, 134, 136
  municipal 24, 30, 48, 53, 67, 73, 97, 129
  provincial 24, 31, 48, 53, 61, 62, 63, 67, 71, 73, 74, 78, 79, 97, 103, 107, 119, 123, 129, 136

Graham and Lam 181

Graham, John L. 181

Grandall Legal Group 89

Grasslands 117, 118

Grease payment 108

Great Firewall 161

Green card 39

Greenhouse gas emissions 122

Greenpeace 113, 119

Green Wall of China 117

Gross Domestic Product (GDP) 4, 6, 7, 84, 107, 111, 146, 202, 203
  global 7
  provincial 14

Guangzhou 13

Guanxi 102, 103, 183, 184, 194

H

Hacker 156

Hainan 61, 79

Hainan Higher Court 61

Haley, George T. 27

Haley, Usha C. V. 27

Han 35

Handley, Meg 122

Hangzhou 36

Han, N. 118

Hardware 66

Harris, Dan 45, 81

Harvard Business Review 26

Hays, Jeffrey 115

Head hunters 40, 41

Health care 43

Heinze, Bill 77

Higher People's Court 52, 54, 74, 79l

Highways 21, 133, 142, 143, 144

Hilton 10, 15

H&M 20

Hochberg, Frank 133

Holidays 96

Hong Kong 14, 127, 147

Hong Kong's Bank of East Asia Ltd. 128

Hospitals 40, 143, 144

Households
  Australian 147
  wealthy 13

Housing 135, 144
  public 143

Housing fund 91, 95

Howie, Fraser 127

ABOUT THE AUTHORS

Alan Refkin is the chairman and CEO of Thornhill Capital, a global consulting firm. He is an internationally recognized expert on China and has worked on numerous projects throughout China for over ten years. He has spoken on how to negotiate in China, as well as on financial, management, and joint venture topics at the National People's Congress in Beijing and at Chinese government seminars. He currently serves as an advisor to a number of US, Chinese, and international corporations and financial institutions. More information on the author, including his blogs and newsletters, can be obtained at www.alanrefkin.com, twitter.com/AlanRefkin, and www.thornhillcapital.net.

Scott D. Cray has served as the CEO and founder of many US companies. Since 2004, he has provided managerial and operational advisory services to Chinese companies. He has served as the director of operations for a public Chinese company and has served on the board of directors of a number of Chinese companies. He is a member of Thornhill Capital. More information on the author can be obtained at www.thornhillcapital.net.